©1998 R.S. Riddick

THE ARBUCKLE CAFE
Classic Cowboy Stories
by Val FitzPatrick

Yellow Cat
PUBLISHING
Yellow Cat Flats, Utah

Published by
Yellow Cat Publishing
Yellow Cat Flats, Utah

Administrative Offices:
Yellow Cat Publishing
P.O. Box 174
Moab, UT 84532

Design by Alice Sjoberg Graphic Design
Carbondale, Colorado

Printed in Canada by Hignell Printing, Ltd.

ISBN 0-9655961-1-7

LIBRARY OF CONGRESS CATALOGING-IN-PUBLICATION DATA

FitzPatrick, V. S. (Valentine Stewart), 1886–1988.
    The Arbuckle Cafe : classic cowboy stories / by Val FitzPatrick.
        p.   cm.
    ISBN 0-9655961-1-7 (pbk. : alk. paper)
        1. FitzPatrick, V. S. (Valentine Stewart), 1886–1988 Anecdotes.
    2. Cowboys–Colorado–Moffat County Biography Anecdotes. 3. Ranch
    life–Colorado–Moffat County Anecdotes. 4. Cattle Trade–Colorado-
    Moffat County Anecdotes. 5. Moffat County (Colo.) Biography
    Anecdotes. 6. Moffat County (Colo.) Social life and customs
    Anecdotes. I. Title.
    F782.M65F54 1999
    978.8'1203'092–dc21
        [B]   99-23790
                                                                      CIP

★ **Contents** ★

★
Introduction

On January 4, 1886, in a log cabin at a silver mine near Georgetown, Colorado, a baby boy was born and christened Valentine Stewart Parnell FitzPatrick by his Irish/English parents. When young Val was eight months old, his family homesteaded in beautiful but lonely northwest Colorado, about 20 miles west of the town of Craig, a country so rugged and remote it was often called "the last frontier."

In 1894, when Val was eight, the family moved from the homestead to a ranch that was near the postoffice for the tiny community of Lay, Colorado (originally called Lay Over, as it was the crossroads of the military road from Wyoming and the wagon road west towards Utah and a handy place to stop for the night). Val writes, "We were right in the mainstream of whatever traffic there might be in the region. Hardly a day passed but there came ranchers, cowpunchers, an occasional prospector or trapper, a few Indians, and now and then an outlaw. In this same year, 1894, the outlaw Teton Jackson died in a jail break in Idaho. Although Butch Cassidy and his Wild Bunch had not yet attracted much attention, they occasionally stopped for food and shelter."

"But the main change in our lives was closer acquaintance with the most influential people in the country, the cowpunchers and their bosses. Up to this time we had known them as only an occasional rider who stopped for a brief chat. But now, seeing cowpunchers almost every day, delivering their mail, talking with them, having them at our table, we got to know them well."

"Most of these cowpunchers had followed the annual trail herds from Texas, Oklahoma, and New Mexico into Montana and Wyoming. But the new railroads came, making the long cattle drives a thing of the past and leaving these men without jobs. Many of the cowpunchers stayed permanently with the herds they'd helped drive up. When Ora Haley brought his Two-Bar Cattle Company herds from Wyoming into northwest Colorado, the men who came with them were these same seasoned, cattle-wise riders, the cream of the crop. They ranged from tough young lads to graying old-timers, and from uncouth, shy, and awkward youths to men with some education, ambition, and intelligence and who later themselves became big cattlemen."

At the ripe old age of 13, Val got a job at the K Diamond Cattle Company, and at 14 he went to work for the prestigious Two-Bar, the goal of nearly every young man in the area. Val says he got the job only because the Two-Bar foreman, Heck Lytton, "was sweet on one of my sisters." Thus began Val's career as a cowpuncher, the foundation for the stories in this book.

Val's other careers over the years included geologist, civil engineer, and newspaperman. Twice he was made Grand Marshall of the Craig Ride 'n Tie Days Rodeo, once at age 98, and again at age 100. Val FitzPatrick's story-telling was enhanced by a daily journal he kept from the age of 10 until he died, on July 3, 1988, at the age of 102.

The stories in this book, all first-hand accounts, were compiled from Val's "Last Frontier" series and his "Back Trail" journals, now out of print. We hope you enjoy these authentic and classic accounts, truly vintage and one-of-a-kind insights into the lives of the old-time cowpunchers.

Yellow Cat Publishing
Yellow Cat Flats, Utah

★

Preface: Arbuckles, the Buckaroo Brew

by Marjorie Miller

Even though I grew up in the cattle country of northwest Colorado, it wasn't until just a few years ago that I had my first sip of Arbuckles' Coffee, the original "buckaroo brew." After a mellow day of trail riding, we'd decided to kick back around the campfire for a spell, warm-up some canned beans, and see who could spin the best yarn. This turned out to be an appropriate setting for learning about the java that "won the West."

As the evening wore on and the pinyon fire settled down to a comfortable glow of hot embers, one of the old-timers posed a tricky question:

"Go back one-hundred years. Who do you suppose was considered the most famous and best-known hero in the Old West? Whose autograph was most valuable?"

We each had our guess—maybe the Governor of Colorado, Alva Adams? Was it Cleveland, the U.S. President? Chief Ouray of the Utes? Otto Mears, the road builder?

After we'd exhausted every name we could remember, we gave up and the old-timer answered his own question. "It was Arbuckle. Everybody—men, women, children—knew of Arbuckle. His name was known in the lowliest dugout and in the best log house, in freighters' camps, on roundups, in trappers' tents, and in prospectors' shelters. Arbuckle's signature was the most treasured autograph ever known. Everyone drank toasts to him."

"Who was Arbuckle?" we asked.

The old fellow, enjoying his role as historian, answered, "Arbuckle was the man whose signature appeared on the one-pound paper packages of coffee used by everybody. Arbuckles' "Ariosa" was the only coffee known on the frontier for many years. The price was 20 cents a pound, and Arbuckle was the first merchandiser to offer premiums."

He paused as if to remember, then continued, "On each package of coffee, running lengthwise, was the scrawled signature of Arbuckle. Cut out the signatures, save them, and in due course for a certain number of signatures and a little money you could get such things as scissors, jackknives, mirrors, comb-and-brush sets, razors, and perfumes, not to mention mouse traps, jaw harps, napkin rings, and mustache cups."

That old-timer indeed knew Arbuckles well, for he was Val FitzPatrick, once a cowpuncher for the famous Two-Bar outfit at the turn of the century. He'd had his share of the strong brew, we were sure.

Valentine FitzPatrick was a good friend of my grandfather, Corrin ("Corny") B. Davidson, one of northwest Colorado's early game wardens. Val and Corny spent many hours together prospecting around the West and trading old stories.

From the Beginning

Since that evening around the campfire I've been fascinated by this famous coffee and the lore that surrounds it. I've talked to old-time cowpunchers and toured some of the old trading posts in the Southwest that still have Arbuckles memorabilia on display. And much to my delight, in 1994, Francis Fugate (an even more ardent Arbuckles fan) authored a book called "Arbuckles, the Coffee that Won the West" (published by Texas Western Press). In it, Fugate presents a complete history of Arbuckles' Coffee and its founder, John Arbuckle. To my own research I've added tidbits from Fugate's book about the buckaroo brew.

So, if you're inclined, lean back against that log, close your eyes, feel the fire warming up the cuffs on your Levis and the bottom of your boots, have a sip of hot steamy Arbuckles, and listen up. Here's how the story goes:

Up until the end of the Civil War, coffee was sold green, in bulk. The green beans had to be roasted on a wood stove or in a skillet over a campfire before they could be ground and brewed—and one burned bean ruined all. Many a batch had to be thrown out or "drank anyway," depending on your "financials." Sometimes even the wealthy had to "drink it anyway" or do without.

And as any coffee aficionado knows, roasting is the key to good coffee, as green coffee has little or no flavor. Back then, roasting coffee was a task that called for ingenuity and high levels of experimentation. Coffee roasters were usually make-do affairs, consisting of a variety of devices, including skillets, cookie tins, dutch ovens, and stove-top popcorn poppers. Sometimes even a bed-warming pan was used.

To roast the coffee, you started out with a single layer of beans placed in your "roaster," then you constantly stirred and shook the beans over the fire to prevent burning, gradually adding another layer and repeating the process. Some creative cooks added spices, salts, or oils in an attempt to improve the flavor of the beans, which often came from Mexico and were of questionable quality. Coffee was also sometimes "adulterated" with a variety of substances, including mesquite beans, chicory, barley, oatmeal, and even beets.

Once roasted, the beans had to be ground and quickly brewed, for they soon lost the volatile oils that gave the coffee its aroma and flavor. Once brewed, sugar and cream were rare additions, at least out on the range. There's the story of a Texas cowpuncher working in Montana, who, when someone passed him the sugar, replied, "No thanks, I don't take salt in my coffee." He'd never seen processed sugar. As for "canned cow," most cowpunchers usually declined, afraid they'd have to help milk the cow later.

But even before the days of the cowpunchers, coffee was one of the staples of the early American frontier and often helped make meager rations tolerable. In 1849, while surveying a military route through the Southwest, Lieutenant William Whiting noted in his journal that coffee was "the great essential in a prairie bill of fare." It was said that many of the Indian attacks on early wagon trains were motivated by a desire for coffee and tobacco. The Sioux called coffee "kazuta sapa" (black medicine).

The Indians' love of coffee helped the fur companies prosper. From 1833 until 1859, the American Fur Company would trade Indians one cup of coffee for one buffalo robe, a price that they later "generously" increased to three cups. The company then turned around and sold the robes for three to four dollars each. Coffee was considered by Indians and traders alike as a superior trade item, equal to or better than whiskey or gunpowder.

A Pennsylvania Innovator

While America suffered poorly roasted coffee, this early version of what would later become the national drink, an entrepreneur was in the making. In 1860, back in Pittsburgh, a young John Arbuckle left college to join his brother in a wholesale grocery business. John was an inventive type, and he soon became intrigued with finding a way to roast coffee and preserve its freshness. He knew a huge market existed for such a product, and it wasn't long until he'd patented a method for glazing coffee beans to seal the pores against deterioration of flavor and aroma. Initially, his glaze consisted of Irish moss (a seaweed), gelatin, sugar, and eggs. He later modified this recipe to just sugar and eggs.

After getting the glaze down to a science, Arbuckle began packing the roasted coffee in one-pound packages, an innovative idea that allowed for easier transport than the current bulk methods. He ignored the derision of those in the coffee trade who said his coffee reminded them of "little bags of peanuts." He soon had invented an automatic packaging machine to support his new and sky-rocketing sales. It wasn't long until he'd moved to the heart of the coffee industry in New York City, where he was again ridiculed for being hopelessly "middle class." An article about him in "Cosmopolitan" said that "he likes pie, and there are awful indications that he has not entirely outgrown the fried steak habit."

Also a creative marketer, Arbuckle presented the coffee marketing world with its first color ad in 1872. It read: "It is cheaper to buy Arbuckles' Roasted Coffee in one-pound airtight packages than to buy green coffee and roast it yourself...You cannot roast coffee properly yourself."

Arbuckles called his coffee "Ariosa" and put a flying angel on the label. Supposedly, the "A" stood for Arbuckles, the "rio" represented a type of low-altitude coffee, and the "sa" stood for Santos or South America. The Rio type of coffee was considered to be hearty, and the Santos type was milder. Arbuckles' was a blend of both, giving it a rich and mellow flavor.

But the coffee industry didn't take well to this new competition, and the Arbuckle Brothers were soon in a battle with another major company, the Dilworth Brothers. John Arbuckle didn't even flinch at having the "big guns" out to get him. One Arbuckles' advertisement had a drawing of the Dilworth Brothers' plant with a crowd looking in through the door and saying things like, "No wonder I have been sick," and "I see what killed my children." The dispute finally wore out and both companies agreed to ignore each other.

The Company Warms Up

Arbuckles' Coffee prospered, and during the 1890s, John Arbuckle, by now considered a marketing genius, began to give premiums to his loyal buyers. Each coffee package had his signature printed on it, and this signature could be exchanged for items in a catalog, including belts (20 signatures), window curtains (65), watches (90), and revolvers (150). Over 100 million of these signatures were traded each year for Arbuckles' premiums.

Out West, the new coffee was an instant success with chuck-wagon cooks, who were faced with the task of keeping cowpunchers supplied with plenty of hot "mud" out on the range. As further enticement to buy Arbuckles' Coffee, a stick of peppermint was included in every package of Ariosa. This became a powerful tool for the camp cookee to bribe cowpunchers to help with chores. The chuck-wagon cook was well-respected, for anything otherwise might lead to "dehorned coffee" or "water that's been scalded to death." Sears carried bags of the coffee in their famous mail-order catalogs at 20 cents a pound.

Arbuckles became so common that by 1890 it had became a generic name for coffee. It was common to hear cowpunchers ask for a cup of coffee by saying, "How about them Arbuckles?" And a good cowpuncher was "worth his weight in Arbuckles." One old cowpuncher said he made "cowdog coffee" out of Ariosa. When asked what "cowdog coffee" was, he replied: "It's just like cowboy coffee, you boil Arbuckles in a pan over a fire for a few hours, then you throw in a hoss shoe, and if it won't sink, it's done. Add a little whiskey. Makes you howl." Variants on this recipe were once found across the West (often you'd throw in a six-shooter). Another cowpuncher said, "Most people don't realize how little water it takes to make good coffee. Probably not all that nutritious, though, without much water."

The Navajo Indians loved Arbuckles' Coffee, which they called "Hosteen Cohay" (Mister Coffee). Every camp or hogan had a blackened coffeepot hung over a bed of juniper or pinyon coals. Traders at the Indian trading posts sent coupons to Arbuckles in packets of thousands, brought in by the Navajos and traded for goods. The traders then redeemed the coupons for more goods for their shelves. Arbuckles used shipping cases made of Maine fir. These were also prized items, used for everything from furniture to cradles. Many of the old trading posts, including the Hubbell Trading Post and the Old Red Lake Trading Post (both in Arizona), still have Arbuckles' crates proudly on display.

Although the Navajo were generally loyal Arbuckles' fans, Fugate tells the story about Arbuckles' competitor, Lion Coffee Company, who sent a salesman to the reservation to drum up more business. The man went around telling the Indians that the picture of the lion on the coffee package meant that they'd have the strength of the lion if they drank Lion Coffee.

To the alarm of the Arbuckles' salesman, the Indians began buying Lion Coffee. But the Arbuckles' representative, being likewise creative, took his turn and told the Indians that the Ariosa brand, with its flying angel on the label, would give them the strength of ten-thousand lions. The Indians switched back to Arbuckles. The salesman later said that "if Lion Coffee now wants to beat Arbuckles, they'll have to put a picture of God himself on the label."

In 1912, John Arbuckle died, and with him went the driving force behind the coffee empire he'd built. His estate was valued at 37 million dollars, left to his sisters, who continued the company's operation. Just after Arbuckle's death, the company introduced what had been his private blend, called Yuban. Prior to this, Yuban had been available only as a gift to friends or at Arbuckle dinner parties. The coffee was a success, and General Foods purchased rights to the name in 1944.

Fortunately for Arbuckles' fans, in 1974 the trademark Ariosa brand was revived by Denny and Patricia Willis, who also revived the Arbuckles' Coffee Company, now based in Tucson, Arizona. Arbuckles is now produced in a variety of gourmet blends, each package containing a peppermint stick.

The label is an accurate replica of the original, complete with the flying angel. Although no one really knows what the original Arbuckles tasted like, the new company has a blend that fits the descriptions in historical accounts—a coffee that's robust and flavorful. Arbuckles is once again finding a following across the nation.

Completing the Circle

But back to the campfire, this time to a more recent conversation, one that John Arbuckle would probably approve of:

The old-timer asks, "How about them Arbuckles?"

The youngster replies, "What do you mean, how about them Arbuckles?"

The old-timer snorts, good-naturedly, "What! You've never heard of Arbuckles? Why, it's the coffee that won the West! The buckaroo brew! Pass me a cup."

The youngster replies, "Oh, you mean Arbuckles' Coffee. The company in Tucson. I've had their coffee before—in the espresso shop in Seattle. It's good. I especially like the French Vanilla Cream, although the Prickly Pear and the Ethiopian Sidamo are good, too."

Now it's the old-timer's turn to look puzzled. "Arbuckles' Coffee, in a college espresso shop? Whatever happened to plain old Ariosa? What's the world coming to?"

The fire settles down to a comfortable glow of hot embers, as each ponders history, but from different directions.

And truly, the most widely known man on the frontier, even more well-known than General Custer, was Arbuckle. And many a cowpuncher and many a waddie spent many an hour telling tales by firelight at the Arbuckle Cafe, served by a surly waiter called Cookee.

I sincerely hope you enjoy this collection of stories by Val FitzPatrick and have many pleasant evenings at the Arbuckle Cafe.

(This story first appeared in Western Horseman, *May, 1999.*
For more information on Arbuckles' Coffee, call 1-800-533-8278.)

★
Dogies, Dust, and the Drink

"**S**omebody's shore goin' to have to tell me a hull lot 'bout this kind of cowpunchin'," Al Hurd chuckled as we rounded the south end of Cross Mountain and headed west. "How 'bout it, Joe? You know I ain't never done no trail herdin' of no caows."

Joe Sainsbury, the wagon boss, kind of grinned and told Al, "Well, myself I ain't no Frenchy McCormick nor Ol' Man Chisum. But I been on trail herds, hoss wrangling."

"I heard Old Thorne and Bill Pratt arguin' about trail herds," Antelope Anderson told us. "Jest like a Chineyman and a Chickasha Injun arguing. Neither one understood the other."

Antelope was right. You still hear such talks once in awhile when one of the few old timer cowpunchers happens to get to talking cows with some fellow who runs some cattle today. The changes have been so great they don't have a basis for comparison. What old timer knew about mechanical chutes, serums, feed pellets, or artificial insemination? How many present-day cattle handlers ever followed a trail herd a thousand miles, stood a night guard, or rode before a stampede?

Trailherding was an experience you'd never forget. Of course the big trailherds, such as from Texas to Montana, had ceased before I was born. But after I came 'long in 1886 there were still some small trailherds handled. I helped a little with one of them. That is where we were headed when Al Hurd asked Joe Sainsbury about trail driving.

The K Diamond, K Ranch, and some of the small ranchers had thrown in together and bought some steers over in Utah. I think the cattle were raised in Nevada and later moved up into Utah north of Cedar City. We picked them up near Park City, where the east and west running Uinta Mountains butt into the north and south running Wasatch Range. We were going to bring them across country to Green River, Utah, pretty well up in Brown's Park, Colorado, then to Snake River, where some would be split off for the Snake River Association and the rest go on over somewhere on Bear (Yampa) River.

Because he knew about trail herds, Joe Sainsbury was boss of the drive, although some of the others were better cowpunchers. Fatty Smith was the cook. The mess wagon had been taken over in Brown's Park and left on the river about where we figured on hitting it with the cattle where the old Indian Trail used to cross.

It was a big picnic for me. I was only 14, and all the others were about twice as old. Al Hurd was the youngest of them, and he always looked as if he had just had a shave, but I never did see him shave. Joe, the boss, was a big rangy man with a heavy mustache, whom I'd seen more times on the handle of a pitchfork than on any trail drive. Antelope was a big amiable cowpuncher, and a good one. He had some whopping stories to tell. One about roping antelope got him his nickname. Another big old boy, Doc Chivington, from up Snake River, had a long mustache and was always kind of solemn, but knew cattle inside out. We picked up two more cowpunchers at Tom Morgan's, and a couple more overtook us before we got to the cattle. The "cattle," was a herd of 1,200 steers of every color of the rainbow, but mostly reds and yellows. They were kind of scrubby but had lots of room to put on fat and weight.

The drive was made in July. The high country was beautiful, with flowers everywhere. There were some deer flies and horse flies to pester the horses, but they didn't seem to worry the cattle. We took it easy, making maybe 10 or 12 miles most days.

At first, the steers were very hard to manage. They were of a wild and skittish breed, distrustful of man, and ready to scare and run any second.

The nine men were hardly enough for the job the first few days, and we rode our horses to a standstill trying to keep the herd strung out and moving. The country was timbered. Let a steer take fright at a flurrying grouse, a scurrying deer, or maybe just a big old spruce tree blown down, with its big root and the hole it had left, and a dozen more would follow him on a mad race into the tangle of quakers, chokecherry bushes, and dense undergrowth including wild parsnips up to the saddle skirts.

It was a new and strange experience, even to the boss, so we had to work out a technique. We finally found that when one of those runs started, which was virtually a stampede on a small scale, it was best for two men to follow. One man rode beside the steers, the other near the lead steer, quirting it over the head and turning it and its followers to run in a circle. By circling the small running bunch, we could actually run them down to exhaustion. Then we threw them back into the herd. For a day or two they would be docile enough.

Another thing we learned before many days was which spooky steers repeatedly started these breaks. There were only a few, but they were natural trouble makers. A big old yellow steer was the worst. Once we got the mean ones identified, we had the remedy. The moment one of them bolted, the man nearest him, with his lariat ready instead of strapped to the pommel, looped it out and dropped it over the renegade's head. The busting the steer got when he came to the end of the rope, tied hard and fast to the saddle horn, civilized him for quite awhile.

It all may sound simple and easy. It might have been, too, if we had been in open country, with good footing and nothing to impede. The trouble was, we were working nearly all the time on steep mountain slopes, strewn with rocks and boulders from fist-size to big as a house. We were going through growths of juniper, pinon, spruce, pine, quaking aspen, bushes of chokecherry, sarvisberry, buckbrush, alders, and willows, all intertwined with the profusion of weeds and grasses that grew in such country in those days. Add to these impediments the tiny rivulets, small creeks, swamps, muskeg, and beaver holes, and you had hazards that made the riders' lives a burden.

The wagon had been left on the river bank near the ford in Brown's Park. We therefore had a string of pack horses to add to our difficulties. Fatty Smith, the cook, was no slouch as a cowpuncher himself. He punched cows with Wils Rankin in the early 1880s. When he got too fat to do hard riding, he started doing cooking and ranch work. But with beds, dutch ovens, pots, skillets, dishes, and food, on a half-dozen horses, he had more than his share of troubles. So, we had to give him a hand pretty often in order to keep the pack string untangled and moving. Even so, packs were ripped on snags and rocks, pack horses slipped off steep banks, got mired in sloughs and sinks, and got stuck in between trees.

The only thing that gave little trouble was the saddle string. There were about 35 head of saddle horses. If anything, instead of being a burden, they were a help. Nearly all were fairly well-broken horses. Most of them kept pretty well up front of the cattle, the others scattered through the herd. They could travel faster than the steers, but stopped more to graze, so it came out about even. They helped to break trail and keep the herd pointed up front. Those toward the rear were not adverse to nipping the rump of a laggard steer.

Two men rode point. They kept the herd headed in the right direction. The herd was about a quarter-mile long. On each side, spaced front and rear of the herd, two men rode "swing" to keep the herd from bulging in the middle and to keep the column of steers about 100 feet in width. On the two corners which brought up the rear were two more "drag" riders. Theirs was the job of keeping the stragglers, the lazy ones, the tired ones, and even the sick ones, in motion. The cattle they urged forward really set the gait for the drive. If they dragged too much, the line of cattle stretched out too long and thin, making the side-riders lose control, and anything could happen. I think it was mostly luck that between the starting point and Green River, in 10 days of trailing, we had to abandon only two animals that became too weak to travel.

Tom Morgan, the trail boss, usually rode ahead. Well-mounted, he could go faster and farther to reconnoiter the trail for the herd to follow.

We looked forward to the day when we would reach the river, get out of the infernal trees and brush, and have no more grief with the pack string. Little did we know what was in store for us.

We hit Green River about two in the afternoon. Tom and Doc and some of the others held a quick pow-wow and decided to make the crossing right away, even if it would be late in the day before we could make camp. We could see the wagon on the other side of the river and knew that meant better chuck.

I had two good friends in the outfit, or it might have been that that day's bright July sun would have shone on my finish. The friends? Antelope, the big amiable cowpuncher, and Coal Oil Johnny, the small gray horse on which the year before, at the K Diamond Ranch, I had really got my education in riding buckers. Albert Gent, a big cowpuncher at the K Diamond, had made me "thumb up" Johnny and make him buck. Your thumbs, run up a horse's neck clear to his ears, would bring out any buck if it was in a horse.

All through the drive my position had been second swing man on the righthand side of the herd. Antelope was first man, up toward the point. In the river crossing we were to keep to our regular positions.

In the cavvy was a bright-eyed dun horse that wore the bell. He had a lot of savvy and proved it when we came to the river. Tom had half the saddle string brought up ahead, with the rest left back at the end of the line.

We rounded up the pack horses, untied the diamond hitches, shoved the packs up in piles on top of the horses, tied them, and hoped they wouldn't turn and get in the water. There wasn't much food left, but all our beds were on the cayuses.

Tom gave the word and we pushed the loose horses down to the end of a sandbar. The shiny-eyed dun just moseyed right out into the river as if swimming rivers was an everyday thing. I doubt if he or any of the rest had ever had to swim before, but they all followed him right in. Soon they were all swimming, some with strong strokes and noses up out of the water, some fighting the water and terrified. But at least all were headed for the farther shore about 400 feet away. And, joyful to behold, the cattle, responding to the yowls and leg-slapping of the cowpunchers, followed the horses into the stream.

Each man held his position, but we closed the space between us a little. When my turn came to slip into the now-swirling waters, I just remembered Antelope's instructions and let Coal Oil Johnny have his head. He didn't need any help from me. An older and wiser horse than when I had "thumbed him up" on the K Diamond a couple of years before, he breasted the waves with steady strokes. But I wouldn't have been surprised if the smart little gray had remembered those "thumbing ups" and let himself and me sink out of sight to pay me back.

The current was fairly fast. I noticed the herd drifting downstream. The horses were just going out of the water on the opposite shore about 100 yards lower down the river than where they went in. This wash of the tide kept the cattle crowding those of us who rode on the down-river side. I noticed Antelope having trouble. Some steers drifted against his horse and nearly upset him. The horse became alarmed and started to faunch, but Antelope soon had him quieted down. That is, I guess he did, for about that time that big mangy yellow steer that had given us trouble from the first hour of the drive decided to bolt. He turned straight downstream. A dozen more fell in behind him.

We had talked about just such a situation beforehand, so I knew what to do. Being only 14, and Antelope about 25, he had sort of taken me under his wing and given me some good pointers. So now, steering Johnny as well as I could, I shifted my quirt to my left hand and began to lace the big yellow steer across the nose and eyes, trying to turn him back into the herd.

It happened so quickly I don't rightly know how to this day. They told me afterward that two steers tried to go behind my horse, and one bumped into the other. One sank out of sight, but came up right under Johnny. The next I knew I was drinking and breathing water, and looking down along my leg I could see the sun shining. The thing was, Johnny was on his back and I under him.

I can't swim a lick. Maybe by giving it all I've got I could stay on top for 20 feet.

Anyhow, by some miracle, Johnny righted himself, and I'm in the water with a hold on the saddle horn and trying to get back in the saddle. Every time I lurched and pulled, I turned Johnny on his side. Then, above the bawling of the cattle, I heard the powerful voice of Antelope:

"Stop it, kid, stop it! Damn it, I say listen to me! Turn loose of that horn and grab him by the tail. Grab his tail!"

I wasn't about to turn loose of that saddle horn. Antelope swam his horse in close, leaned over and lashed out with his quirt, taking me across the hands and neck. I got the message. I turned loose of the horn, and as Johnny swam past, grabbed his tail. We were both now upright and he was swimming. "Crawl on him from behind," Antelope coached. I did, and landed in the saddle, darned near drowned, but happier than I can remember being before or since. In spite of the fact that I've always been lucky, I fully expected to drown.

"Now get to hazin' cows," Antelope yelled, and suiting the action to the word, shoved off to do some cow hazing himself.

By that time, the big yellow steer and his cohorts had made it back to the shore from which they had just come. One of the corner drag men behind took after them, got them to circling and ran them down until they were plumb fagged. Then he quirted them

into line, and they got in and went to swimming like good little
dogies.

Fine! Bully! Hot stuff! Our troubles were over. We scattered
the herd on the good grazing in the bottom, and leaving without
even a guard, high-tailed it to the mess wagon, where by now Fatty
Smith had a big fire going and the dutch ovens were putting out
smells like food. Fatty cautioned us though, that this might be our
last meal for a spell. While we were making the circle around by
Cross Mountain, Vernal, and so on, some scalawag had raided the
chuck wagon and taken just about all the food. That was something
they just didn't do in the early days—or, so you've heard. Anyhow,
they'd done done it. After the big feed, the main thing we had left
was a big old round yellow cheese, all wrapped up in stuff like mos-
quito-bar. It was about all left, as nobody seemed to care much about
big old yellow cheese.

The older fellows talked it over and figured that maybe in the
morning Fatty could get some grub from J. S. Hoy's ranch. It was
about 40 miles over to Bear River where any kind of grub could be
bought. Hoy's was just a couple of miles or so. Tom Morgan figured
we'd make it to a spring in Douglas Draw the next day. The spring
wasn't very big, so it would take the cattle all night for all of them to
get a drink. They'd be fagged out for the next day, so it would take
two more days to make it to Snake River. That was the next water
that amounted to anything.

I stood second guard that night, riding the way a clock goes.
Doc Chivington was the other night-guard, riding the other way.
When we'd meet we'd stop and talk. The cattle were either grazing
or lying quiet, so we didn't need to be too busy. Doc was a tall old
puncher, with a big droopy mustache, and always kind of solemn.

"I don't like the idea of these next three days," he told me.
"What if that spring on Douglas is so low it won't water all the cattle. No steer ain't goin' to go three days without a drink."

I reminded him that Tom had scouted the country and the
spring a week or two before we started and said it was all right.

Doc was in a pessimistic mood.

"Well, maybe," he admitted. "But we could lose some cattle if
it ain't. Besides that, what if old J. S. hasn't got enough grub to let us
have any? Or what if he won't do it? He's an ornery old cuss, and he
don't like the cattle outfits anyhow."

He must have been right, for next morning after we had the steers on the trail for awhile, Fatty Smith caught up with us.

"Old Hoy wouldn't go for no borrowin' or sellin' no grub," Fatty told Tom.

"Said he couldn't haul grub a hundred miles and then let it go and go hungry hisself."

Tom was probably expecting something like that. He told Fatty to take off for Pete Farrell's over on Bear River at the Thornburg Bridge. If Pete had any grub we'd get some of it at least. Pete and Sally Farrell were good folks.

"If you can't get grub at Pete's," Tom told Fatty, "keep on goin'. Fog them old pelters on the rump and make 'em step out. Get back as quick as you can, Frank. We won't die of overeatin' while you're gone."

Food wasn't our only trouble. All the way, until we had hit Green River, we had been in country where there was timber and brush, moist soil, and not bad going. Now we were on the bald flats of Brown's Park. This was the old "Brown's Hole" where the "Mountain Men" trappers used to be. The soil of this whole area is derived from a gray-white calcareous rock and from pumecite, which is nothing more or less than powdered natural glass.

Old Doc opined that it hadn't rained there since Noah's flood. The hundreds of hooves stirred and powdered the soil until like so many ashes, it filled every wrinkle on our faces, and choked eyes, ears, and nostrils. A gentle breeze was blowing—in exactly the same direction we were going, up Vermillion Creek. So, no matter how or where you rode, you were in this stifling maelstrom of dust. To add to our tribulations—and no doubt those of the animals too—thirst soon began to nag us. Thermos bottles, canteens, water bags? If they had even been invented, we had never heard of them.

Before leaving Vermillion Creek and pushing off up Douglas Draw, we had managed to get the cattle all down to the creek for water. We had all taken on all the water we could hold. It was five or six miles to the spring on Douglas Draw. Before we had covered half the distance, the west walls of Lodore Canyon were already dark with the lengthening shadows. It would be nightfall before we reached the spring.

It was—but what matter? It was supper time, but scanty supper—the few scraps and morsels of food we had left, plus all you could (or would) eat of yellow cheese. For with only a few swallows of water before the cattle roiled it, the cheese clung to the roof of your mouth and you could hardly swallow it.

But not even that was the worst. Twenty minutes after the dust-choked herd reached the spring, it had been sucked dry of its last drop. It might have done more, but there was no keeping the cattle out of it long enough for its pools to fill. They waded in, churning the scant water and the mud into a loblolly quite undrinkable.

We guarded them as usual. It wasn't necessary. Tired, choked by dust, bedeviled by thirst, and tortured by the clouds of tiny black gnats that swarmed along the trail and with only sparse tufts of grass for feed, they were milling and churning all night. The gnats subsided when darkness came, but their stings remained. It was bad business. Even Doc, as we met on our rounds, was beyond complaint or dire prophecy. I guess he was afraid to talk of our prospects for fear it would come true.

Next morning we broke our fast—on yellow cheese. We got the herd pointed up the narrow valley of Douglas Draw, and by midmorning were headed down East Boone Draw.

It was about 15 miles to Snake River. There, we knew, would be plenty of water for men and animals. There too, we hoped would be Fatty Smith with the wagon and grub.

The farther we went, the slower we traveled. Lack of water, lack of rest, shortness of feed, the choking dust, and the vicious gnats were getting in their work. Even the loose horses dragged, and our saddle horses were spiritless under us. All we hoped was that the steers would not falter and come to a full halt.

A tiny spring at a mudhole at East Boone served only to accent the thirst. The loose horses bolted ahead, and by the time the herd got there it had been stirred beyond use. We had to use the quirts cruelly to force the cattle away from the moist seep.

Noon came, but the yellow cheese went begging for takers. That drive down East Boone Draw was a nightmare. I'll bet every man relived it in after years. The piteously bawling cattle, the loose horses with drooping heads, the trembling of the mounts under us, are things not easily forgotten.

But of all the things to remember, the heat was uppermost. The heat of that day is worth a chapter in anybody's book.

Many who have been in that country know the heat of a mid-July day in the Colorado high desert. The rare air makes it seem that the sun is perched on your shoulder. In Brown's Park and all the territory where the Brown's Park Formation of rock and soil prevail, there is added glare. it comes from the nearly white soil and rock of the area. The glare of beach sand is as nothing compared with it.

But worse, far worse, than all of this, was a thing of which I had never before heard—the heat generated by the living things around us. Twelve hundred struggling, laboring, sweating animals gave off heat like nothing describable.

As all finite things must finally end, so did our tortured drive across the sweltering expanse. They had thought to take three days for the trip. We were doing it in two, because now we felt that we had won. The herd-point was emerging from the gray-white hills where East Boone Draw converges with Sand Wash. Before long we were clear of the hills and on the flat within a half-mile of Snake River. Then it happened!

The big yellow steer, the one that had all but drowned me and had been a curse from the start, was near the point. He must have caught a whiff of the smell of water. With a bawl I could hear where I rode my post near the middle of the herd, he bolted. In an instant, like a long freight train taking up the slack, steers here and there all along the line must have caught the waterscent. They lunged forward. From a tottering, barely moving mass of spiritless flesh, they were in an instant galvanized into a sea of fast-flowing yellows and reds, the rattle of hooves and the crash of horn against horn mingled with the bawling to drown out all other sounds.

There was no time for plans. There was no time for orders. It was every man ride and ride on his own. And he rode for his life if he was one of the three on point and in the path of the mad stampede. I knew that Doc Chivington and Al Hurd were up there, and with them Tom Morgan, who had not been needed to scout trail since we hit East Boone.

As the steers surged around me and I was swept forward in the mad race, I caught one glimpse of the three, now all on one side of the point, their quirts splitting the air as they tried to turn the thirst-maddened steers. For they knew, as we all knew, that directly ahead lay an abrupt adobe bank of the river, 30 feet of a drop. We had talked of how we should approach the river by swerving the herd to the west to a gently sloping gravel bar that gave easy access to the stream.

There was little I could do. I was on the wrong side of the herd. Besides, no man could stem that tide nor change its course. A feeling of horror arose in me as I realized the three men at the point must be within a few yards of the brink. At that moment—although I could not see it—Tom Morgan raced to his left, waving his arm as signal for the other two men to follow him. The herd swept on by. I saw Antelope ahead of me pull to the right, and once clear of the cattle, stop. I drew away from the herd and joined him. As the stragglers and weak ones caught up with us, we rode toward the river. Well we knew what we would see.

It was worse than we could have imagined. The big yellow steer must have been buried under scores of his fellows. They had gone over the bluff like a torrent of water. It was a heavy loss. It was augmented by a few that mired and drowned, and some that died from the effects of too much water after so long a thirst.

We rounded up on the sagebrush flat beyond the river. Darkness soon settled down on the contentedly grazing cattle and horses, and on us. Fatty Smith had not shown up yet. Antelope and I volunteered to ride to meet him and give him help if needed. We forced down our supper—yellow cheese. But we met Fatty only a couple of miles from camp. You can guess the rest.

But you can't guess for how many years I hated yellow steers and yellow cheese.

★
Never Been Throwed

An aura of romance has been built up about the old time cowhand. I'm not sure the old time waddie saw his job as romantic. Of course he realized he was a different kind of critter from the "town dudes." But that his job was romantic—well, not any of the punchers I knew or rode with gave any hint of it. My brother Vern did a lot of riding and he is of the same opinion. My brother Art rode the range, and it took 40 years for him to find out his job was romantic, and that only long after he had quit the range.

The average cowpuncher's life was one of privation, poor compensation, and frustration. Billy Higney could tell you that.

Billy Higney's forehead was easily spanned by the one-inch band of his battered old hat that had come with him from his paw's scrawny ranch in Texas. Billy's brow may not have been lofty but his ambitions were. To Billy these ambitions seemed quite reasonable. All he wanted to be was a cowhand exactly like Ed Sizer. Ed was his idea of a top hand. Tall, handsome, wise, amiable, courageous, and never bucked off. That was Ed Sizer.

This morning, shivering in the pale light of the coming day, he had Ed in mind as he struggled to get the saddle on his horse. He had the saddle gripped by the pommel in one hand. With the other he held tightly to the cheek-piece of his bridle. Inside the bridle headstall was the Roman-nosed head of the cowpony Billy was supposed to ride on circle that day.

"Whaoe, y' gol-danged hook-nosed whelp uv hell," Billy pleaded, as the horse kept stepping over just far enough that Higney could not swing the saddle to his back. Already they had a circle tramped in the dust as Billy tried to back the animal into a brush, the mess wagon, or anything to stop its elusive tactics.

"Jawny, hey Jawny," Billy yelled at last. "Why daon't y' give me a hand with this here crowbait. Cain't y' see I'm having trouble?"

Johnny Slates was to be Higney's partner on circle today. Johnny had his horse saddled and, holding it with a tight but not too tight rein, let it sidestep, back, step forward, and circle so as to get the hump out of its back and the bucking notion out of its head. This particular broomtail was going to buck today. He did every day. But Johnny hoped he would hold it until it was later and warmer. A man can't make his best ride when it's cold and the daylight isn't all come yet.

"Well give him a kick in the belly and shove him over against the bed wagon and throw yer hull into the middle of him," Johnny counseled. "Don't back him into the mess wagon or among Thorne's kittles if you wanta stay healthy."

"Gol-dang it Jawny, tain't advice I need, it's he'p," Billy whined in the nasal twang that was a cross between his mother's Yankee and the Texas brogue of his dad. Billy had come up with a cattle drive from New Mexico, had tackled the Two-Bar foreman, Wils Rankin, for a job and been taken on a trial basis. Johnny, not much older than Billy, but already a seasoned cowpuncher, reminded Higney of this, as well as his ambition to emulate the example of Ed Sizer.

"If yew figger to keep Wils from giving y'a little piece of paper with his name on it and the pictur' uv a bank, y' better get that there pony saddled and get in the middle uv him. How long do y' s'pose Ed Sizer takes to saddle his bronc?"

"If this here is the kind of old bench I gotta ride I'd jest as soon Wils *would* fire me," Billy declared, resting for a moment from the sashay with the coffin-headed roan. "Ed Sizer rides somethin' that anyways *looks* like a hawrse and not no gol-danged brawnk like thissun."

"Oh well, I guess I gotta hold yer head and feed y' some pap like a baby so I jest as well get at it," Johnny said resignedly as he took hold of the cheek of the bridle of his horse and swung to the ground, pulling the horse toward him to keep him out of the notion of ripping loose a kick as he stepped down. He tied the bridle reins pretty tightly to the stirrup, pulling the pony's head around so that when released he would be drawn into a circle, instead of taking off on a high run.

"Don't fool yerself, I'm goin' t' saddle him fer y'," he cautioned Billy. "I'm jest goin' to stand on the other side and he won't have no place to go without runnin' over me or you, one. Get that old cactus on 'im!"

Billy did indeed slip the saddle onto his mount, reach under and grab the swinging cinch, jerking it under in the nick of time to miss the forward kick the bronco aimed at it. He tightened the cinch, but before he could secure the latigo he and the horse gyrated in a cloud of dust. Before he got the horse gentled down a little, Billy was winded, one of his ankles was full of prickly pear stickers and he had lost his hat. Johnny grudgingly twisted the horses's ear while Higney got on, urging Billy to hurry as all the other riders were already out of camp and headed for the circle.

Johnny leading in the early dawn, and Billy trailing, they had gone about a half-mile when John's horse came uncorked. He wasn't a hard bucker and Johnny had little difficulty in not only sitting him, but hitting him over the neck with the quirt at every jump, pouring forth a stream of profanity aimed at this cowpony, all cowponies, all cowpunchers, foremen, cattle, and particularly would-be cowboys like Billy Higney.

But Billy heard none of this. He had troubles of his own. At the second jump Johnny's horse headed for Higney's. Not wanting to be mowed down by the pile-driver in a horsehide, Billy unthinkingly dug the spurs into his mount. About the fourth buck jump of John's horse, Billy's joined him. It was a beautiful duet—until the fourth jump of Billy's horse. The rider was doing all that Ed Sizer could have done up to that point. The next he knew the horse stumbled and Billy, feeling the animal going down under him, kicked his feet free and prepared to unload easily. He unloaded, but not easily. The horse regained his feet, went up sunfishing, came down with a side-swipe and Billy joined the birds.

When Johnny finally circled back to Billy, he found the budding top hand gathering up his hat, Bull Durham, RizLa papers, and a few cents in change and cursing the same array of objects that he himself had so recently given the profane treatment.

Billy's horse was just disappearing in the direction of the cavvy, alternately running, stopping to buck a few jumps, and kicking like a ballet dancer as the stirrups, lariat, and saddle-pockets flopped and gyrated.

"Get up behind and we'll run him down some time," Johnny told the groaning Billy.

Billy had no very keen desire to ride double as he knew it would take some skillful hanging on. But he didn't want to walk a half-mile or more in his high-heeled Cubines, so stuck his foot in the stirrup that Johnny kicked free, swung on and gripped John's waist with both arms.

As expected, the pony resented this two-man riding business and started to faunch. Johnny jerked the reins and spurred him and just about had him convinced when he stuck a hind foot in a badger hole.

Nearly thrown from his perch, Billy instinctively gripped the pony with his legs, jabbing both spurs into the bronc's flanks. Billy lasted several jumps, nearly squeezing Johnny in two in the middle while doing it and all but pulling him from the saddle when an extra flip of the pony's rump sent Billy spinning.

Heck Lytton, once the Two-Bar foreman, was known from Bastrop County, Texas to Custer County, Montana and back to Bear River for the variety, power, and rhythm of his profanity. But now he stood to lose his crown as Higney and Johnny combined their voices in praise of all broncos and everything connected in even the most remote way with the livestock industry. This went on as Johnny took off in pursuit of the horse Billy had lost, and Billy hobbled, mad, bruised and perforated by cactus, toward the wagon.

As Billy hobbled along, at the rate of about a mile an hour, he ruminated on the cattle business in general. This morning's harrowing first half-hour was only the start. If and when he got his horse back and when and a big if, he could set the beast long enough to *get* on circle, it would be the same old day's work. Rawhide all day over gulches, ridges, pup holes, and bog holes, eating dust and dirt and listening to the bawling of stupid bulls, stupider cows, and calves without sense enough to keep track of their mothers.

Then branding and more dust, and finally good food, but too tired to know whether it was good beefsteak or badger meat and then tumble into bed on the hard ground and maybe in a downpour of rain and in just a few minutes it seemed pile out and stand two hours nightguard, singing even if you sang like a crow to keep the cattle company. Then back to bed for a few minutes and up and through the whole shootinmatch again. What for? thought Billy gingerly fingering a knot on his noggin where he had bumped a greasewood root.

Just so he could get $30 a month and get to be like Ed Sizer, the only one in these parts who'd never been throwed.

★
Cowboys and Cowpunchers

The person who reads about our kind of cowboys may take issue with us, because our cowboys do not conform to the accepted pattern. They are not like the movie cowboys, they are not like Milt Hinkle's rodeo cowboys, not like Helen Clark's American cowboys, and they are not like Walt Coburn's Montana cowboys. And let us agree here and now that Walt Coburn certainly knew his cowboys. None better. And few could equal him in telling about them. Walt's cowboys rode fine horses and came to love them. They rode fine saddles, often trimmed in silver. In Montana were many big cattle outfits, with extensive ranches and herds of several thousands. They were founded in the 1870s. By the 1880s they were well established. In our country, northwest Colorado, the cattle business was just getting a good start.

Helen Clark wrote of a kind of cowboy I did not know. The painter Charles Russell was much the type. Charlie Russell never had an equal for portrayal of the rough and rugged side of the West, and he was a first-rate drinking man, but as a cowboy he was a fair-rate horse wrangler. Helen's cowboys had "a truly magnificent, hardy physical makeup, the primary attribute of the working cowboy." Sent into the mountains alone to round up cattle missed in the roundup, her cowboy took along horse, pistol, knife, coffee pot, frying pan, bed roll, slicker, and maybe his dog. "Once a man gave his heart to an outfit, he worked for that spread as if it were his own. No movie can over-emphasize the value of the cowboy's loyalty." Clark's cowboy who managed to become a cattleman often did so because "he fell in love with the rancher's daughter and papa helped set the newlyweds up in business." (I'm quoting from Helen Clark's writings.)

"The regard the cowboy had for his employer was matched by the love he had for his own particular mount. Charlie Russell had this regard for the horses he owned and never let them out of his life. They remained his as long as they lived. A cowboy's finest possession besides his horse and maybe his dog was his saddle, a saddle made to order. The waddies' trousers still in popularity on the range today and still known as Levis were worn until they wore out and they rarely knew a scrubbing. He wore chaps of leather or sheepskin, and a neckerchief knotted at his throat to pull up above his nostrils or eyes to keep out the dust or the sleet of winter."

"His belt was hand-tooled and its buckle probably hand-engraved silver. His pistols rode in scabbards attached to his belt. His rifle rested in another scabbard attached to his saddle. He also carried a knife in its scabbard, this at the waist and attached to his belt. Twin saddle-bags hung from his saddle or were built into it." Mentioned are bacon, mutton, and hardtack candy. The cook was supposed to have whisky in the jockey box to administer to sick cowboys.

Now, why all this preamble and quotations from those who have written about cowboys? Certainly not to either dispute the writers' accuracy or to make light or make fun of what they have written. I will venture to say that the pictures they have drawn of cowboys is just the way they saw them. Maybe even the cowboys we see in the movies, with beautiful girls in camp, all gathered around the campfire at night, strumming guitars and singing "Get Along Little Dogie," or "Good Bye Old Paint," actually existed. Let's let it stand that way.

But the cowboys I write about are the ones I knew. I will write of them as I saw, and knew, and worked with them. They won't be like the cowboys described above, because they were not like them. I don't know how it came about that our cowboys were so different, but different they were. I can't change that, so if I write about cowboys, I'll simply have to write about them the way I knew them. They won't be like the cowboys you've seen in movies nor about which you have read in most stories.

Some readers may not like my kind of cowboys. But at least I think you'll find they are different, genuine, down to earth, and honest. I'll picture them the way I saw them, and I'd better, because among my readers will be northwest Colorado cowpunchers and cowgirls such as Roy Templeton, Whitey Hindman, Bill White, Ole

Barber, Ivey Blansit, Edna Haworth, Belle Hodges, Myrtle Van Dorn, and Maude Wilson, as well as my own brothers, all of whom know what our old-time cowboys were.

First off the reel, we'll change the name. Our cowboys were cowpunchers, waddies, hands, or riders. The only time a cowpuncher referred to himself or others as "cowboys" was in derision.

In the Yampa, Snake, and White river valleys in which our sabe of cowpunchers was acquired, the ordinary ranchers seldom made the big time. They had small herds of never more than 100. At first, the giant Two-Bar outfit, owned outright by Ora Haley, dominated the entire scene. The outfit had about 40,000 head of cattle. Other outfits, with a thousand or two were the L7, K Diamond, Pot Hook, Sevens, Keystone, and Two-Circle Bar.

On big roundups each outfit sent a mess wagon, with cook, who drove the four-horse team, and a bed wagon, which carried the bedrolls brought to the roundup on "bed horses," with a "cookee" or assistant who drove the bed wagon team of two horses. With the two wagons went from five to a dozen riders, each with eight or 10 saddle horses, one of which carried the rider's bed and wore a bell. Any rancher was welcome to join the roundup to help with the work and see that his own cattle were "gathered." On lesser roundups the Two-Bar, and sometimes one or two other outfits, sent the wagons and riders, but the others sent only one, two, or three riders. These were called "reps," as they represented their company. Their job was "repping" for their outfit.

The cowpunchers were a mixed breed, varying from the type of Ed Miles to Billy Higney. Most of them could read and write in a way but seldom did either. Most of them had come from the cattle countries of Texas, Oklahoma, and New Mexico. They knew cattle and horses and not much else. If they married it was usually a rancher's daughter. Her dowry was most likely to be a lot of spare bedding and cooking kettles from the family's meager supply.

Of all the cowpunchers I knew, only a couple were a little "good-lookin." The rest were an assortment of gangling beanpoles, awkward beefy fellows, and shorty-sawed-off-and-hammered-down chaps.

I never knew of a lone rider to be sent into the mountains or anywhere else to round up strays for more than one day. He would have preferred starving to carrying along food and a lot of cooking paraphernalia but would do it in a pinch. I never knew of a working cowpuncher to carry a rifle, a knife, or have a dog. Settlers tied their

20 ★ The Arbuckle Cafe

dogs when cattle were passing, for fear they'd stampede the herd
and end up dead with some cowpuncher's bullet in them.

Everybody wanted to work for the Two-Bar for two reasons:
you had to be good to work for the Two-Bar which meant prestige,
and Ora Haley kept his good men the year around. Other outfits
were likely to lay men off in winter. As far as love or loyalty for the
outfit, I never heard of it. The men knew that if they were crippled
or killed it was no skin off Haley's shin. He might pay the doctor bill
and the fellow's board for awhile but that was it. Loyalty was no
great thing for a fellow who might have to go through life with a
short leg, a crooked spine, or a wopper jaw. And all for $30 a month.

It was a fact that the regard a waddie had for the owner was
about the same as his regard for most of the horses he rode. He
loathed, hated, and despised them. They'd kill him if they could.

The cowpuncher, like Billy Higney, went through that routine day in and day out. Each day he rode the grass-fat and soft pony
to a standstill, turned him out to recuperate and graze with the
cavvy until his turn came again in a few days. Each time the pony
knew what was coming and did his best to avoid it.

Once in awhile maybe one horse out of 50 might show some
horse sense and be developed into a good rope horse or a good cutting horse. The rider might actually like such a horse.

There were good horses in the country, but the ranchers
owned most of them, not the cow outfits. Most cowpunchers owned
a horse or two, but most of them were gentle old things, too fat and
dead on their feet to be of much use on circle or working a herd. So
what they rode was the string given them by the company. They'd
vary in size from 750 pounds to 1,150 and were every color of the
rainbow—excepting pintos. Indians and Mexicans rode "paint" horses but not any self-respecting cowpuncher. Likewise, no cowpuncher rode a mare and neither did they ride a horse with a long tail.

There were made-to-order saddles, but not many. Usually, a
rider went to a saddle shop and bought a saddle that fitted him. A
small man could do with a 14-inch tree and a big man might take
even a 17-inch. Fancy tooling and silver mounting cost money and
no waddie at $30 a month had money. What money he had went
either to the saloons, poker games, and floozies, or into a jackpot to
buy a team, cow, wagon, plow, some fence wire, and cooking-and-
eating tools so he could take a homestead.

I never heard of "Levis" until I was about 40. They were
"overalls" and the denim jacket was a "jumper." They were washed

if they got filthy, and each washing faded them more until they were a sort of bluish white. I never saw a pair of sheepskin chaps, although angora goat chaps were bought by punchers who got staky, through good luck in a poker game, or otherwise. The bandanna around the rider's neck was to keep the gnats from crawling inside his collar, mostly. If he wore a belt at all it was a simple leather cartridge belt with one six-shooter.

A knife attached to his belt would have been an invitation to disembowelment if his pony stepped in a pup hole and rolled him. Saddle bags, or saddle pockets as they were called, were mostly for ranchers, coyote trappers, and soldiers. Bacon was seldom seen around a cattle outfit, milk not at all, excepting at headquarters ranch, mutton never. Even when cowpunchers killed hundreds of sheep in the sheep-and-cattle wars they didn't eat any of them. Candy? I never was in a camp when the wagonboss passed it out.

So, as you read of the cowpunchers and cattle people I knew, you will be forewarned that they were quite unlike the movie cowboy, the Montana rancher-cowboy, or the ideal and romantic cowboy who has become a legend. Our cowpunchers were just a hodgepodge lot of guys from far and near who knew cattle, horses, and what was necessary to hold a job at starvation wages under foremen who knew how to get the last lick of work out of them under the most trying conditions. If they were indeed romantic, they didn't find it out until they were old broken-down men and it was then too late.

I think that most of you are reading this book for the pleasure of seeing what kind of people, and what kind of life, existed in those early times in the 1880's and after up to about 1900. That is the real reason I'm writing it. I could soup it up, draw on imagination, and make real thrillers and heroes and villains out of some of those people and events. But my choice and my chore is to just give the facts.

Cowboys

If a sailor wants to ridicule the bosun, he calls him the "boat swain," which is the way it is properly spelled. If a rider of the range wanted to ridicule himself, or another rider, he called him a "cowboy." Otherwise, he was a rider, a cowpuncher, a waddie or, in the southwest, a vaquero, which means a herder of animals.

In the same vein, all saddle horses he used were "ponies," the throw rope he used to catch animals, called "la riata" by the

Mexicans, was a lariat, a rope, twine, hard twist, snare, or catchin' string.

His saddle was a cactus, or a hull, or maybe a Fred Mueller, the name of the maker, or Ross, Wagner, Hartke & Sheets. If he was lucky his hat was a Stetson and his boots Cubines.

Beefsteak was buffalo chips, coffee Arbuckles, and the water gravy often seen had a name not admissible in any decent society, although eight-year-old Chick McKnight asked for it by that name in the high-class Baker house in Craig.

Cowpunchers

When fellers took to punchin' cows
Instead of herdin' sheep,
The first thing that they learned was how
To do without much sleep.

They crawled in bed as soon 'twas dark
But sometime in the night,
Crawled out again to stand night guard
Two hours, 'twas no delight.

Later they got a few more winks
But rolled out long 'fore dawn,
Had beefsteak, gravy, spuds—such stuff
Is what they're livin' on.

The nighthawk brought the cavvy in
With ropes they made a corral,
No posts, just men to hold the ropes
They done it just as well.

An' so most of the summer went
All work, no fun, no playin',
But sometimes to the ranch they're sent
To help with the damn hayin'.

A puncher hated all ranch work
But sometimes he might plow,
But waddies balked at just one thing
They wouldn't milk no cow.

Squat on a stool, start jerkin' teats
The bucket careful place,
The cow's long tail drags in manure
Then switches in your face.

No sir! No man with self respect
At milkin' aims to shine,
Instead, his wages he'll collect
And hit the old chuck line.

Somewhere he knows there's got to be
A safe place for his ilk,
Where all them cattle will be steers
Without no cows to milk.

There were plenty of things the cowpunchers wouldn't do, but there were a great many more things they would, and did do. For $30 a month and their food, they worked the longest hours, under the worst conditions, at the most dangerous tasks, in the most unattractive surroundings of any working men I ever knew or saw on the five continents and seven seas. As the rhyme points out, they were up long before dawn, be it summer or winter, fair or foul, bolted their food, then caught the horse they were to ride that day.

Picture a hundred or more horses, held in a compact bunch by the corral formed by men holding ropes stretched between them and milling in the half-light of predawn. Out of the hundred, your "string" numbers probably eight horses. Some of these eight you may have never seen until a week before. Yet, you are supposed to be able to recognize the horses of your string, maneuver to get a moment's chance at one to put a noose on its neck and drag it from the cavvy. Try it sometime.

The puncher saddled the unwilling pony—all riding horses were "ponies," and that was usually a chore. The animal was cold and ticklish and had no taste for the job of packing a man all over 20 miles of hills and gullies and big sagebrush and pup holes. He knew, just as well as his rider, that any second he might get snakebit, harpooned by a prickly pear or a snag, or might have to make a race to head off some wild and stupid steer and maybe stick his leg in a badger hole up to the shoulder and break a leg or twist his neck in the ensuing tumble. Not to mention the sweat and dust and stink of cattle.

It always ended up by the pony submitting to the saddle, even if it took some kicks, quirting, or ear twisting to accomplish it. No wonder the horse made a vow (and carried it out) to come uncorked sometime during the day at the opportune moment when he had the rider foul. The least he hoped for was to jar the rider clear back to his grandmother's pickled green tomato preserves; the best to leave him with a broken leg dragging his way alone over the hot sands toward the camp 10 miles away. It all could and did happen.

There was no bonus, no pension, no workman's compensation or unemployment payments. If you got a promotion, it came as the result of your proving you could ride anything that wore hair, and then you got a raise of $5 or $10 a month and the privilege of riding the "rough string," the meanest and most murderous nags that none of the other hands could or would straddle.

That, and a string a mile long of other evils that went to make up the life of a cowboy was the lot of the oldtime cowpuncher. And they loved it! I guess.

The "beef roundup" occurred any time from late summer to early fall. Sometimes it occurred late in the fall, even to mid-November. But, whenever it came, it meant a big time for somebody. After the cattle were rounded up and sorted over to separate out the fattest steers, the resulting herd was trailed to the railroad. This might be Rawlins or Laramie, Wyoming, less frequently Rifle, Colorado, and still less often, Wolcott, Colorado. This of course is before the Moffat Railroad was built into the country.

No matter where the herd was trailed, after the cattle were on the train, the men spruced up in their good clothes, got bathed and shaved and hit the row of saloons and sporting houses on the far side of the railroad tracks. Of course there were saloons on the near side of the tracks, in the business district. But they were more toney, permitted but little ribaldry, and closed early. Across the tracks they ran as long as anybody was there to buy. The girls from the nearby or adjoining red light houses circulated freely in the saloons, accepting free drinks from the saloon's customers and drumming up business for their own establishments.

It was a lucky cowpuncher who survived the ensuing 24 hours and came out broke but with his head intact. The unlucky ones emerged from this gala not only broke but with their heads damaged as well, as it took a good diplomat to avoid fist fights and other forms of mayhem. The unluckiest punchers were also in debt to the company for a month's or more advance wages. The wine was potent, the women were shrewd and heartless, and the songs ribald and monotonous. In one saloon in Rawlins an old-fashioned gramophone played a single record for 28 hours with stops only to set the needle back to the start. The song ran:

It's mighty strange, yes, mighty strange
No one ever says "Sylvester just keep the change."
I try to do as folks tell me to, but
They get absent minded when my day's work is through.

Try as I may, from dawn and all day
Never do a tip I see coming my way.
It's time I blew, to some place that's new
All I get here is "Much obliged to you."

Cattle trailed to Rawlins or Laramie were loaded directly on the trains and the cowboys were free. If loaded at Rifle or Wolcott, or later when shipped from this area to Denver, a certain number of lucky riders were assigned to accompany the cattle. Two men to each car of cattle was the rule. They were carried free of charge, but their "luxurious Pullman" was the caboose of the freight train. It was called the "Crummy," and well named, because, since sometimes hoboes also were allowed to ride in it, it was often infected with a batch of lice or "crumbs" as they were called. Hence the name "Crummy."

The men in the crummy actually earned their ride. Each time the train stopped, they swarmed out of the crummy, each man carrying a prod pole of some kind. Some were broomsticks, pitchfork handles, or similar wooden rods. With these they reached through the slats of the cattle cars and prodded any animals that were not on their feet. Stops were frequent, and it was well they were, for a lazy or weak animal could be trampled by its fellows and dead animals had no value on the market. These men were soon referred to by the train men as "those cow punchers in the crummy."

One November, with a shipment of cattle on the Moffat Railroad, the crew turned out at Corona in 40-below weather to do their "cow punching." When we came back inside the crummy, there was a Negro boy, about 16, who had slipped in from the tender or "coal car" where he had been bumming his way. If he hadn't been black he would have been blue with the cold. How he had endured the cold that far I'll never understand. He had only overalls and jumper and a ragged old coat six sizes too big for him. The knees of his overalls were worn through to big holes.

"What you got them holes in yer pants fer, boy?" one of the cowpunchers joshed him. "Don't they let the cold in?"

"Yassuh boss, Yassuh," the shivering lad answered good naturedly. "Dem holes sho' does let the cold in. But dey let it out too and let de warm in now," as he hugged the pot-bellied stove.

When he had stopped shivering he started out to climb back on the top of the train and make his way back to the tender behind the engine, but the men wouldn't let him go. He was kept in the crummy until we got to Denver, when he was taken up to the hotel along with the crew, persuaded to take a bath, given some warmer and better clothes, and sent on his way grinning happily.

"In days of old when men were bold," as old cowpuncher Andy Stephens might say, men were divided into various classes. The bottom layer of the cake was made up of serfs and the top of knights. Of these there were various degrees of chivalry. Well, the cowpunching world did not have quite such sharp lines of difference between classes, but they were there, just the same.

Among cowpunchers in our county, the least was the rancher who attended the roundups, riding his own self-broken horses, and shoving most of the skilled work off onto the top cowhands. Next above him came the old cowboys who may have been top hands in their day but whom hard rides, wet beds, and wetter sprees had stove up to where they rode only the gentler ponies.

Young ranchers and others aspiring to be real cowhands came next, being tolerated if mediocre, but encouraged if they showed signs of becoming good hands—provided they were not smart alecs and too lippy.

Above those riders were the all-around hands who could make a hand at anything pertaining to cattle and horses, would tackle anything thrown into their strings even if they couldn't ride them all, and willing to do anything the professional cowhand did.

Next above them came the "elite" of the fraternity. These men were like the class next below them, with the exception that they could ride almost anything that wore hair. They were at the top of the pile.

In a different category entirely were two other classes of riders. One was the bronco snapper. He might not be the best all-around cowhand, and he might fall short in several ways. But one thing he did and did well was to ride the meanest horses in the cavvy. Offtimes, when no roundup was in progress, he devoted most of his time to breaking broncs. In roundup time if he joined in the work his was the "rough string" into which was thrown all the horses that the top hands couldn't or wouldn't ride.

Bronco twisters were usually good men and fitted in well on ranch or range. But a lot of them were ornery cusses, disagreeable, lazy, and sometimes plain unsociable. Most of these bronco twisters naturally took part in the "bucking matches" that later became "rodeos." Those days they "rode them to a finish." The beating the riders took must have affected their minds, as a good many of these rider's lives were ended by their own hands.

The other special group might be found in any class above the aspiring young riders. These were the men who had made a study of cattle and horses and related subjects. They had good business sense, got along well with men and could get the last lick out of the men if put in as strawboss, which they usually were. From this class, too, came foremen and eventually a good many cattlemen. Some of them with political leanings became stock detectives, sheriffs, U. S. Marshals, and even governors and senators. A few even became merchants and bankers and more than one became a preacher. Such preachers could portray the evils of such sins as profanity, adultery, gambling, inebriety, and gluttony from first hand knowledge.

★
Hired Killers and Winter Underwear

Billy Sawtelle's reputation outran him and got here before he did. So when he showed up in this area it was already the talk that he had notches on his gun like sawteeth and that he'd been sent for to wipe out some cattle thieves.

When Sawtelle first stopped at our place we all wondered about the reports that had preceded him. He was a quiet and amiable fellow and seemed far from our idea of a hired killer. He was handsome, too. Medium size and build, black hair and mustache, and eyes that seemed to snap fire. They were the only thing about him to indicate that he might be a cool and deadly customer.

He didn't kill anybody right off the bat. In fact he just took a job like any other cowpuncher. He got along well with other men, and women reacted to him as they would to any youngish, handsome, agreeable male. As months passed and Sawtelle gave no indication of being what rumor had said he was, the whole thing was mostly forgotten. The alleged "hired killer" appeared no different from other range men. He could make a hand and did, he liked to play poker and did. And that was what led to the killing.

Strangely enough, the fellow who got killed wasn't a cattle rustler. He wasn't even a rancher, but a Mexican rider who had been working on some ranch up the river. He didn't get killed for stealing cattle, but for being suspected of stealing a king from the discards. Sawtelle accused him of it. He went for a gun. But before he could press the trigger, Sawtelle had his gun out, fired, and the other fellow was dead.

He didn't even emit a yell before he died. But an innocent bystander did. Billy McCune, standing back of the Mexican, got the slug after it passed through the Mexican. It nipped McCune in an arm, cracking a bone.

I don't think Billy Sawtelle ever killed anybody else around here. But I do think his presence and reputation kept the fear of guilt in a lot of fellows who had been stealing calves from the Two-Bar and other outfits.

One fellow who was said to be marked for slaughter by Sawtelle was Jeff Dunbar, a big man who spent most of his time on Snake River. Dunbar had a ranch, a few cattle, and a penchant for whisky and poker. One night in the Ledford & Kittel saloon, Jeff was having a drink and some talk at the bar. Billy Sawtelle came in. He asked for a beer and was drinking it, standing close to Dunbar.

Presently the big rancher set down his glass and turned to Sawtelle.

"You Billy Sawtelle?" He inquired.

"Yes, I am," Billy answered.

"I'm Jeff Dunbar. You know me. I'm one of the fellers on your list, I hear. You're supposed to dry gulch me."

"I never saw you before," Sawtelle said evenly. "Why should I kill you?"

"Because I'm supposed to have stole some critters from the people that hire you," Jeff said without raising his voice. "Maybe I have stole some calves and maybe I ain't. But if like I hear tell I'm on your list, why don't you get to earnin' yer money?"

"I've got no quarrel with you," said Sawtelle, fingering his beer glass and keeping both hands above the bar.

"'Tain't a question of no quarrel," Dunbar pursued. "Men kill each other in quarrels, they got an excuse. But killin' men fer money is different. That's why I say you don't need to wait to catch me in no dry gulch. I'm right here, you're here. We both got guns and know what they're fer. So if yer out to kill me, get to doin' it."

Sawtelle finished his beer, very slowly reached into his vest pocket and took out a couple of folded bills, laid one on the bar, waited for his change, picked it up and dropped it in the same pocket. Turned and without hurrying, walked from the saloon.

Everybody there knew that if Sawtelle had made the fatal mistake of going to his trousers pocket for money, Dunbar would have killed him on the spot.

Which was the nerviest man? The subject was good for an argument for many a month afterward.

In course of time, Billy Sawtelle moved on to other ranges. Whether he was the hired killer he was reputed to be, or whether he had the notches on his gun it was said he had, was never known here for sure. My best guess is that he had killed a man or more, had a reputation, and was hired by the cattle people more as a threat than for actual killing.

Some figured that he had "shown the white feather," when he failed to take up Dunbar's dare and that he was a coward. I don't think he was a coward, nor a fool. If by some freak of luck he'd killed Dunbar, the chances are he'd never have left the saloon alive. If Dunbar was a rustler, he wasn't the only rustler in that barroom.

Actually, Jeff Dunbar was mostly a gambler and saloon frequenter. But as well as having a lot of raw courage, he had a heart. My brother Art tells of an incident that proves this.

A lad named Dean had a job at the big livery barn in Craig, Colorado, that stood about where Dr. Booren's office is now. On the corner was the Ledford & Kittel saloon.

Young Dean had the job of caring for the barn stalls and the livestock on a shift that ended about nine in the evening. He was a cheerful sort of chap and went about his work happy and whistling. In fact, he whistled so ceaselessly that he was dubbed "Whistling Dean."

Dean had another habit. This habit added nothing to his happiness and kept him broke. He loved to play poker. They wouldn't let him play and lose his money in the regular games. But there was one fellow who was glad to help out. "Poker Sam" was an older man. He also loved to play poker. Not, like Dean, to improve his game, but to improve his bankroll.

Poker Sam and Dean engaged in a friendly poker game in the office of the livery barn every time Dean got his paycheck. As a result, Dean was always strapped. So much so that he wore the shabbiest and raggediest clothes of any young fellow around. This in spite of good advice given him by older men.

Came late fall and one evening Jeff Dunbar, coming in from a trip and taking his horse to the livery stable to be cared for, noticed Dean shivering as he went about caring for Jeff's horse.

"You better be gettin' you some warm duds, boy," Jeff told him.

"Yeah, I been thinkin' 'bout it," the boy replied.

Jeff didn't say any more but went on over to the saloon to see if he could rustle up a poker game himself. No game was going so he stood at the bar, chinning with John Ledford, the owner, who was on shift bartending.

"John, I noticed that there Whistling Dean kid ain't got no proper clothes fer cold weather."

"I guess not," John agreed. "He ain't likely to have. He stuffs off what money he gets playin' draw with Poker Sam."

"Oh, so that's it?" Jeff ruminated. He didn't say anything more about it until the next day. Then he told Ledford, "John, I want you to let that kid play a little poker. In the back room after reg'lar hours. C'n we do it?"

"I don't get the drift," John told him.

"Well, that kid needs clothes. First he needs money. Poker Sam has been takin' all the kid made. So we get them and me and you in a game. Get it?"

John "got it" all right. He knew Jeff pretty well.

So, the next night, Jeff, at the barn just before Dean came off shift, told him, "Kid, you like to play poker, don't you?" The lad said he did. "Well, let's get in a real poker game. At Ledford's."

"They won't let me play in those games," Dean said truthfully.

"I been talkin' to John," Jeff explained. "He says it will be all right if we have a little game after closin' time. Jest me and you and maybe Sam and Ledford. You play pretty good, don't you?"

"I play good," the boy said eagerly. "If Sam wasn't so lucky I could win most of the time. I do win pretty often."

"Okay, I'll see you after closin' time."

Jeff was a pro. He not only knew how to size up the other players, how to judge a hand, and how to play it, but he knew a lot of things that Hoyle, an honest man, didn't put in his rule book. So as the game got in progress, Whistling Dean began to get good hands. It wasn't long before the self-satisfied smirk vanished from Poker Sam's face. He used every trick he knew and still the boy won. Jeff wasn't doing much better.

Every time Sam or Jeff went broke they bought more chips. All the time, the stack of chips in front of Dean grew higher. Sam just knew that his luck had to turn. But at the strike of 12 John declared the game ended.

Sam raised a holler and the kid didn't want to quit. But John and Jeff wouldn't deal any more cards and John insisted on closing.

So the game broke up.

"I just don't have the money to cash your chips," John told Dean. "I went out and paid some bills tonight and didn't expect to have to pay off so much on a poker game."

Sam insisted that John ought to pay off but John had the better of the argument. He didn't have the money. He told them though that he would pay off first thing when he opened next day.

Whistling Dean was waiting at the door when John opened. Jeff Dunbar was right behind him.

"I don't have the cash," John told them. "But I'll give you a check and you can go across the street to the Bank of Hugus."

"I'll go with you," Jeff volunteered. "Bankers are kind of funny and you might need a witness."

At the bank, when Dean got his money, it was $125, a fortune in those times and that place. The bank was in the Hugus & Co. General Store.

"Let me go ahead and talk to the bank feller," Jeff advised. In a moment he signaled for Dean to come to the wicket. Before the cashier handed over the money, Jeff told the boy he ought to get some better clothes while he was flush.

"Yeah, I been thinkin' about it," the boy said. "I'll see about it some time when I'm off work."

"No time like now," Jeff told him. "It's cold and you'll be freezin'. Right now while you're right in the store, get you some clothes. I doubt if the bank will cash your check if you don't do a little tradin'. You ain't no depositor in the bank are you?"

Dean said he wasn't.

"All right. First thing you need is shoes."

That was the start. Jeff was the kind of person it was hard to dispute. He was big and solid-voiced and paid no attention to the boy's protests that all he needed was a warm coat.

By the time the shopping spree was over, Dean was fitted out from head to toe with a good cap, shirts, underwear, socks, shoes, overshoes, gloves, and anything else he might need.

After he had paid the $79.85 bill, he asked the clerk, "If some of this stuff don't fit or I change my mind I can bring it back, can't I?"

"Oh, sure," the clerk told him. "Anything that don't fit, you can bring back and swap it for something that does fit. But you can't swap it for money."

That was what Jeff wanted to hear. Poker Sam was foiled.

★
Out on Strike

The great union organizers Walter Reuther, George Meany, and Jimmy Hoffa hadn't been born when labor troubles broke out in Moffat County and the region's first "strike" occurred.

It was early November and for several days rain, sleet, and snow had been falling. The Two-Bar outfit, with 2,500 head of fat dogies, was camped on lower Elkhead Creek, waiting for a break in the weather so they could proceed up through California Park, across Slater Park, down Slater Creek to Snake River and so on through to Rawlins, Wyoming, where the cattle would be shipped.

Heck Lytton, the dynamic, irascible, and profane Two-Bar foreman was in charge. Among the cowpunchers on the drive were Bill Flannagan and George Long, top cattlemen themselves and both later to be foremen in their own right.

Heck didn't like the delay. He was for going ahead, storm or no storm, but with such high-power men as Long and Flannagan counseling delay, he couldn't move.

But finally he could stand the pressure no longer, and going out to where the herd was being held, he told the men he intended to take the trail next morning.

Next morning, with sleet and snow coming down in sheets, along about daybreak, the last night guard was holding the herd. The other men would be showing up before long. Heck showed up and gave orders to head the herd up Elkhead Creek. The men objected.

"All, right," Heck told them. "If I've got a crew here that can't take a little weather, I'll get a crew that can."

The men took him at his word. To a man they headed for Craig. Cursing a blue streak, Heck arranged to put the herd in a rancher's pasture for a day or two, where no herding would be needed.

The "cooling off" period of the Taft-Hartley law didn't come along for a generation after that, but Heck knew all about a "cooling off" period. He gave the men a day and night in town, enough, he no doubt thought, to let them all have time to get drunk if they wanted to and spend all their money. Then he appeared at the saloon in Craig where most of the waddies were gathered in the warm and dry. He was quite pleasant.

"Well, them cattle have just about cleaned out all the grass in that pasture, so we might as well get going," he told the men. "I guess you fellers have had your good time. We can finish up the party in Rawlins. Plenty of saloons there."

The men must have talked it over beforehand, for they had a ready answer.

"We ain't in no humor to get out in no blizzard," the spokesmen for the "striking union," told Heck. "We aim to sit right here 'till the weather breaks. Old Man Haley ain't goin' to lose no money on them there steers even if they are a week late gettin' to Rawlins."

There was some discussion, the temperature rising with each interchange. Finally the punchers told Lytton, "We're staying here, Heck. If you want them Two-Bar ponies we rode in, they're in the livery stable. Just go get 'em."

Heck was stopped but not beaten. With his slicker pulled up around his ears, he sloshed his pony through the mud to hunt up every boy he could find between the ages of about 14 and 18. Among the number was Harry Hindman, Bob (Pea) Green, Jim Robinson, Dave Davis, and several others.

In those days it was the dream of almost every young fellow to be a cowpuncher. They hoped that if they could learn to ride and rope, get jobs with small outfits and acquire a "rep" as riders, they might some day, in the dim future, attain the distinction of being a rider for the Two-Bar.

So, to be plucked, as it were, from the bosoms of their families, and catapulted into a job with the Two-Bar without the preliminary years of apprenticeship with lesser outfits, nearly left them all in shock.

All of them managed to rustle a slicker but otherwise they were poorly clothed for the time of year and the weather. Whereas the mature cowpunchers had heavy woolen underwear and socks, heavy coats and gloves and skull caps, the young chaps had only such sketchy winter clothes as their parents could afford.

But though the boys' knees might be knocking together from the cold, opportunity also was knocking, and the hardy lads were not going to let cold, sleet, or hard work keep them from grasping this golden chance to be "Two-Bar cowpunchers." So they buckled in, listened to every word of instructions Heck gave them, and in due course the herd was delivered to Rawlins and loaded on the cars for the trip to market.

The boys were not so young or green but they had heard of the high old times cowpunchers had after loading a shipment of cattle. So, true to tradition, and under the watchful eye of Heck Lytton, they made the rounds of the saloons—some of them even landing in jail for a night to sleep off the effects of gazing too often on the wine.

Back in Craig, Heck paid them off whatever they had coming above what they had drawn in Rawlins. By that time the weather was fine again and the old adult crew had had their vacation and was ready to go back to work. So Heck took them on, as he was too shrewd to let a little disagreement stand in the way of business.

But although he did not keep the boys on the payroll, he did keep them in mind, and whenever opportunity offered, and the boys developed into good hands on other outfits, he gave them jobs. Some of the boys turned out to be among the top hands in later years. Heck also asked his successor as foreman, Hi Bernard, to keep the boys in mind when hiring. With all his faults, Heck had a lot of good spots in his makeup.

Of course many adventures had befallen the young fellows during that memorable cattle drive. Typical was a mishap that befell young Dave Davis.

Dave's father, also Dave, had a prejudice against big cattle outfits and forbade young Dave to work for any of them. But when the chance came and the other boys were rushing to accept Heck's offer of employment, Dave ran away from home and "joined up." Later his dad forgave him.

But on the drive, one pitch-dark night Dave and Billy McDonald were on the second night guard, eight to 10. Rain and sleet were coming down in torrents and the ground was a mire. In making his round around the herd, Billy came to the point where he should have met Dave, circling in the opposite direction.

No sign of Dave.

Halted and listening, Billy heard a sort of wheezing, coughing sound. Urging his horse toward the unusual sound, he raised his voice to find the cause.

"Hey! What's going on?" he shouted.

"Here. Get me out of this!" came the reply.

Dismounting, Billy approached the sound, to find Dave lying in the sagebrush emitting grunts and wheezes.

"What are you doin' there, Dave? Are you hurt or somethin'?" he asked.

"I think my back is broken," Dave groaned.

Billy knelt beside the injured lad, inquiring why he thought his back was broken and how it happened.

"Because I can't move. I can't get up. My leg seems to be paralyzed. My pony stepped in a badger hole and fell with me."

"Do you have much pain?" Billy asked solicitously.

"No, but I can't straighten out my leg and I feel numb all over," Dave gritted.

"Gosh, we got to get you out of here and get you home," the bewildered Billy sputtered.

"I don't think I'll ever get home," Dave whined, "But I'll bet if I do, they'll never get me on no roundup again."

All this time, Billy had been running his hands over Dave's body, trying to find out what was broken and if he could be of any help.

"I don't think you got no broken back," he finally told Dave. "You got one foot tangled in the front of your slicker. Wait 'til I get the slicker unbuttoned and see if you can straighten out your leg."

It took a struggle for him to unfasten the slicker. Dave's knee was against his chin and Billy had to force the leg still farther upward and unbutton the slicker. When he did so, Dave straightened out his leg, twisted his body to see if he had any feeling in it, and presently sat up, realized he was alright, grinned sheepishly, then stood up and clambered onto the patient pony which had been standing by.

As a sort of afterthought, this strike reminds me of a "strike" in which I took part a few years after this one.

Irvin Green owned the fine Yampa River bottom ranch just beyond the county line past Elkhead. He had lots of alfalfa, timothy, and redtop hay, and a crew to put it up.

Otto Schraeder, Bill White, Bill Covey, Charley Taylor, Black Bill Johnson, and an older man called White and I made the hay crew, with Irvin himself and his father, R. H. (Whispering) Green.

The first morning before we went to work, Irvin told us, "I might as well tell you fellers I'm one hell of a hay hand. I reckon you are pretty good men, too. But I don't figure you can keep up with me. But I sure expect you to try."

He wasn't boasting. He was a hay hand and no mistake. In fact he was quite a man all around.

We didn't disappoint him. We had all been toughened up by ranch work before haying. Irvin had good horses. So, instead of letting the horses take a brisk walk from the stack to the field with empty slips, we trotted them. A "slip," I might mention, was a flat wooden affair like a big barn door. The horses dragged it. On it was placed a contraption of wooden bars and rope, called a sling. Hay was piled on the sling by using pitchforks to pick up the bunches or "shocks" of hay. At the hay stack, a Mormon stacker was used. This was a tall derrick. A rope-and-pulley arrangement lowered a big iron hook. This was lopped into rings on the slings and the hay-loaded sling swung over the haystack and dumped. A man on the stack spread it and so "built" a stack.

Most of us were young, full of fire, and liked to work. We made a sort of game of this. Before the team could come to a stop in the field we were off the slip and forking on the hay. There were three slips working and we raced to keep our turn at the stack.

Irvin was happy to sic us on. He was getting more hay put in the stack in a day than any hay crew on the river.

And he was a good boss. Come Sunday, and no matter what, the crew knocked off and went to town to the ball game. Irvin did some pitching and his speed ball was hard to hit.

After the game, in town, we got to talking to other hay crews. We found that our crew was averaging nearly double what any other crew was averaging per man in tons of hay put in the stack.

We talked this over in the bunkhouse. So, one evening we tackled Irvin for a raise. He laughed.

"Why, you're gettin' same as all other crews," he said truthfully. "You get better grub than most. We knock off for Sunday. What d'you mean more money?"

We agreed with him on all points. His wife was a McDonald girl and all the McDonald girls were super cooks. We did knock off for Sunday. But, we were rolling in about twice as much hay as any crew. We thought we ought to have $2 a day instead of the standard $1.50.

"No, can't do it boys," Irvin told us. "Do that and next thing I know you'll be wantin' $2.50. So no go."

"Well, all right Irvin. No hard feelings," we told him. "We'll just mosey on down the road and you can get another crew."

He hit the ceiling. But we stood firm and finally he agreed. And we responded by putting even more hay in the stack each day.

And when in September there came an early snow that laid low the fine stand of oats he had, we pitched right in, without a murmur, and after Whispering Green had shown us how, hand-tied the straw after the oats were cut with a mowing machine. And Irvin gave each of us an extra five-spot when he paid off at the end of the season. I continued to work for him for quite awhile.

That's all about strikes.

✬
This is your Church

Mr. Kohler was one to remember. A tall, gaunt, eccentric German, he lived in a small log house in Craig. He was a talented musician and taught all kinds of instruments. I was one of his violin students. He was exacting and severe. Your lessons had to be mastered or he raised the roof.

One Sunday when I went for my lesson, two girls 14 years of age came to their lesson late. Kohler always spoke in a peculiar manner. In his toothless jaws he always had a long-stemmed pipe. A wad of string bound around the end of the stem kept the pipe from falling from his mouth when he spoke. It also gave a peculiar sound to his speech, which frequently included profanity. "Christ Almighty" was an expletive he used when excited. "Why, why?" usually preceded a sentence.

"Why you come late?" he barked at the two girls.

"We had to go to church," the girls told him, timidly.

"Church! Church! Why for you go to church?"

The girls stammered, confused.

"Why, to learn about heaven and Christ and God Almighty," they finally managed.

"Why, why, so you learn about Christ and God Almighty," he said quietly. And then in a voice that shook the rafters, he howled at the girls, "Church, Christ, God Almighty. This is your church, the violin is your Christ, and I am your God Almighty!"

In two steps he reached the cringing girls. Seizing them by the scruffs of their necks, he banged their heads together and escorted them to the door, warning them to never be late for a lesson again.

In 15 minutes the door flew open and the mothers of the girls stormed in. Almost before they could say a dozen words, Kohler drowned them out.

"Shut up!" he bellowed, nearly losing his pipe. "Don't say a word. I am the master teacher. Nobody teaches like I do. I give your children something nobody can steal from them. They have it all their lives. I do not charge too much. So you go home. See that your girls are here on time. Shut up!" as one of the women tried to interrupt. "Why, why, get out or Christ Almighty I will bang your heads together too."

They "got" and Kohler turned calmly to me.

"We will now proceed," he said mildly.

Years after studying under Kohler, I took instruction from several violin teachers, some of them eminent. But none of them equaled Kohler for thoroughness and results. Eccentric he was but musician too. So eccentric that he once returned a box of matches for refund.

"What's the matter with them, Mr. Kohler?" asked Pete Howard, one of the store owners.

"Why, why, they are a fraud," Kohler averred. "They say on the box five hundred matches, full count. I count them and there is only 493."

Crazy, you say? Yes, no doubt. Crazy enough that he carried wood on his back from the cottonwoods on the river south of town. Also, because he had two cats, a small one and a large one, he cut two holes in the lower part of his front door. "One for the big cat and one for the small cat," he explained.

One night on the stage of the theater that stood where the Craig Drug Store is now, he played a violincello solo. During the piece the instrument emitted a sudden loud cracking sound, probably caused by cold air from the opening of a door. The music stopped abruptly. Kohler arose and kicked the cello across the stage.

As he stalked off the stage he grunted, "Crack when I am playing solo, will you? I crack you!"

The Foreman, the Waddie, and the Cook

Dressed in cutaway coat, Homburg, and carrying an attache case, you would have known him for an ambassador, or at least a foreign minister. In less formal dress he could have been identified as the bank president, the head of a university, or a man of letter. The last thing you would have expected him to be was the rugged chief of even more rugged men. But that is what he was.

Wils Rankin was the foreman of the Two-Bar cattle outfit. To riders and ranchers and buyers today the names "Two-Bar" or "Ora Haley" mean almost nothing. To those who dwelt in northeast Utah, northwest Colorado, and southern Wyoming in 1886, they were the most widely known names in the entire region. Ora Haley was owner of the Haley Land & Cattle Company, and the Two-Bar was his brand. Cattle bearing that brand could be seen on every hill, in every gulch from Green River on the west to the Continental Divide on the east, from Snake River to Bear River and even beyond. There were other important cattle companies, but the Two-Bar dwarfed them all.

Of this vast empire, with 40,000 head of cattle and many ranches, Wils Rankin was the overall boss, the foreman. Rankin succeeded a man named Kelly. We should not pass by Kelly without giving him a well-deserved niche in history. We did not know much about Kelly, but one reliable story will serve to identify the kind of man he was. It was told by Nick Davis, who was the cook.

"We were not far from Meeker," he related, "and Christmas was comin' on. We had been fightin' the cold rawhidin' every day tryin' to get the job done. It looked mighty dreary on Christmas eve, as we huddled over the fire, takin' on the same old sowbelly and beans. Next mornin' we rolled out same as usual. Nobody says anything about it bein' Christmas. Didn't want to make the others feel bad."

"While we was chokin' down the sowbelly and sinkers at breakfast, Kelly says in a kind of joshin' way, 'How'd yuh like to have turkey fer Christmas dinner?' Some said nothin', some laughed kind of sour like. Two or three yells right out loud how they'd enjoy some turkey."

"'All right," says Kelly the foreman, "turkey it will be. Wash yer faces, put on yer best bib-and-tucker and we'll go into Meeker for Christmas dinner.'"

"That's just what we done. We had drinks, turkey dinner, and packed away enough turkey with us fer another feed. Kelly, knowin' how tight Haley was, paid fer the whole works out of his own pocket."

Wils Rankin had to fill Kelly's shoes, which he did, and then some.

M. Wilson Rankin left his home in Pennsylvania in 1876 and the same year arrived in Wyoming, going to Rawlins, where his uncle, Joe Rankin, was located.

That was the day of movement of big herds of cattle. They were brought into Wyoming, drawn by the lure of limitless grasslands and abundant water. Big herds were pushed in from the plains of Texas and Indian Territory, the mountains of Montana, and from Idaho and even California. From this flood of cattle a tiny trickle had found its way over into Colorado, this being the small herds of some who had squatted on land in the domain of the Uintah Utes. Rankin was soon taking an active part in trailing some of these herds, one of the biggest being a herd brought from Raft River, Idaho.

Within eight years Rankin was foreman of the biggest cattle outfit in northwest Colorado, the Two-Bar, an outfit that had grown explosively as soon as the Indians were removed from the area and it had been thrown open to settlement.

We had not been on our ranch long when Wils Rankin first visited us. It seemed to be the custom for the Two-Bar foreman to get acquainted with all new settlers. There was probably more to this than just a neighborly call. Even at that early date there was friction between the big outfits and many of the settlers. There were two main reasons for this.

First, the settlers were locating and fencing in the best springs and waterholes in the country. Second, a good many of the settlers were preying on the big herds, some stealing calves from which to form the foundation of cattle herds of their own, and others killing fat young critters to feed their families. It would be safe to say that about half of the settlers either mavericked or beefed other people's cattle. The other half was either restrained by conscience or liked to hunt wild game so well that they left other people's cattle alone. Ora Haley, shrewd operator that he was, estimated the situation about that way. Living in the middle of it, we knew it to be a fair estimate.

Rankin and our parents became good friends. Like all the cowpunchers, he had problems trying to keep his clothing clean. Although it meant extra work of the hardest kind, mother washed and ironed not only Rankin's clothes, but clothes of some of the cowpunchers who worked under him.

The cowboys who were in Moffat County when we came in 1886 were professionals. Most of them had followed the trail herds out of the Southwest and had been "born in the saddle." When railroads had penetrated to the heart of cattle country and trail herds were no longer necessary and the plains became populated with settlers, many of the erstwhile trail herders and general cowboys drifted into Montana and Wyoming. When cattle moved into Moffat County, Colorado, these professional cowpunchers came with them. With them too, were a few like Wils Rankin, who though not from cattle country, had learned, and learned well, the crafts of the range in a hard school and under hard teachers, the pros of range and trail.

As it is with pros in any profession, the professional cowpunchers disdained to do other work. Out of a job and threatened by hunger, in wintertime a waddie might now and then assist with cattle feeding. But they milked no cows, slopped no hogs, nor did they repair fences, cut cedar posts, haul manure, nor rip-rap creek or river banks. Neither would they, when summer came and there was riding to be done, take part in haying.

Their place was atop a horse. So wedded were they to this position they seldom walked more than a few feet. If they had to go, they went horseback. There was sense to this, too. For one thing, the high-heeled boots they wore made walking a misery. Another thing, on the range a man afoot was the target for attack by any cow, steer, or bull near. A man mounted was something for cattle to respect and fear. A man afoot was neither feared nor permitted to live if cattle could get to him.

Later, toward the turn of the century, a crop of local ranch boys had developed into riders. Some of them, broken in by the old hands, became capable riders, top hands, good cowmen, bronco busters, and even contestants and sometimes winners in bucking matches. But unlike the old time waddies, these later cowpunchers were not averse to taking a turn at plowing, handling a pitchfork, milkpail, or manure fork. In winter time you might find them climbing telephone poles, hauling lumber, subbing as bartenders, swamping in saloons, or even fiddling for dances. Anything to make a dollar to tide them over until roundup time came in the spring.

With the coming of the homesteaders and the consequent shrinkage of the open range and of the range herds, the need for cowpunchers lessened. The breed dwindled and before the 1920s had practically disappeared. There are still cowboys employed mostly by owners of huge ranches and of purebred herds. They are often knowledgeable cattle men, skillful with pickup truck or jeep, and some ride well and even rope. Their hours are not as long, they sleep on springs and mattresses, eat from tables, using silver and regaling themselves on all sorts of ready-mixed, fancy foods. If an old-time waddie from the 1890s, raised on beefsteak, spuds, yeast powder biscuits, gravy, and coffee, should come back to earth, he'd be as lost as a frog at a pelican convention.

They were probably not very bright, those early day cowpunchers. They risked their very lives nearly every minute of a sixteen-hour day for $30 a month and furnished their own bed. But a man had to eat, and what else was there to do? There were no factories, no offices, no job insurance, no unemployment compensation, no peace corps, no job corps, no social security, retirement pay, or pensions. All there was was a multitude of cattle, owned mostly by very greedy men who paid as little as possible and sold for all they could get. Thereby they accumulated fortunes to hand on to sons and daughters who in many cases squandered it all in high living.

The old time cowpuncher did what was to be done and did it well, without hope of great gain, glory, or a place in history. Many, without education or inheritance, and in age without health or friends, lived out their lives in want and misery. Some others saved their money, played all the angles, and themselves became owners of ranches and herds. Life is always that way.

Shorty Doyle was one of those who came from the big trail-herds by way of Texas, eastern Colorado, Montana, and Wyoming. It is doubtful if he ever saw the inside of a schoolhouse. He must have been in the saddle long before he began to shave, as he was still a young fellow when he worked for the Two-Bar. And you may well believe that a Two-Bar cowpuncher had to be able to make a hand.

The one thing that set Shorty Doyle apart was his insatiable love of a practical joke.

The fall shovedown dragged on unusually late. Before the shovedown had moved on westward from Lay, deep snow and bitter weather came. Earlier that fall a cowpuncher had been killed by a boy over a row about a dog, and at night the men were holed up in the half-cellar in which the wounded cowpuncher had died. The preceding summer, this building, half below ground and half above, had been partly filled with straw, with the intention of using it for an ice house, the ice blocks to be packed and insulated with straw, so as to keep them for the next season's use. This straw made a good substitute for mattresses for the bed rolls of the crew. A big stove sat in a box of earth to keep it from setting fire to the straw. In this snug place the men were much better situated than in most cow camps. They usually went to bed about 9, so had a little time for talk and now and then a little poker.

This night a desultory draw game was in progress. Those not in the game were dozing. Unnoticed, Shorty Doyle left the shelter and went out into the stormy night. Presently the men were disturbed by a clanging and clattering in the stovepipe. It ceased as suddenly as it had begun. The poker players had just gotten again absorbed in the game when a pistol shot crashed in the gloomy cellar, followed by a veritable fusillade. The stove began to fly to pieces as the men stumbled over each other, clawing their way to the steps that led to the outside.

As they reached the outer air, Shorty Doyle met them and dived into the cellar, screaming and writhing with gales of laughter. He had dropped a handful of pistol cartridges down the stove pipe and was enjoying to the utmost the mad dash of the men.

Some of the men cursed him, some laughed with him.

The shovedown was about to move on westward a few days later. It was their last night at Lay. Snow was falling again and a sharp wind had a blizzard in the making. Again a poker game was going. And again Shorty Doyle left the refuge. As the men expected, again the clang of falling objects in the stovepipe broke the silence. The men bolted from the cellar as before.

The whole nonsensical performance might have been a film, rerun through a projector, but with one difference. No explosions followed. But Shorty, as in the first stampede, trotted into the warmth of the inside, chuckling and whooping in delight. He had dropped only a handful of rocks into the stovepipe this time.

The film changed.

Coming back into the dimly-lighted hole, the men seized Doyle. Some held him while others stripped him of every stitch of clothing and of his boots and hat. Picking him up bodily, they carried him to the top of the short stairway and with a lusty heave-ho tossed him out into the swirling snow. Then they went inside, closing and locking the door.

Here was a practical joke with which the practical joker couldn't cope.

There wasn't time to think it out or to figure ways and means. Shorty was freezing. He hammered on the door and begged. Nobody paid the least attention. He pleaded, wheedled, promised. Still no response. Calling to Johnny Slates, whom he considered his buddy, he chatteringly shouted that if they didn't let him back in, he would die.

Joe Sainsbury, an older Texas hand, yelled back at him:

"A better man than you died *in* this shack, so you can die *outside*."

They let him shiver and yowl until his voice began to sound weak and they figured he would surely be cured of his nonsense, then let him in.

Cured? Not Shorty Doyle. There are two addictions that cannot be cured—playing practical jokes and writing short checks. Shorty probably never wrote a check of any kind. But he did keep right on with his pranks.

Probably to the day of his death. And *that* day came very near to coming the very next summer, when Shorty foolishly toyed with "Old Thorne" Biggs.

Snowden, the Negro cook, had recently been replaced by another black man, Washington Thornton Biggs. "Old Thorne" had been born in slavery. But he had come west when freed, had worked where he could, and finally found employment with Ora Haley at Laramie, Wyoming, Haley's headquarters before he moved into Colorado.

Thorne was quite young when he first appeared in cattleland. By the time he was 17 he was rated as a good cowhand and a top bronco buster. That was in Texas, where anybody has to be mighty skillful to be rated at all. But Thorne did not like to be referred to as a "cowboy."

"Dem fellers what handles cattle in Arkansas, Missouri an' places like that call theyselves cowboys, and what they rides cowponies," he'd say. "In Texas, we got men and hosses."

In Colorado, and particularly northwest Colorado, the riders were almost universally referred to as cowpunchers. This was varied occasionally by rider, cow waddie, or hand.

In most of the West the horses cowpunchers rode were called cow ponies, no matter what their size. Work horses, used to pull loads, were horses, but all saddle horses were ponies.

Sometimes, in anger or contempt, a rider would call his mount a cayuse, a skate, or a bench. Many an Easterner or even Westerners wondered where the term horsewrangler came from. The standard answer to this question was, "why because he wrangles the ponies." Which still left the inquirer in doubt about the genesis of the term.

The term wrangler started with the Spaniards who handed it on to the Mexicans. A hostler in Spanish is a coverange. Pronounced rapidly in the Spanish way, it sounds more like rangaw. With the high talent most Americans have for twisting up foreign pronunciation, this easily became wrangler. Most pioneers were so inept at the word-business, they found Indian dialect, and especially Indian proper names, so difficult they simply gave up and used an English name. This infuriated the Indians. A case in point is the famous Ute leader A-ca-gat, whom white people called Jack.

No matter from whence cowpunchers came, if they had ever trail-herded, they knew the lingo of that activity. Trailherd was a herd of cattle, strung out in a long, narrow formation. To *keep* them that way, they had men ahead of the herd or on point. Men along the sides of the herd were on the swing, while those who brought up the rear and kept the herd moving were on the drag. This was true whether there were 100, 500, or 5,000 head of cattle.

To Old Thorne, all of this was primer grade stuff. He knew it all, and he knew much more. Including cooking. He could do everything required of a roundup and camp cook. He got along well with the men and was held in high esteem by Haley. He was a big man, good humored, but mighty firm when it came to anything concerning his work. He knew the country well, having ridden it as a cowpuncher. Knew the dim roads, all the springs and waterholes, was an expert at driving the four-horse team that hauled the mess wagon, and ruled the empire of his traveling outdoor kitchen with a firm hand.

That summer, the roundup had worked its way up from the Utah line on its way to the high mountains of Colorado. It was now at the Two-Bar horse camp.

Old Thorne had served the noon meal, washed the dishes, peeled the potatoes for supper, and so to take his regular siesta, he stretched out on his back in the shade of the chuck wagon. Soon he began to snore loudly, now and then slapping with his big hands at a fly or mosquito on his face.

The temptation was too much for the prankster Shorty Doyle. With a stick he collected some of the black, sticky lubricating tar that dripped from the wagon wheels. This he quietly dripped into Thorne's outstretched palms.

With a long bunch-grass straw Shorty tickled Thorne on the cheek. The big man, in his sleep, slapped at the "fly" that was tickling his cheek. Shorty kept it up, rocking with silent laughter. Suddenly Thorne woke up. Shorty faded back out of sight behind the wagon. Thorne put his hand to his face, then looked fixedly at his hand for several seconds. Then he got up, slowly and sleepily. He stepped slowly around behind the wagon as if to get a drink from the water keg slung there. Thorne opened the door of the cupboard that formed the back of the wagon, and took out the long, sharp butcher knife.

In a flash all lethargy disappeared, as Thorne spun on his heel and made for Shorty. The joker took one swift look, did a backwards somersault and came up on his feet running. They went twice around the wagon, the whistling knife within inches of Shorty's back, then Shorty took to the rabbitbrush flat, down into the creek, leaped the narrow stream, fell but recovered, and scrambled up the creek bank and lined out across the buffalo grass meadow. Winded, Thorne gave up. Catching his breath he sauntered back to the wagon. The riders were saddling for the afternoon working of the herd.

"I'll bet he won't monkey with you again, Thorne," Johnny Slates grinned. Thorne didn't grin.

"He sho won't John. No suh, he sho won't," the big fellow said grimly. "Cause if he ever comes back to dis here camp, I kills him. I sho does."

There was no place Shorty could go. If he went to the Haley place at Lay, Charlie Gregory would by then know about the matter and wouldn't let him stay. Old Thorne rated mighty high with Haley.

Anyhow, it went on thus for several days. The cowpunchers sneaked some food out to Shorty, with a couple of blankets so he could sleep in the tall sagebrush. Nobody dared suggest to Thorne that he forgive the sinner.

Towards evening, Wils Rankin, now foreman, who had been away for a couple of days, rode in. Some of the men explained the situation to him. After awhile he talked to Thorne. Afterward, he told Johnny Slates to slip out and tell Shorty he had better continue to sleep in the brush. Thorne still promised to kill him if he came near camp. Johnny sneaked out some cold biscuits and meat to Shorty and told him the cheerless news.

Towards evening the next day, after the men were in, Thorne finally told Rankin that Shorty might come in.

"I knows you boys been seein' that there Shorty," he said. "Well, if you see him agin, tell him he can come on in. I reckon he done learned a lesson by now."

Shorty didn't really mend his ways, but he never monkeyed with Thorne Biggs after that. That war was over and a doubtful peace reigned. The roundup moved on up country and the usual routine prevailed. A couple of years later Old Thorne went to Haley's Wyoming range.

I was too young to punch cows for the Two-Bar while Thorne was there. But I got to know him well, as he often stopped and left us a big chunk of beef when the roundup moved past our place.

I think it was 1926 that I was told Thorne was in Craig, and we enjoyed a grand visit. He was about 80, had given up the mess wagon, and now drove a shiny Model T Ford.

During this visit Old Thorne told me, "I got no call to worry none. Dat Mr. Haley he done fix me up fo' de rest of my life."

And all of this, in a brief way, gives just an inkling of what kind of men they were, and what they did, as cowboys for the Two-Bar under the foremanship of Wils Rankin.

★
The Outlaw Trail

As we travel along a mountain trail, we note, from time to time, small divergent trails forking off to the left and the right. We wonder where such trails lead. We come, too, to where the main trail divides into two equal branches, and unless we are familiar with these trails, we must make a decision. Often I've started along a trail and because of a hunch, or some occurrence or mishap, turned back and taken the other fork. I never do this without thinking of one particular trail on which I almost set foot, but through circumstances abandoned, to take a straighter and safer trail. The trail on which I mistakenly started was the "Outlaw Trail."

The Outlaw Trail was well known over all the West and much of the East. It was the trail ridden by the various gangs of thieves, robbers, and murderers that infested the West before the twentieth century began. It extended roughly from the Canadian line to central New Mexico. Its most important segment ran from the Hole-in-the-Wall country in Montana to the Robbers Roost in eastern Utah.

And how did a simple, inexperienced lad who had never spent a night away from people he knew well almost set foot on the Outlaw Trail? I'll tell you.

The summer of 1895, we had been living a year on the Haley place. That spring, there came into the country the Edge family, looking for land on which they might homestead. Mr. Edge had been a farmer near Wichita, Kansas, and they had lived in the city, too. He was an ordinary sort of fellow. His wife was a somewhat delicate lady but an excellent housewife. They had a daughter, Ada, about 17, and a boy, Eddie, 11.

Since Lay had a post office, they stopped there to mail letters and to ask about the country. Alert to get somebody to stay at the post office and ranch while they went picture-taking, Wallihans, the postmasters, made a deal with Edges to do just that. First thing we knew we had new neighbors. The one I have reason to remember was Eddie. He was older and bigger than me (I was only nine), but we got along well and soon were together about every day. It was always he who came to our place, as our folks didn't believe in letting their kids bother other people.

Eddie didn't bother our folks, as he and I usually took off on some project at a different place every day. This was in spring. Later in the summer I had to work to help Dad so our companionship sort of lagged.

Eddie knew everything. Looking back, I still wonder how an eleven-year-old could stuff so much useless knowledge in one head.

In his time in Wichita he had not missed anything. He knew more about city life and the ways of the human race than I do now. Of course in my callow, country hick condition, nine-tenths of what he told me had no more meaning than if he had spoken in the Phoenician tongue. As a matter of fact he did speak in a peculiar way. He lisped, so that the letter "s" sounded like "th." "This says six" became "Thith theth thix."

But with all his lisping Eddie had big ideas.

"How'd you like to travel all over the country, thleep in good hotelth, wear good clothe, have your pocketh full of money and see lotth of good showth?" he asked me one day.

Who wouldn't like all that, I thought, and told him so.

He lost no time in outlining a plan he'd been hatching up for quite awhile. To steal, in Eddie's lingo, was to "swipe."

"We can thwipe a lot of hortheth from them Morganth," he explained, and went on to elaborate on the plan.

The Morgan brothers, whose ranch was in Morgan Canyon, had hundreds of horses. Eddie's plan was for him and me to "swipe" some of these animals, drive them out of the immediate locality, sell a few for working capital, take the rest far away and dispose of them, and then use the money to tour the country in style. I had seen just enough of the "outside world" to know there were many wonderful places and wonderful things to be seen if one traveled.

Eddie made it seem very attractive, and also the whole project seemed easy, to hear him tell it. It was easy to justify the whole procedure by considering that Morgans had hundreds of horses and we would take only a few.

I wasn't about to embark on this unchartered ocean without a little adult advice. If Dad had been a warmer personality I'd have asked him. But I had no hesitancy in asking Mother about it. I chose a poor time to tell her about it. She was up to her elbows in the washtub.

"Eddie wants him and me to take some of Morgans' horses and sell 'em and go traveling."

"You boys are too young to be handling horses alone," she answered absently.

"I can ride pretty good and I guess Eddie can too," I offered.

"Well, all right, if Mr. Morgan thinks it is all right, and your Father doesn't object."

I don't think she had the slightest idea what I was talking about. I was so full of weird ideas all the time she dismissed anything that sounded different as just another of my growing-up pipe dreams.

I reported to Eddie and he was delighted.

"I knew your folkth would think it ith a good idea," he said, with evident pleasure. So we planned to go the next day. We would not need to take any extra clothes or lunch or anything of the kind as we'd have plenty of money as soon as we could get to Meeker and sell a horse or two. It seemed like a great idea.

Next morning, when Eddie came, soon after breakfast, he told our family we were going over on Lay Creek Hill. They wouldn't be alarmed if we didn't get back for dinner. I said nothing.

Eddie didn't have a saddle horse, so we rode Kitty double. I didn't dare take Dad's saddle as we intended to turn Kitty loose and let her find her way home and I didn't want her to scuff Dad's saddle going under trees or maybe lying down with it on. Kitty's backbone was prominent and sharp and by the time we got to the Morgan place, near noon, our seats were raw.

There was a pasture about a mile square with the Morgan house in one corner. We found a single gate near the house. There was nobody at the house so we just went on in and up to the far end of the pasture where we could see a bunch of horses. There were about 20. We decided we might as well take them all, as it would be too hard to cut out a few with only one saddle horse between us.

That's when our problems began. We got the horses bunched and started along the pasture fence, toward the far end. There would be a gate there. But we were wrong. There was no gate there. We continued along the fence, the herd driving easily, but no sign of a gate could we find. Another thing we began to wonder about was how we were going to catch a couple of those horses to ride. We had no lariat, not even a halter rope. With only one bridle, how could we ride two horses? I'd left the planning to Eddie. Now I began to realize Eddie was no Western ranch boy, even if he did know all about city ways. I asked him about catching the horses and riding so poorly equipped. He had an answer, "Oh well, we'll jutht keep thith mare until we get a couple of hortheth thold. Then we'll buy a couple of thaddles and bridleth."

I knew that was no go. I didn't dare keep Dad's old Kitty. He needed her to work and if she and I disappeared at the same time he'd scour the country until he found us, or her, at least. Another thing, were we sure we could ride those Morgan broncos?

But by this time we had another worse worry. There was no gate to that pasture excepting the one at the house. And, as we got to the top of a ridge where we could see the house, we could now see smoke coming from the chimney. The Morgans were home.

We kept back out of sight and held a quick conference. We knew we couldn't drive the Morgans' horses right past their own house. There was no other way to go. Besides, I was starving, and when I mentioned the fact to Eddie he discovered he too was facing starvation.

So, we decided to abandon the project, at least for the time being. But even that had its drawbacks. To get out of the pasture we had to go past the house. Eddie thought maybe we could just leave old Kitty and sneak out afoot and maybe she would head for home and we could catch her outside. I had to veto that. I knew if we turned her loose she'd go to grazing, being as hungry as we, and we'd have to either walk home or starve or face the Morgans anyhow. So, since we had only one course, we got on it.

It looked as if we might slip by unseen, but at the critical moment the house door opened and Charlie Morgan came out. I had seen him before and knew who he was. I hoped he didn't know me. A brilliant thought hit me. I'd not utter a word.

"Hello there, you boys," Morgan said as he stood in the road blocking our way. "What've you been doing up there?"

"We been chathin' a kayote," Eddie said, with admirable presence of mind. People did chase coyotes.

"Chasin' a coyote?" Morgan said in wonder. "How'd you chase a coyote through a three-wire fence without gettin' scratched up?"

I thought we were sunk. But I underestimated Eddie.

"Thith wath jutht a thmall one. It went under the fenth tho it didn't get thcratched."

"I don't mean the coyote, I mean yer horse."

Again my heart sank, but Eddie was equal to the emergency.

"We didn't ride the horth through the fenth. We come in through thith gate."

Brilliant thought.

"Well, I don't know," Morgan pondered. "I ain't sure I savvy you. You talk funny. How about you, boy?" turning to me.

"He'th thick," Eddie explained. "He'th got a thore throat and can't thpeak a word."

"Whose boys are you, anyway?" Morgan wanted to know. "Where you come from?"

"We're the Thmith boyth. Our folkth are camped in Akthial Bathin."

"Yuh'd better come in an eat. 'Course yer hungry."

Now I knew we were done for. Staunch as Eddie was, I knew he never could withstand an hour of grilling while we ate and washed the dishes.

"Oh no, thir," Eddie came up nobly. "Our folkth will expect uth back for dinner. Tho we can't thtay."

"Well, all right, but yer welcome to eat. Next time you boys come monkeying around here come to the house and let us know. We don't like fer people to be in here without us knowin'. We got horses in here and don't want 'em scared through the fence."

"Yeth thir," Eddie said quite deferentially. "We'll come and thee you if we come again. Good-bye."

As we took off, I was torn by two conflicting emotions. For one, I felt intense admiration for Eddie. He had coped with a potentially tragic situation. But my other feeling was no less strong. Smart or not, I wanted no more of his leadership. Only while he talked to Morgan did it occur to me that it was a common custom, so I'd heard, to hang horse thieves. And even if Morgans had a thousand horses, taking even one without their permission would still be stealing.

So, as we sped along homeward, my thoughts were divided between our narrow escape from hanging and the misery of my rear. Because every step old Kitty took was a misery. Her walk was not so bad. Her trot was pure hell, not only slithering our raw bottoms back and forth along her ridge pole, but sending shock waves up our spines at each clopp-clopp of her feet. So we compromised by sending her into a gallop, which was comparatively smooth, then letting her walk until she could recover her breath. By thus alternating slow drag and mad dash we made it back by about four o'clock. I left Eddie at Lay, rode around behind the hill, and left Kitty on a grassy patch beyond Uncle Jack's grave. I knew she'd stay there until her belly was full and by that time she'd be dried out from the ride. The folks didn't show much concern about my tardiness.

It may sound funny now. But its implications were not funny at all. Had we found a gate and made away with the horses, it is not likely we could have gotten far. Ranchers those days were quick to notice anything unusual. Two boys riding double and hazing a bunch of horses would surely have been spotted by some of the Colloms, Taylors, Shavers, or Seilaffs. They'd have gotten on a horse and investigated.

Even if Eddie's glib tongue and inventive brain had been equal to the occasion, how could we have sold a horse with the Morgan brand? Even dumb as I was, I should have known that. But I had done what many others have done—let the vision of a rosy future blind me to the present hard facts. That sort of business is what still keeps phony stock dealers, dishonest salesmen, and mining promoters fat.

Caught abducting other people's horses and trying to sell them, we may not have been hanged. But there is a fair chance we would have been sent to the reform school. The best that could have happened would have been that the whole community would have known of our escapade and come to regard us as guilty in spirit, if not in fact, of horse stealing. With such a "black eye" to bear, there is better than an even chance we would have eventually "gone wrong" and joined some outlaw gang. A good many outlaws got their start in much the same small way.

There was a saying those days that if anyone had a lucky break, they should "thank their lucky stars." It was just a saying, or "pisherogue" as Dad would say. I did thank my lucky stars when I got back in the safe atmosphere of our home. But not yet did I realize that I had lucky stars. Maybe not stars, but lucky something.

So, when this trail divided, and I started down the wrong line, the Power that watches over me guided me back onto the right trail. The experience convinced me of the folly of taking that which is not your own.

⭐
Eddie and the Bullfight

Eddie was tall for his age and big compared with me. He was rather skinny, tow-headed, with wide pale blue eyes, and he lisped. Every "s" was to him "th." Sometimes he called his sister Thith (Sis), that is, to her face. To me he always referred to her as "ol' Thpout Nothe" (Spout Nose). Her nose was rather long, like his own, but hers was somewhat flat. He spoke respectfully of his mother, but often his father was "Ol' Judath Prietht" (Judas Priest, whatever that meant).

His most vehement expression of anger, disgust, or surprise was "Tholoman Amen" (Solomon Amen). When extremely upset he might say "damn" or call things and me a "bathtrood" (bastard).

To me, he seemed to know everything. With one exception. He had evidently never seen a kerosene lamp until he saw ours. So what did he do but clasp the burning lamp in both hands. Of all the yowls and dancing and "Tholomon amens" you ever heard and saw. That one experience with the sizzling hot lamp chimney taught him a lesson.

Eddie came up one day and we went over to the Little Peak and watched the chipmunks play for awhile, then went down and dived into the warm pool and sat on the bank until we got dry.

"We'll buy a boat, then we c'n thail on thith pond," Eddie remarked.

"That would be nice," I agreed. "But a boat would cost a lot of money."

"No odds. We'll have plenty of money after the bullfight," he said.

"After the what?"

"The bullfight, of courth."

"I don't know what you're talking about," I told him, mysti-
fied.

"I'm talking about the bullfight. *B-u-l-l* fight. Are you deef?"

"No, I'm not deaf. But I don't know anything about any bullfight. What bull? And what's he going to fight?"

"You and meth going to fight him, of courth."

I was as far at sea as always when he broached some new and
outrageous idea.

So he explained, somewhat impatiently, that he and I were
going to train one of the bull calves we had, dig things into him and
make him mad, and Eddie would be a "tordor," and I would be a
"picdor." He elaborated on the duties of this proposed toreador and
picador and finally got it through my head what he had in mind.

We had other projects on at the time so it was about a week
before we could begin the training of the little bull.

"When we get him tho he'll fight," Eddie explained, "we can
get practithed up and then people will come from all over the plath
to thee thith bullfight. We'll get rich."

I was dubious about the whole idea, but you couldn't remain
dubious around Eddie. At least I couldn't. He usually ended up by
convincing me, either by talk or by resort to physical persuasion.

So we began training. We hazed the milk cows around from
the barn where they were lying in the shade and over into the creek.
We didn't want them to begin a ruckus and alarm my family, which
we knew they would when we began to work on the bull calf. Then
we put the other calves in the barn and left this near-yearling in the
corral.

We had made some "darts" out of willow sticks by cutting the
head off some nails and sticking them in the end of the sticks. On
the other end we tied a bit of rag like a sort of flag. Eddie had a book
showing a bullfight in Spain he let me look at. The darts we made
looked much like the ones the picadores used to make the bull mad.

Eddie had just a willow stick for a sword. But since we didn't
plan to kill the bull, or even to seriously injure him, he had no need
of a sword. That could come later, I suppose. He was vague on that
point. We had a bayonet, off of Dad's Long Nine rifle, but Eddie did-
n't think much of it as a toreador's sword. Too straight.

The little bull stood, switching flies off himself with his tail.

"Thlip up to him and gig him in the flank with the dart,"
Eddie instructed. I did, hesitantly and without enthusiasm. The calf
kicked with one foot and trotted across the corral.

"Gig him, gig him," Eddie said impatiently. "He'th got to be mad."

He planted himself in front of the puzzled calf. I eased alongside and gave the calf a jab with the willow stick. He kicked with both hind feet and let out a bawl as he darted straight ahead, nearly knocking Eddie off his feet as he bumped him in passing.

We had forgotten the cows. When the calf bawled, the cow that was his mother must have heard him. First thing we knew she was at the corral gate, all excited, shaking her head and mooing in a low tone.

We were in position and Eddie told me to "gig him." I gigged, the calf bawled and ran towards the gate, and the cow, with a mighty leap which didn't clear the top rail of the pole gate, crashed through, busting two of the gate poles. She came for me like a tigress, head down, froth flying, and me flying too. I made for the snubbing post in the middle of the corral, it being nearer than the side rails of the corral. I grabbed the snubbing post as I went past and swung to its far side. The cow hit it squarely with her face. She rebounded about two feet, stood weaving, her legs slowly buckled, and slowly sank to the ground.

I stepped back from the snubbing pole and looked around. The calf, staring, was taking in the whole show, as was Eddie, perched on the top rail of the corral. Before the cow could come to herself and struggle up, I joined Eddie.

We sat there, silent, until the cow got up, and followed by the calf trying to get a lunch while the cow was moving, went over the remains of the gate and back to the herd. Only then did we get down, cobble up the gate, and let the calves out of the barn to the corral. Then, still only mumbling and grunting replies to my remarks, Eddie went on home.

★
Rattlesnake Four-in-Hand

I have often wondered what became of Eddie Edge and whether he lived to maturity, so prone was he to paint himself into a corner. That boy! Horse stealing. Bull fighting. Training a rattlesnake. Oh yes indeed, he barehandedly tackled the job of subjugating one of the vipers.

We had heard Emerson tell about Ben Morgan and his "team" of rattlers. I guess it really happened. Anyhow, Emerson told that one time when he went to Snake River to get a couple of horses that had strayed and been taken up by the Morgans, he visited their ranch. Nobody was there but young Ben, about 12 years of age. Ben was out near the barn, playing with something. Emerson walked out to tell the boy he had come for the horses, but Ben met him halfway. Before Emerson could say anything Ben blurt out enthusiastically, "Want to see my snakes, Mr. Emerson?"

Emerson, a born Irishman, had no more time for snakes than had Saint Patrick, who, it was said, chased all the snakes out of Ireland. But out of curiosity and good manners he told the boy yes, he wouldn't mind seeing his snakes.

What he saw would have horrified anybody but a snake charmer—or Ben Morgan.

The lad had two rattlers, each about two feet long, rigged out with a sort of "harness." A little pad made of buckskin and stuffed with cattail fuzz was held on the back of each snake a few inches back of the head. A similar pad was farther back. From these pads led the "traces" which led back to a little wagon, made with sewing thread spools for wheels. Two "lines" enabled Ben to control and to turn the "team."

How he had ever arrived at this result without being bitten, Emerson didn't wait long enough to find out. As soon as he could, he got his horses and left.

Soon everybody in the country, including Eddie Edge, knew about this. But Eddie was the only one who got the big idea of going Ben Morgan one better and having a four-snake team. This design he confided to me the first time I saw him after the go-around with the bull calf.

I wanted no part in it. From as far back as I can remember, I had loathed snakes. I think I was about five when I killed my first rattlesnake. From then on, it was an almost daily occurrence for some of us to kill a snake. That cliff of ours was a veritable snake den, and almost anywhere on the ranch you'd come on them. Our dogs were bitten repeatedly and even cattle and horses were struck.

So now, this character wanted me to take part in his four-snake-team project. Not me. So, the argument was on. I remembered the campaign he had put on to induce me to be with him to steal the Morgan horses. So I was forearmed.

We finally settled the debate lasting three or four days by my agreeing to go with him, but to take no part in the catching, subjugation, and training of the serpents, to say nothing of putting them in harness.

So I went along. And we caught a snake. A brownish two-footer. It was full of fight, but Eddie got a wire loop over its head and finally got it into a wooden box, such as apples came in. In spite of his pleas that I be a close spectator, I stood back, aloof. He kept the snake box in the sagebrush, about a quarter of a mile from their house. It was a place to which we could sneak without being seen. He called the snake "Buzzer" or "Buther" the way he said it.

It really seemed that he was making progress. Instead of coiling and making its rattles fairly sing, the snake grew less demonstrative and even let Eddie push it around in the box without striking at the stick. Eddie assured me that in just a few days he was going to put his hand in the box instead of the stick. I mentally resolved that that was going to be the day I wouldn't be there.

So we went out this morning as soon as the sun got high enough to warm things. I always let Eddie go ahead about 50 feet. Just as he reached the box I heard a shrill screech and heard Eddie shouting "Tholomon amen" as fast as he could repeat it and yelling for me.

I darted forward and he met me, pulling up one of his overalls legs as he got nearer.

"I'm thnakebit, I'm thnakebit," he yelled. "Solomon Amen what'm I goin' to do?"

"Suck the poison," I yelled in return, the coaching I'd had over the years coming to me without thought. "Suck the poison."

He fell to the ground, trying to get his mouth to a point on the calf of his leg. He lacked about a foot of making it.

"Here, you thuck the poithon! Thuck the poithon!"

I recoiled in horror. Me suck the poison and poison myself?

"Thuck the poithon, thuck the poithon!" he screamed.

He was frantic. I just stood. He bounded up, wrenched a dead and rotten sagebrush stick loose and descended on me, yelling, "Thuck the poithon, damn you, thuck the poithon."

I backed off. He swung the club and brought it down glancing off the side of my head and hitting my shoulder. The club shattered into smithereens but its mere weight put me down. Before I could scramble to my feet Eddie had me by the front of my shirt, had grabbed a short stubby piece of sagebrush wood and was digging me in the ribs with it, as he screamed, "Thuck the poithon, you bathtrood, thuck the poithon!"

His superior weight and size had me. I couldn't escape. The blows of the prodding stick were hurting worse than I'd ever been hurt, I thought. Desperately I pressed my lips to his leg at the spot where two drops of blood stood out like twin rubies. I sucked and the blood spurted into my mouth. I took my mouth away, sick.

"Go on, thuck the poithon," Eddie said more calmly. "Don't thtop. Get all the poithon out. Thpit it out."

I don't know how he, a city kid, knew so much about the matter, but his knowledge was sound.

"Let'th thit a while and thee if I begin to die," he said, in a trembly voice. The thought flashed through my mind that he must be weak from loss of blood. Actually, I don't suppose I had drawn more than two or three ounces.

"What about me?" I asked him. "Do you think that poison will kill me?"

"Holy Tholomon Amen," he sputtered. "You didn't thwaller it, did you?"

I didn't think I had swallowed any. But I wasn't too sure.

So there we both sat, the sweat pouring off us, half whimpering, and waiting for what we knew not but imagined would be some sort of horrible agony.

After a while, Eddie's leg began to hurt, and on a closer look we could see a little swelling. Then he really began to whimper and bawl. I wasn't feeling so well myself.

"Why don't we run to your house so your folks can do something?" I asked him. Between gulps he whined, "They'd do thomething all right. Oh God, why did I have to monkey with that damn thnake, anyhow?"

I just sat, while he passed through a paradigm of crying, cursing, and vilifying the snake.

All the time we watched the wounded place on his leg. It swelled more and hurt but didn't seem to be getting greatly enlarged. And then, I had the thought that I should have had long before, "Why don't we run to the creek and put your leg in the black mud. That's what the dog does and it always cures her snake bites."

Eddie bounded up as if stung again.

"Run, run," he sobbed, "Run, you bathtrood. Why didn't you think of that a week ago, you fool bathtrood? Run, run."

I ran and he at my heels. At the creek bank he plunged his leg into the thick black mud that bordered every creek, until his overalls were wet to the waist. Then he just sat, whimpering. I watched him for awhile, then wandered off, scaring frogs to see them leap into the water, until after a half-hour or so I heard Eddie call and went to him.

He was actually grinning.

"I gueth old big me ith goin' to make it," he said amiably. "I gueth your old dog knowth more than we do. It'th jutht about quit hurting."

He pulled the leg out of the mud, washed it off, and we inspected it. It was still swollen but no worse than before.

So he took off his overalls and we washed them in the creek and hung them to dry on a bush. We talked the situation over, and since it was near noon I went to our house to dinner. Eddie sat with his leg in the black mud. After dinner I got my sister Hortense to one side and told her the gist of the story. She spirited out a couple of slices of bread with a couple of antelope steaks between and I took them to Eddie, where he still sat with his leg in the mud.

His folks never seemed to worry if he didn't show up for a meal.

Along about midafternoon, examining his leg for about the twentieth time, we noticed the swelling had gone down a bit. So, being that it no longer hurt very much, Eddie said he thought we had better go see about the snakes.

"Not me," I chided him. "I'm through fooling around snakes, only to knock their heads off."

"That'th exactly what I'm goin' to do," he surprised me by declaring. "Maybe I'll jutht turn old Buther looth. But I'll beat that other bathtrood's brainth into the earth."

"What other snake?" I wanted to know.

"Why that one that bit me, of courth. You know, that bathtrood that bit me?"

I didn't know and said so. So he told me. He had walked up to the box to work with the snake and another snake was on the ground near the box and he stepped on it and it bit him.

"Of course, why every snake has a mate," I told him. "We always have to watch for the mate when we kill one."

He almost screamed, he was so mad.

"You littlc meathly, crawling fool bathrood! Why didn't you tell me that a month ago?" and he made a grab for a big dead sagebrush club and began to twist it to get it loose.

I didn't wait to see or hear more. I lit out on a beeline for our house, a half mile away. Eddie didn't follow. I guess he disposed of the snakes. I never found out. I didn't see him for a week. Then he sauntered up one day, all smiles. As soon as we got under the bank, down by Mopadeeny's tree, he rolled up his overalls leg and showed me his calf. It was still swollen slightly but all round it the skin was a sort of blue color. For some reason, Eddie was not concerned.

"I gueth I'm jutht modrifying," he said cheerfully. "I looked in our doctor book and it thayth people modrify. But it don't thay anything about it killin' them. Tho I gueth I'm all right. I got an idea, though. You and me is goin' to make uth a dugout tho we'd have a plath to take thtuff when we thwipe it."

He elaborated on the plan. But he had an audience not in sympathy. I had no intention of digging any dugout with him and maybe having it cave in on us. Nor did l intend to be a partner to any more of his stealing projects. So I just kept still and listened. And the next time I saw him he had forgotten all about the dugout and had some other wild scheme in mind.

I was thankful he didn't resurrect the idea of the four-in-hand of rattlesnakes.

About that time the Wallihans came home, Edge's took a homestead on North Fork, and we saw them no more.

★
The Great Elk Migration

It was a momentous event. Probably unlike anything that ever occurred on this continent. Yet I doubt if one person in a thousand in our own county today ever heard of it. And, although this event was amazing, unique, and had far-reaching consequences, there is nothing about it to make a long story. It can, and shall, all be told in a few pages.

Since there is no written record of this event, I must depend on memory and the help of my brother, Arthur, who like I, talked of the Great Elk Migration with several who saw it.

I think it was the autumn of 1889. At that time our father was going each fall to Aspen to work in the mines during the winter for the cash stake needed to operate our ranch. Since he left in early November, he could "lay in" a few buck deer for our winter's meat. But it was too early for elk, so if we had elk, which we usually did have, we bought it.

This fall, we learned afterward, the cowpunchers had noticed an unusual number of elk in the Sandhills, west of where Craig is now. Usually, when driven from the high mountains by deep snows, elk became numerous on Pine Ridge, in the Sandhills, on Iles and Duffy Mountains, and even on westward to Elk Springs. In fact, Pine Ridge seemed to be a favorite wintering spot, and as late as 1906 hundreds of shed antlers could be seen on the ridge and nearby.

But this fall of 1889, the elk came down early. Tom Wisc, who had a ranch a short distance up Williams Fork, having a day or two free, slipped out in the Sandhills and got four.

A few days later, Riley Hamilton, whose ranch was a short distance up Moor Rapids (Morapos) Creek, stopped at Tom's and noticed the four carcasses hanging.

"Kind of rushing the season aren't you, Tom?" he asked. "Ain't you afraid they'll spoil? How come you hunted so early?"

"Well, I had a couple of days with nothing else pressin' me," Tom explained. "And somehow I just got a hunch to get my winter's meat. You know the elk are down here unusually early. Never saw anything like it. They're thick out there."

"Well, I think I'll wait until about the usual time. It's pretty warm before the middle of November to keep 'em."

Riley went on up the river, but when November 20th came he did go to the Sandhills as usual with sled and team to get his elk. It was late when he got back as far as Tom Wise's, and at Tom's urging he stayed all night. So they had plenty of time to discuss the elk situation. And there was plenty to discuss. Riley had not seen a single elk.

"Tracks, tracks, tracks, everywhere. Hundreds of 'em," he exclaimed. "And over toward Horse Gulch the snow and ground are beat down like a well-traveled road. But not an elk could I find. Do you reckon there'll be more comin' in from the high country?"

Tom didn't have an answer for that. The sudden absence of elk in the Sandhills had him as badly puzzled as it did Hamilton.

Another one who got his meat early and helped his neighbors do the same was Ol Haughey. Ol had a ranch a few miles up Fortification Creek. He was a horseman, and most of his animals ranged in the Sandhills. Riding in that area, Ol noticed the early arrival and the concentration of elk. He told E. A. Farnham, a neighbor, "There's one whale of a lot of elk in the Sandhills. Do you reckon that hard winter last year stirred 'em up and they are goin' to the lower country early?"

Farnham didn't know, but after some more talk on the subject, the two agreed to let some other neighbors know and to harvest a few elk just in case. This they did, four neighbors loading a big sled full and piled up with fat carcasses that would see them through the winter. Many another rancher wished afterward he had done likewise. It became apparent that something very unusual was in the wind.

With the lack of communication in the country at the time, it took forever for news or rumor to get around. So it was probably a year before Tom and Riley learned the truth of the situation.

Art and I got our information from such ranchers as John Ledford, Andy Saunders, Charlie Duffy, and Pete Farrel, and from cowpunchers such as Wils Rankin, Fatty Smith, Hi Bernard, and Ed Miles.

Ed Miles happened to be picking up some stray cattle after the shovedown and when he got his little bunch headed into the Sandhills, suddenly found himself in the middle of a concentration of what he estimated to be hundreds, and maybe thousands, of elk. Miles said the main body of animals filled the basin formed by the Sandhills and seemed to be just holding, like a bunch of roundup cattle. But more elk were coming in from the direction of Black Mountain and from Iles Mountain.

Ed shoved the twenty or so steers he had gathered west to Lay Creek and rode over to spend the night at the Two-Bar horse camp. There were only a few elk seen on Big Gulch.

But the next morning, when he went back to pick up his gather and head west, he found that the cattle were scattered from Lay Creek to Wet Gulch. Evidently the mass of elk had passed westward in the night, sweeping the cattle along for a few miles. Only a few straggling elk were to be seen, but the ground, in a path a half-mile wide, was beaten down as if by myriad hooves.

It was that same day Pete and Sally Farrel and their family saw the passing migration. When they got up in the morning, they could hear the drum of hundreds of hooves. Wondering, when daylight came they saw the mass of moving elk. The animals had come almost straight west, but a couple of miles east of the Farrel house, about at Boston Hill, the elk herd had turned an almost perfect right angle, again crossed the river and headed north.

Other ranchers and riders saw them, and like Ed Miles and the Farrels, were as puzzled. For weeks the people watched and waited to see the elk come back. They never came back, but kept on until they reached the Jackson Hole country in Wyoming, as we heard later from residents there.

For many a year, a favorite topic of talk in this whole area was, "why did the elk leave?" The answers to this question were almost as many as the departed elk. The elk had not been under much hunting pressure, so that could not account for the migration. Winter had not really started and that particular winter was not severe, although the previous winter had been a bad one.

The most logical solution to this problem I had ever heard was that the inroads of the cattle on the elk ranges had posed a threat of short feed and starvation. Actually, feed was not short. But, this was the very period when the country was filling with cattle. Within three or four years the ranges were loaded.

Do you suppose instinct warned those animals of conditions that were to come? But granting that, what caused the elk to concentrate in the Sandhills? What elk was the leader? How did that elk know where to go? The questions can be multiplied.

All we know for sure is that hundreds and maybe thousands of elk came out of the mountains early, gathered as if by agreement in that certain area, headed west, made a 90 degree turn and headed north and never came back.

Astounding? Yes. Puzzling? Yes. Animals all over the world migrate. But they always go back. Moffat County's early elk migrated and stayed away!

★
Good as Dead

District Court was in session at Hahn's Peak. A number of jurors had been summoned from all over the county. Among them was Andy Saunders, who owned the ranch across the river northeast of Maybell which later became known as the HX ranch.

Andy Saunders had no desire to do jury duty. Early the morning after his arrival at "the Peak," he went to the courthouse. In the main court he saw on the bench a tall, dignified man, busy arranging papers. Approaching, hat in hand, Saunders made his plea to be excused from jury duty.

"Y' see how it is, Judge," he explained. "I got my taters to dig, my winter firewood and coal to get hauled, and some cattle to gather. Now Judge, would it be all right with you if I just go on back to the ranch?"

The tall man looked up. Saunders noticed that he had only one eye. On the rancher he fixed this one orb in a kindly manner.

"Why yes, Mr. Sanders. Sure and it will be all right with me if ye get on back to the bosom of yer fambly."

Saunders lost no time in saddling and departing for his ranch, a hundred miles away, full of gratitude to the judge and to fate for relieving him of the odious chore of serving as one of "twelve good men and true." He was not so well pleased, though, when Sheriff Hank Campbell, a brother of Jim Campbell, early game warden in Moffat County, appeared with an order for Saunders to return immediately to Hahn's Peak. Back there he was taken before stern old Judge Rucker.

Asked to explain why he had left the jurisdiction of the court without permission from the presiding judge, Saunders explained in his slow, drawling way, "Why Judge, I did have permission. From the other judge."

"What other judge?" Rucker thundered.

"Why that other judge that was here on that very seat where you are sitting. He was a lot taller than you. He had only one eye. But he told me it would be all right with him if I went on home."

Judge Rucker turned to Sheriff Campbell. He spoke only two words, "Bring Leahy!"

In a few minutes Campbell was back, herding before him a tall, one-eyed Irishman.

"Leahy," the judge said severely, "Did you tell this man he could leave the environs of this court and go home?"

Leahy shuffled his feet, looked up, and then down, but answered, "Shure an' I did yer honor. He axed me would it be all right with me if he went home and I told him it would."

Judge Rucker scowled for a moment at the blotter on his desk.

"Ten days in the county jail. Take him away, Sheriff!"

To Saunders he said, "This court will be merciful to you, Mr. Saunders. You must remain and serve on at least one jury. Then see me, not Leahy, who is the janitor of this court house, and maybe I'll let you go home."

That afternoon, as usual, court was adjourned at three. Within a few minutes most of the officials, including Judge Rucker, were absorbed in a poker game that would run until early morn. After awhile, Rucker leaned over and whispered to Hank Campbell, "There's an even number of men in this game, Hank. That's bad luck. We need another man. Bring Leahy."

So the sheriff went to the jail and brought Bill Leahy, who gladly sat in.

In 1918 I roomed at the Sheridan Hotel while working in Steamboat Springs, Colorado, for the newspaper, the "Steamboat Pilot." Bill Leahy was rooming there also and told me the story. Jim Campbell, at the hotel, vouched for it.

"Sure an' I'd a been better off had I stayed in jail. I lost a month's wages in the game. I was a sad man when Hank took me back to me cell in the early marnin," Leahy concluded.

The liquor law at that time permitted the shipment of two quarts of liquor per month per person. Dell Gee, one of the Pilot editors, sent for two quarts of 22-year-old whiskey for Christmas, which would have been his allotment for the month of December and therefore must arrive in that month. But a cave-in on the Moffat Railroad delayed the shipment more than thirty days, so it was confiscated by the sheriff and turned over to the local hospital.

But while it lay in the depot and before the sheriff took it, Ralph Irwin, the express agent, sneaked the package out, took the whisky from the bottles, and replaced it with strong tea. He told me about it and even gave me a drink, as he also roomed at the Sheridan.

About that time Bill Leahy went to the hospital with pneumonia. At his age of near 80 recovery was slow. One day he told Doctor Willett, "Docthor, I belave if I had a swig of good whishky it'd do me a world of good."

The doctor thought it might, so told Bill he'd bring him a drink like he'd not had in a long time, a swig of 22-year-old whiskey. He opened one of Dell Gee's quarts contributed by the sheriff, and poured a generous glass. Bill fairly grabbed it from the doctor and took a huge swallow.

He batted his eyes, smacked his lips, shook his head, and handed the whisky back to the doctor.

"Doc, sure and I'm good as dead. There is no hope."

He didn't smile when he said it and Willett hastened to ask why this mournful statement.

"I'm tellin' ye, Doc, that when 22-year-old whiskey tastes to me loike weak tea, I'm just the same as dead."

I guess he later got some real whisky, as he didn't die.

★
A Deal with the Infinite

I had been talking to a neighbor about a trapping expedition. Oscar Ames had a homestead between Yampa River and Lay Creek where they met near Juniper Canyon. Os was a young bachelor and lived alone in his cozy cabin.

In winter time, there was little that could be done on a homestead, excepting to grub sagebrush to clear land for other crops. So Os told me he planned that the coming winter he would go over back of Juniper Mountain, and maybe on down toward Crooked Wash and Coyote Basin, where most of the vast numbers of deer wintered, and trap coyotes. He invited me to go along.

"Just come down most any time," Os told me. "I got horses and all kinds of traps. Bring a little grub and your bed and any traps you've got. We'll make it fine."

Since the deal was to be on the profit-sharing basis, it sounded good. Can you imagine a 14-year-old lad being charmed with the prospect of camping out in winter when the thermometer was at 30 below almost every night, without a tent or other shelter, cooking on a campfire, and tramping miles in deep snow every day? No, I suppose not. We didn't know any better. My parents seemed to approve of the plan. My brothers were entranced at it and would have gone along if permitted.

So, the day after Christmas, Dad took the team and wagon, and loading in my bed, gun, traps, food, and other necessary paraphernalia, took me down to Os Ames' cabin. When we got there it was kind of late in the afternoon. Ames was not at home. But we could see sleigh tracks a short distance from the house, and there were tracks of horses and men at the house, so we concluded Os had just gone away for the day. Dad had chores to do, so we unloaded the equipment, and he took off for home.

I stood in the lee of a shed and soaked up what heat the lowering sun afforded. Soon it was gone and the purple frost ring began to rise in the east. That denoted a frigid night coming. I devoutly wished Ames would get a wiggle on him and get home. The only other ranch of which I knew anywhere near was that of Jim Nutt. I didn't like Nutt. He was a red-muzzled, reserved, frigid Quaker, and it chilled my blood still further to think of going to him for shelter.

I think it was probably nearly nine o'clock before the intense cold drove me to action. I tried the door of the cabin. It was locked, but a shove of my shoulder opened it. Soon I had a cheery fire going in the old iron stove and prepared enough supper for two, but Ames did not show up, so I ate and enjoyed a restful night of sleep.

In the morning, when I looked out the window, a fat, chunky gray mare was nibbling at the sparse herbage near the house. After breakfast and washing the dishes and tidying the house, I began to wonder about Ames and did a little investigating. First, I inspected the cupboard and other places where food would be kept. Old Mother Hubbard's cupboard was a well-stocked larder compared with Young Bachelor Ames. His cupboard was really bare. Next, I went to look at the roads leading various directions from the house. None of them had been used in weeks by any kind of vehicle. Then I began to get mad.

"A fine kind of man he is," I told myself. "Talk a boy into going to all this trouble, when he knew he wasn't going to be here when I came."

Besides that, he had left the mare without hay or any way to survive excepting the sparse and poor bits of grass she might find among the sagebrush. Decent people didn't do that kind of thing. It was not hard for me to make my decision. Since Mr. Ames had quite unfeelingly left both me and the old gray mare in the lurch, what more right or in the way of poetic justice than for me and the mare to go in cahoots and work out our own survival.

I knew the mare would be better off almost anywhere than on the infertile and sandy flat. How she had managed to stay so fat so far into the winter puzzled me, but I concluded that if she were that good at rustling a living she and I were going to get along famously. So I turned my attention to planning and to action.

First of all I tried to catch the mare and tie her up. She had other ideas, but by putting a handful of my precious store of oatmeal in a pan along with a few small gravel stones and shaking the pan, I baited her into coming near enough for me to slip a rope around her neck. I tied her in the shed and rewarded her with a generous part of my oatmeal and some sugared bread. I knew that even if I ran out of food I could live on meat, as deer were to be had where I was going and my 30-30 was with me, as well as some traps for coyotes. They would serve to catch a rabbit if necessary.

I went to work with what little I had and could find, first fashioning a harness for the mare and a sled on which to transport my dunnage. A big piece of canvas, found in the shed, folded several times, made a pretty fair breast collar. Barbed wire, with the barbs hammered flat, answered for traces. A canvas backband and other necessary parts completed the harness. I was quite proud of my resourcefulness.

There was plenty of rope in my pack, and from it I rigged up a bridle. All our team bridles had blinders, so to cut up a tomato can I found and bend it into a pair of blinders was the next step. These were secured with baling wire.

Next came the sled. There was no other course but to dismantle some of Ames' furniture for this. But since I was going to restore everything after my trapping trip was over, I could see nothing wrong in this.

Side pieces from Ames' homemade bedstead were excellent for runners for the sled, after being shaped with the ax. Lumber from his table provided the platform. Nails were abundant. The table legs, nailed together in pairs, were just the checker for shafts. My luck was good, as I found an old singletree.

It must not be thought that this took no more time than the telling. By the time I had this much accomplished, it must have been about nine o'clock in the evening. The patient mare had been served most of my remaining oatmeal and bread as she seemed to have a good appetite. I led her to the river, about a quarter-mile away, and from a hole in the ice she drank her fill. I then ate a hastily prepared supper, deciding to leave that night for my intended camp. There was a bright moon and before storm came was the time to be on the way. For two hours I loaded and secured the sled.

But now a problem I had not anticipated confronted me. How on earth to get the loaded sled out of the cabin? It now became apparent that I should have moved it outdoors and then loaded it. But it was so nicely loaded, and the load tied on so well, I hated the thought of unloading and reloading it. So, I decided to bring the mare inside and to let her take it from there.

The mare was gentle and easily handled. But she soon demonstrated that she was not house-broke and that she knew her place. Go in the house she would not. Even the sugared bread routine failed in this crisis. Was I going to have to stevedore all that junk off and on again just to humor a contrary horse? I didn't think so. I still knew a few tricks she didn't. So I turned her tail to the door, where she couldn't see to the rear on account of the bridle blinders and proceeded to propel her backwards into the door and right in between the shafts. It was the work of only moments to fasten the shafts to the backband and make the traces fast to the singletree. All set! I looked around hastily to make sure the stove door was closed and opened the house door. The next few minutes are still a blur.

Just as I opened the door, the mare turned her head to look behind, and her tender nose touched the hot stove. With a loud neigh she reared. Her head crashed into the low ceiling, splitting the boards and opening a great hole through the flimsy board-and-tar-paper roof. Yelling "Whoa, whoa," I leaped towards her but a blow from one of her flailing forefeet sent me spinning.

With a loud snort she bolted. The sled crashed into the door frame, knocking that and a section of the wall galley-west. The sled careened, going on through the door but overturning in the yard, scattering food, blankets, traps, and kerosene. The last I saw of the mare, she disappeared in the bright moonlight over a low ridge, kicking every jump at what little remained of the cobbled-up harness, her mane and tail flying in the wind.

In my contacts with cowpunchers, trappers, and some ranchers I had learned some cusswords. These I used as best I could, inventing a few on the spot. What I lacked in facility and glibness I made up for in volume and repetition.

If I had been less tired, I might have tried to follow and bring back the mare. But I was beaten. I had worked under excitement for perhaps 17 hours. So I decided to sit by the stove and rest until daybreak, before trying to retrieve the mare and go through all that agony again. My determination to go through with the trapping trip had not abated a bit. I built up a good fire and propped my chair back against the wall to wait the dawn. The next thing I knew somebody was shaking me by the shoulder and demanding who I might be, what I was doing there, and what was going on.

It was Andy Haskett, a fellow of whom I had heard who had a cabin near the river at the mouth of Juniper Canyon. To my horror I learned that the mare was his. When he found her at his gate, adorned with my barbed-wire-and-canvas travesty of a harness, he had back-tracked her and discovered me sound asleep, in a cold cabin with its roof punctured, part of a wall knocked out and camp equipment scattered all over the yard.

Half awake, cold, and confused I could only think to tell Haskett the truth. As he listened, he shook his head in wonder. When I came to the part where the mare had bolted, he began to chuckle. When I told of the final outcome, mirth overcame him and he sat down and rocked and roared with laughter. I could see nothing funny about the situation.

Finally controlling his mirth, he said, "Well kid, I don't know whether you're lying to me or not. But anyhow, come along with me."

I could feel the sheriff breathing down my neck. But I felt no sympathy for myself. My only worry was what my parents and brothers and sisters would think.

Haskett took me to his house, a half-dugout roofed with cedar logs and earth, but as warm and clean as any habitation I had ever seen. His wife was a small dark-eyed and really beautiful woman, little more than a girl. Their small baby was as pretty as its mother. Haskett was not a bad-looking fellow himself.

I had to endure the agony of hearing him repeat my story, with some additions of his own and a few assists from me. His wife laughed a little, but I could see more sympathy than mirth in her eyes. We had a fine warm breakfast. After that I helped Haskett with the milking and feeding of a few animals, including my late lamented friend the gray mare. I thought she cast a reproachful glance at me. Back at the house, with the milk strained through a cloth and set away in large shallow pans for the cream to rise, Haskett brought up a subject that held only dread for me.

"I don't know anything about you kid," he told me. "It doesn't make sense that a kid of your age would be going out trapping alone."

I explained about Ames.

"Well, that could be," he reflected. "Os was called away by some of his folks being sick over where he came from. Somehow, I think you're telling the truth. Now I don't suppose you are rarin' to go on back home beaten like you are. So I'll make you a deal. I need some cedar posts cut. There are a lot of kiotes around here. I don't have any traps. So why don't you just stay here with us. You can cut posts and I'll pay you a little for them. We ain't got much money and have to scrabble pretty hard to get along ourselves. But you can ketch some kiotes and maybe make a little money and that way all of us, your folks, you and us, will not be all upset. I ought to turn you over to the sheriff, I know that. But somehow I don't think you're a bad lad. Are you?"

I hadn't expected that. It floored me. All I could blurt was, "Well—well—I don't know, Mr. Haskett. I don't intend to be bad. But I guess I'm not very good."

I bethought me of the times I had snitched a few things on purpose. Oh I knew it was wrong all right, I guess.

"Well, we'll see," Haskett said. "One thing, you didn't lie. That's good. If you had of lied you'd be on your way to jail right now. You just stick to that kid. Don't lie, and maybe you'll amount to something yet."

I loved the Hasketts right from the first. They were young, jolly, used good English and he seldom used profanity. Neither of them reminded me after that morning of the circumstances of our meeting. I worked hard every day, leaving early and returning late from the nearby Juniper Mountain where I set our traps and cut cedar pasts. Some days I didn't go to the mountain, but stayed at the house and helped Haskett with some of his work.

They were trying to make a ranch of their holdings. I did not see how they could ever succeed, but they had hope and industry.

We didn't do much more than the regular chores on Sundays. So one Sunday I told Haskett I thought I'd better go down and put Oscar Ames' furniture and house back together. He went with me and it didn't take long to get the crude bed and table reassembled and the door and roof fixed. We found some tar paper in the shed to patch the roof. It took us until about two o'clock to get it done, so we appreciated the hot dinner Mrs. Haskett had ready.

About three weeks after my advent into their midst, Haskett told me one evening that the next day he was going to Craig for some supplies. Next morning I helped Andy get started for town.

Before I climbed the two miles to the post timber patch on Juniper, Mrs. Haskett asked me, "Please come home a little early. I will have the milking and most of the chores done, but I'm afraid to be alone when it is dark." I could understand that. She seemed so little and timid to be alone in the darksome maw of that wild and gloomy canyon. I promised I'd be home early and told her not to do the chores as I'd allow plenty of time for me to do them.

The day was clear and cold and I got in good licks on the frozen, brittle wood of the cedars. With an eye on the sun, I quit what I judged to be a half-hour early. There was about two feet of snow on the mountain but I had tramped a good trail through it, as it wound along the precipitous slope. I stuck the ax in a juniper tree, the sharpening stone in a crotch, shouldered the rifle, and headed for the river. I hurried, although it was rather funny to me that a grown woman and mother would be afraid of the dark when she was inside the house. But she was so nice to me, acted more like a mother than some stranger, and I wasn't going to let her get scared through my fault.

Well, I'm hustling along the trail when above me I hear the yap-yapping of a coyote. I look up and there, on a sort of point of jutting rock I glimpse Mr. Coyote. I kneel, pull a good bead and the 30-30 cracks. The coyote jumps right out into space and lands in the deep snow below the ledge.

I lever in another cartridge and turn to climb up to bring down that $1.50 worth of fine fur. When I look up again, here comes the coyote to meet me. He had struggled a little and started the snow to moving. A sort of slide of snow is bringing him right on down, but if it keeps coming I'm in the wrong place to grab the coyote as he slides past. So I judge the distance and light out on a run. That judgment nearly cost me my life.

As the coyote and the snow come rushing, more snow moves and in just seconds a snowslide is roaring toward me. I turn to run, but before I take three strides the avalanche strikes, throwing me flat. Tumbling, struggling, blinded, I'm swept 100 feet down the mountainside and over the edge of a cliff.

I didn't have time to think of all this as it happened. Looking back today, I realize I had no chance to escape. Only a miracle kept me from being dashed down among the huge boulders at the foot of the cliff. As it was, I was swept over the lip of the cliff and began to fall. About 10 feet down, growing from a cleft in the sheer rock face of the cliff, as only junipers grow, a sparse trunk jutted a few feet. On this I landed. The breath was knocked out of me, my ribs ached, my rifle was gone, but I was alive.

After feeling myself over to see if there were any broken bones and finding none, I eased to a more comfortable position on the jutting juniper and assessed my situation. Born in snow country, raised on a mountain ranch, it did not take long for me to realize my situation was not only critical, but desperate.

In the east the purple frost ring was already above the horizon. Each night for two weeks the thermometer had been dipping to more than 30 degrees below zero. Perched on this exposed cliff face, dressed in only such clothing as would keep me from chilling while working or walking, without a chance to move about, I was doomed. Toughened though I was, and inured to cold and hardships, I knew mighty well that I could not last more than maybe four or five hours. Already the cold was eating into my bones, and the sun had hardly set yet.

The rock wall above me was at least 10 feet high. Balancing myself on the tree limb, my extended fingers were still a good two feet below the edge of the rock. Even if I could leap high enough to get my fingers on the rim, there was no fingerhold, but only smooth, frosty rock.

Downward the prospect was no less terrifying. A 40-foot drop into those jagged boulders meant either instant death or such crippling impact that death by freezing would be the certain end. I had heard of men in such circumstances taking their own lives. The rifle was gone, beyond my reach. I could see its stock projecting from the snow, lodged among the rocks on the side of the narrow defile where the avalanche had left it.

To add to my misery, a fine, dissipated stream of snow constantly came over the brink, powdering me with its frigid coldness.

It seemed like forever, but it was probably an hour, I crouched, now shivering, on the tree trunk. I have heard that facing death, an entire life may pass in review by the doomed one's mind. It was not so with me. The burden of my thoughts was my family. How the boys would miss the good times we always had together. How my sister would mourn the one who had shared with her so many precious secrets. I even thought of my elder sister, Eva, who had been out in the world on her own for several years. The tears of my mother and the sadness on the face of my father passed across the mirror of my mind in clear relief. I gave a thought, too, to poor Mrs. Haskett, alone and frightened in the dark.

We were what you might call a religious family. There was always "grace" at table and evening prayers. But somehow, this had never seemed much more to me than a ritual required by the rules of the church. If the words spoken had much meaning, that meaning had been lost to me in the endless repetitions. Anyhow, praying for help did not occur to me now when I needed help so desperately.

I had my own ideas about things religious. My dad had taught me enough about the heavens and astronomy that I had a good idea of the immensity of the universe. That such should be ruled by a man-like being on a throne didn't make sense to me. But believe in a Creator, in a Supreme Power over all, I did, with all my heart.

So now, in extremis, with slow but certain death riding that frost ring and aimed for me as surely as any bullet of death, I thought of my belief, of my convictions. Strangely enough I found my thoughts good, and maybe a mite comforting. My body was already stiffening with the cold and it seemed that the shivering penetrated deep to shake the very vital organs within me. Despite this, my mind was racing with heat and desperate speed.

Then suddenly I was saying, "I know I deserve what is going to happen to me. I have been bad. But, I swear my dying oath that if You will get me out of this, so my folk won't be sorry and cry about me, I will never, never steal anything again as long as I live."

For quite awhile I crouched there, thinking of that plea and promise. After awhile, as if in derisive refusal of my ridiculous prayer, the snow from above began to run anew, the trickle coming over the cliff brink increasing to shower me with an increasing source of cold and misery from which there was no escape.

I had barely time to shift to try to avoid this chilling cascade when it increased and grew into a stream of icy horror as large as my body. Then came from above that seething roar that had accompanied the first avalanche, and over the rim came an ocean of white horror, engulfing me and all but sweeping me from my perch.

It was over in a minute. The snow and debris went roaring away down the gully in the mountainside. I was battered and drenched anew, cold to the marrow of my bones. Only the instinctive wish to live kept me clinging to the tree. It was dark, but the afterglow in the west lent an uncanny light to the snow-covered scene. In this dim light I dared to look down. The shock all but knocked me from the tree. I blinked fiercely and looked again. No longer was the heap of boulders beneath me visible. They lay buried under hundreds of tons of snow and rubble, piled up by the avalanche until the topmost part of this pile reached almost to my aerie.

Gingerly, I lowered myself by my hands, feeling with my feet. They touched a fairly solid surface. Dropping, I crawled across the gully, retrieved the rifle, and took off at a dog-trot down the trail.

And oh, did poor Mrs. Haskett give me the dickens for fooling around so late. She had been scared.

★
The Hermit of Yampa Canyon

We've all read narratives of the early settlers who were workers, builders, and good neighbors. They helped to develop and to create. But another kind of settler sometimes came and often left little mark on the county other than such legends as might remain.

Such a one was Pat Lynch. Pat brought nothing with him, created nothing lasting, and left nothing significant, but he was probably talked of more widely and had more written about him than many who made significant and lasting contributions to the canyon country of northwestern Colorado.

Pat Lynch, if that was his real name, is said by some to have been in this area in 1869 when J. W. Powell made his voyage through the canyons of the Green and Colorado Rivers. According to Pat's own story, he was born in Ireland and went to sea in the British Navy when 14. He was shipwrecked off the coast of Africa but managed to get to shore, made friends with a native tribe and lived with them for four years. He did not come to an end like "The Man Who Would Be King" in Kipling's tale, but remained alive and was taken off by a British merchant ship which was headed for India. His term of enlistment in Her Majesty's Navy was not served out but he, in a way, "went over the hill," made his way to the United States and enlisted in our Navy. In an engagement, likely with pirates, he was wounded.

After his wounds were healed, Pat did a sudden chameleon act and changed his name to "James Cooper" and was accepted into the Army, during the War Between the States. After the war he came westward and in time reached the canyon country in northwest Colorado now known as Dinosaur National Monument.

Whether he was hiding from the law or from Indians is not known for certain. He told later that he had killed a man and came to the mountain fastness to avoid prosecution. Many who knew him and his talent with a juicy tale doubted this. Somebody improved on the story and told that Pat had killed his own mother.

But at any rate, Pat found one of the most inaccessible places in the region, in the depths of Yampa Canyon below Lily Park, where he holed up on Pool Creek. His habitation was a natural, open-faced cavern in the sandrocks. During the 19 years he occupied it, he did little to improve it or to make it more habitable. Only when the Chews, a Mormon family, came into the canyon and took a homestead on Pool Creek, did Lynch move. His next roosting place was in Echo Park.

There, by sinking four posts into the ground and fashioning walls of willow brush and mud, he built his "house." The cabin in which Pat later lived in "Pat's Hole" was built by some cowboys, of which Charley Clawson, who told us the facts, was one. Charley was a long-time friend of our family. About 1927 he was game warden and spent a good many nights at our deer hunting camp on Cold Spring Mountain. He told us what Pat Lynch had told him about his first months in Yampa Canyon.

"Pat told me he came into this canyon country with nothing more than the clothes he wore," Charley recalled. "There was some wild fruit dried on the bushes and little else in the way of food. One night Pat heard the screams of a cougar high among the cliffs. Listening and thinking, the idea came to him that the lion was calling to him. Next day he climbed the heights and in a little park near the top of the rimrock came on the carcass of a deer. The animal had been eaten with the exception of one ham. This Pat took, and it provided him with good food for many days. From then on, he listened for the call of the big cats and did not lack for meat."

This story of Pat's may or may not have been entirely true. We do know that Pat either had hallucinations or told tall tales. Possibly both.

He told Charley that he killed a man aboard ship, but leaped into the water and swam ashore and was a fugitive.

"Old Pat was quite a hand to wander," Charley told us one time. "He wandered into this country and afterwards wandered all over it. One of his trips in the middle of winter took him up the canyon, across Lily Park and on up Snake River."

"The reason for such a trip must have been that he simply became bored and irked by the sameness of every day in his canyon retreat and went looking for contact with other humans. The river was frozen over, so he would have good walking on the ice."

"Old Pat probably took along some jerky. In fact, I think he told me he did. He holed up in caves in the rock at night. In two or three days he made it to the ranch of George and Maggie Baggs, where the town of Baggs, Wyoming is now."

"Pat told me he had a good time on the trip. Old Maggie insisted that he stay several days. The way Maggie could cook, it wasn't hard to coax Pat into staying. George and Pat could swap yarn for yarn, too. After a few days Pat headed south, following the freight road. This was the road Dennis Cologne built and went down Fortification Creek to Little Bear then over the hills to Elkhead. That's before the government bridge was built south of Lay. The Hulett Ranch was then right there on Elkhead. Pat finally came to Huletts."

"'Sure an' I was fair shpent, wid all the walkin' an' traipsin',' Pat told me," Charley continued. "'Then suddintly I shpies a bit of light in the darkness, for it was night by now. Before I could navigate the distance the light winks out.'"

"Pat kept on to where he thought the light should be and came to the Hulett cabin. His lusty knocking, though, failed to bring response. After debating with himself for awhile, he knocked again. When nobody answered he unhooked the door latch and went in. It was the work of only moments to strike a light and get the kerosene lamp going. The lamp chimney was still warm and fire glowed in the stove. Pat could not understand the sudden departure, unless it had been perhaps someone on the dodge from the law, who like himself thought to find a haven for the night."

"'I surmises, for some raison unbeknownst to meself,' related Pat, 'that whoever it is, is gone fer the noight. So then, castin' me eyes about I shpies on a shelf a bottle. It is tall like this, it is fat across and in it is a beauchous somethin' that raysembles naught so much as whisky. So I takes it down, withdraws the cork, shmells it and the shtuff shmells loike whisky.'"

"Pat debated the possibility of the stuff being poison, but thirst overcame caution, and he tasted it. It was whisky. What followed is left to your imagination."

"At any rate, the owners, or any others, did not show up that night. Pat could probably have stayed a week if he had cared to. He cooked himself a good breakfast, washed the dishes and piked on down Bear River. He no doubt left a note of thanks at the cabin."

I've heard it said and have seen in print the statement that Pat could neither read nor write. Not true. Bruce and Marian MacLeod of the Whisky Springs Ranch on Douglas Mountain have letters written by Pat concerning the pensions he got in his dual names.

On his way back to Yampa Canyon he would not lack for places to get a meal or spend a night. There were ranches at intervals and their lonely occupants would welcome a visitor, especially since Pat was an amiable old boy and always had a good story on tap.

Pat was no doubt the recluse he was reputed to be. But he had some business sense, too. He contrived to draw pensions under each of the names he had used in the Army and Navy service.

There was a story to the effect that Pat rode into this county on a fine stallion that later fathered what grew into a sizable herd. This herd was supposed to be the nucleus of the wild horse herds that ranged on Douglas Mountain. Some few of them are still to be found. Whether any of this is true we do not know. Around such a character as Pat all sorts of fables and legends are sure to be built.

Roy Templeton told us of a cattle drive in which he took part. The crew of which he was a part brought a considerable herd of cattle from the Lynch habitat and took them into Brown's Park. Pat's cattle and horse brand was the "Ox Shoe." An ox shoe consisted of two plates of steel or iron nailed to the cloven hoofs of the oxen used as draft animals to protect them against injury by sharp rocks and wear on the gritty roads.

Pat spent a good part of his time at the ranch of Henry Shank in Lily Park. Mrs. George Rinker, a daughter of the Shanks, has written comprehensively of Pat Lynch from first-hand knowledge. He also visited protractedly at the home of the Barnes family. Frank Barnes was manager of the big ranch owned by the White Bear Land & Cattle Co.

All I personally know about Pat Lynch (or James Cooper if you prefer) was learned in the summer of 1901 when I worked on a haying crew in Lily Park at the White Bear Ranch. Frank Barnes was ranch manager. One of the Barnes' sons, Waller, was about my age. He and I went swimming almost every evening in Bear River. Among other things, Waller told me about a funny old fellow called Pat Lynch.

I was intrigued by his description of Pat. So I was delighted when the old recluse showed up at the ranch one evening. He arrived in time for supper and remained for the night. He was a good-looking and amiable old gentleman. We kids had been taught to have respect for older persons, but the Barnes family did not appear to take Pat very seriously and during the meal his remarks were frequently cut off by somebody "butting in" with their own talk and interrupting him.

Inwardly, I resented this, as I felt that Pat's observations would be more interesting than what the others had to say. But probably, in the way of oldsters, Pat had retold his stories to the Barnes family until they had lost their charm.

Many who knew Pat agree that, while Pat Lynch has most often been pictured as a sort of "wild man of the canyons, existing much like an animal," the real Pat Lynch was an intelligent, clean, liberty-loving, companionable man who delighted to be with others, to listen as well as talk and to give attention to the small herd of well-bred horses he accumulated and to an extensive orchard.

Says Mrs. Hoover, who grew up in Lily Park and knew Pat well, "Pat had deep beliefs in Providential direction and that he could talk with spirits and hear their voices. But he had a good many common-sense skills and could use materials at hand with dexterity. He cached bits of food at strategic places in the canyons in case he got benighted away from home. He tied strings around his pant legs below the knees to catch anything that might fall through a hole in a pocket. He never passed our country's flag without stopping, baring his head, bowing low and saying, 'In reverence to my flag and my country.' He would not go to an old-soldiers' home, as he thought it would restrict his liberty. He did, though, accept the military pension of $30 a month and $270 back pay, which Mr. Barnes helped him to get. This enabled him to live without charity."

Henry Templeton, who had a ranch on Bear River near Cross Mountain, said he first knew Pat in 1870 when Pat worked for Templeton's father in a rock quarry at Colorado City, at the foot of Pike's Peak. Pat drifted on to the Hahns Peak mining country, then to Brown's Park, and finally into the canyons.

Pat told me a little of this when I met him at the White Bear Ranch. There was rain during the night and it was too wet for haying the next morning. So, after grinding the mowing machine sickles and repairing some harness, we just waited for the hay to dry. Pat was down by the barn, using curry comb and brush on the coat of his horse. I wandered down that way and stood watching him, hoping he'd talk to me of some of the things I had heard he could tell.

After awhile he turned and asked, "What's yer name, b'y?"

"FitzPatrick, sir," I told him.

"Oi mane yer whole name. All of it."

"Valentine Stewart Parnell FitzPatrick, sir," I answered, giving him my full baptismal name.

The old gentleman staggered back as if I had hit him with a club.

"Howly saints alive! By me sowl an' body! Shmall wonder that ye ain't no bigger than a pound of scapl, packin' around the weight of a name loike that!"

I didn't know what to say, so said nothing. Pat regained his poise and talked to me at length, kindly. He found out all about my family and told me much of the lore of the canyon. Presently, eyeing the sky, he remarked, "Sure an' I got to be gittin' down the canyon, 'fore the rain begins."

The sky was cloudless and I remarked on it.

"Yes, I know," Pat replied. "But Frank says it will rain widin' two or three hours, an' Frank ain't ever wrong on weather."

By "Frank" I thought he meant Mr. Barnes. I had heard Mr. Barnes say a short while before that he thought the storm was over and the weather would be fair for a few days. I reminded Pat of this.

"Yes, yes," he answered, "Misther Barnes may think he knows about weather. He knows no more than me er you. But Frank knows. I never seen a horse like this one, me lad."

I saw nothing unusual about the long-legged bay and told Pat so.

"It ain't what ye see, son, but what no man but meself sees an' hears. Frank and me talk wid each other. Have ye iver seen a horse that shpakes the language? Have ye iver set yer peepers on a horse which predicths the comin' weather?"

I had to admit that conversing quadrupeds and prognosticating ponies were quantity X to me.

Pat patiently explained that Frank indeed had the power of communication, and had what today we would describe as ESP.

"Goin' beyant down the canyon, one beaucheous day like now," he related, "Frank cocks an ear back and says to me over his shoulder, says he, 'Pat, ease up on the bridle reins an' let me go. A shtorm has been behint us an' the wather will be rollin' down this canyon.'"

"I aised up on the reins an' Frank and me goes fast. An' none too soon. Fer soon a great hoother ov a tremenjus lot of wather comes an' 'tis only by galloopin' an' splashin' an' shtrugglin' we raich the bank an' presarve our lives."

Pat finished saddling Frank, then sat on his heels against the barn and told me he hoped to meet my father some time.

"Ye might say he is like me, a seafarin' man. Him an' me could shpake ov things ov the fo'csle, ov shinnin' up shrouds in black ov night, reefin' an' makin' fast the sails, ov the voices that shpake to sailors aloft along the yardarms an' on the studs'l boom."

I knew exactly what he meant. Many a night I had lain in a camp bed beside my father while he talked of the sea. Before I was eight I could name every mast, spar, and sail of a four-masted schooner. So I reported to Dad later my confab with Pat Lynch. They never met, as the 50 miles that separated them was in that day as far apart as the oceans they had both sailed.

Anyhow, Pat soon rode away, headed for the canyon. Three hours later a veritable cloudburst raised the river to a raging flood!

Pat died in 1917 at the home of Fray Baker near Elk Springs. He was buried in Lily Park. It is said his grave is marked by a stone bearing the insignia of the U. S. Navy.

★
The Biggest Roundup

For years I heard mention of the Big Roundup of 1909. One day, talking to my brother Arthur, it occurred to me to ask him what he knew about it. To my surprise I found that he knew a great deal. At the time he was only 17, but was a rider for the W. H. Rose cattle and ranch outfit.

Rose owned a ranch on the head of Fortification Creek north of Craig. He had extensive ranch land adjoining the town and a handsome dwelling and huge barn. Art was supposed to inherit this barn at Rose's demise, but some legal sharpers made off with the will and probably most of the property and money. Rose's widow came to the end of life all but destitute.

While Rose lived, Art was employed by him. The last few years of Rose's life, my brother was foreman of his ranches and cattle. It was in 1909 that the Big Roundup occurred.

Up to this time, the big cattle companies had pastured their cattle on forest lands without fee or restrictions. Chief of these companies was the giant Two-Bar outfit. The original Two-Bar Ranch was on the Yampa River near where Craig was later to be. This was in the late 1870s. In 1880, Haley bought a ranch on Big Gulch, two and one-half miles northeast of where Lay post office is now. He also bought a ranch a half-mile north of Lay, and one on Snake River 30 miles west of Lay. Haley had more than 40,000 head of cattle at the peak of his operation in the 1890s.

Things changed when the U. S. Forest Service initiated a plan of charging a small fee for each animal permitted to graze on National Forest land. For a year or two after the fee system was set up, the Two-Bar put their cattle on the forest just as they had always done, ignoring any payment. Probably lesser companies tried to follow suit. But in 1909 the service had a new chief ranger, Harry Ratliff. He was a dedicated forest man and at once set about making preparations to collect the fees. As helpers he chose men who believed, as he did, that the cattle people should pay a small fee for the privilege of letting their cattle eat the grass owned by all the people. Jim Oliphant (for whom Mount Oliphant was named), Ray Peck from Hayden, and Sam Coleman from Steamboat Springs were his key men. With them on prominent and strategic points along the forest boundary Ratliff was all set for the opening day for grazing.

As usual in May the shove-up had reached Fortification Creek extending north from Craig for 26 miles. This shove-up started at the K Ranch near the Utah line on the south side of Blue Mountain. This was low-altitude country with but little snow in winter. Fanned out on what was called the circle, the cowpunchers combed the country, taking the cattle off the good spring grass and moving them eastward, shoving ahead of them a constantly growing herd.

This particular shove-up included not only the Two-Bar, but the other big cattle outfits in the country. Each company taking part in the roundup sent a wagon and crew. The wagon was good-size, drawn by four horses and manned by the cook. It was both portable kitchen and storehouse for the food. Often, too, each wagon was accompanied by a second wagon carrying the bedrolls of the crew, hauled by a single team, and handled, usually, by a young fellow who helped the cook daytimes and night-herded the saddle horses. He was called the cookee. In the case of the Two-Bar, the cookee did not nighthawk, as they had a big herd of cowponies and it took older and more skilled men to care for them.

B. F. "Boston" Shedden, most famous horse wrangler in the West, was for years the Two Bar wrangler. On a roundup such as the shove-up of 1909 he might have 200 head of horses in the cavvy. With horses in that herd from several different ranges, and all eager to get back to their home range, the skill and work it took to keep the herd intact may be imagined.

The six wagons and crews at the 1909 shove-up were sent by the Two-Bar, the Two-Circle Bar, the Sevens (7), the Reverse Four, the OVO, and the Snake River Stockmen's Association. Several smaller cattle outfits, such as the Salisbury, and Temple and Rose interests were represented. These independents rode with one or another of the main crews. My brother Art rode with the Snake River

Association and ate at their wagon. At the end of the shove-up, their wagon was camped just above the Davis Ranch at the Fortification Rocks, the impressive basalt dike that bisects the valley there. Other wagons were at other points on the creek.

The day came when the cattle were to be checked onto the forest reserve by the men of the Forest Service. The Two-Bar was all set with a plan Haley and his foreman had no doubt worked out. Two-Bar cattle, instead of being bunched like those of the other outfits, were scattered for miles along the forest boundary. When the signal came for the cattle to be started onto the forest, the Two-Bar men went into action.

Certain natural trailways had been designated for the cattle to pass along so they might be counted and tallied. The Two-Bar had cattle on these trails, but they also had cattle on every ridge and in every gulch along the line. When the zero moment came, men began to shove Two-Bar cattle over the line in dozens of places.

It looked like a failproof scheme, but Haley had not properly sized up Harry Ratliff and his lieutenants. The Two-Bar herders found checkers at every point. They found these men to be grim, determined, and all set for any kind of fracas that might develop.

It was true that the cowpunchers worked from daylight to dark at dangerous, irksome duty for a mere $30 a month, and in most cases they were somewhat loyal to the company that paid their meager wages. But mighty few cowpunchers let their loyalty extend to the point where they'd risk being shot for dear Old Yale, or dear Old Two-Bar, or any other brand. And it looked as if they might be shot if they didn't hold up their herds and give the pistol-packing Forest rangers and helpers time to tally the cattle onto the National Forest.

It was Haley's first real confrontation with the law. He came off second best. For years he had manipulated his taxes, ridden roughshod over the smaller cattle outfits and small ranches, and gotten away with it. But Uncle Sam was something else.

Art was riding with one of the cowpunchers of the Snake River Stockmen's Association. The name of this puncher escapes me. He was a tall, rangy, leather-faced fellow of about 40. He sat on a horse as if he were a part of the animal. He had been on famous trail drives from deep in the Southwest to such places as Dodge City, Abilene, and Bovina. When encroaching settlers and the extending railroads brought an end to the trail drives, he drifted into Montana where the cattle business was already well established and big ranchers had taken over.

But Montana was too civilized for this rider, so he drifted into the still-raw cattle range of northwest Colorado. Sitting hip-shot in the saddle atop a ridge while the Association cattle poured through a pass onto the Forest Reserve, he and Art could see the valleys and hills covered by slowly moving animals.

"Take a good look at them there cows, kid," the big puncher told Art. "You're probably lookin' at the biggest roundup ever seen in any country."

"You think so?"

"Ah shore do. Ah've knowed of some mighty big cattle drives. Ah've seed 'em comin' out of the chaparral and mesquite by the hundreds and coverin' what looked like half a county. But Ah never knowed of any such lot of cows as this. This here is one hell of a roundup."

Art knew this was one tremendous roundup. His curiosity stirred by the remarks of the big cowpuncher, he later asked Bill Wear, the Two-Bar wagon boss, what the total tally was.

"They tallied in 60,000 head," Bill told him, "But it was more than that. A lot of cattle got in while the fracas with the Two-Bar and the Foresters was going on. I'd put it at probably 62,000."

I have talked with cattlemen from such places as Argentina and Australia and others who had been on trail rides. From all I can gather, that roundup in 1909 may well have been the biggest ever held anywhere on earth. I wish I could have been with Art to see it.

From what has been told, it might be concluded that Ora Haley was a greedy and contemptible character. Far from it. He was hell-bent for making money and would resort to almost any means to do it. That was a rough country, people played rough even in business. Haley tried to outplay them.

He had gotten his start the hard way, working in a butcher shop in Laramie, Wyoming. Before long he owned his own shop. And, seeing the wisdom of raising the beef he sold, he soon had a cattle herd. It was a natural step from the small herd to a big one. But hemmed in by other cattle companies, he needed room to expand. On a flying trip to northwest Colorado, he saw the lush bluestem hills stretching from Black Mountain to the Utah line. It wasn't long until he came with a herd and that was the start of his herds that soon were on every hill and in every valley of what is now Moffat County.

We knew Ora Haley well. When he'd come from his Laramie home to inspect his ranches and cattle in Moffat County, he would spend at least two nights at our ranch home. He could have stayed at one of his cowcamps, but didn't. Being another Irishman, he had a feeling for my Belfast-born father.

Haley was a highly intelligent man, a quick thinker, and a good talker. He and our folks enjoyed the liveliest conversations at meal-times and after. Instead of riding or driving a Two-Bar horse, he always borrowed our horse and cart to travel to his Snake River ranch. Our parents never accepted pay for his meals or for the horse and cart, although Haley always offered it. He did, though, reciprocate. A red calf that had been accidentally left behind by a shove-up was given by Haley to our family.

But of more value was his action in the case of a Two-Bar steer Dad accidentally killed.

It happened one hard winter. Snow was deep and even the coyotes couldn't find dry places to sleep. Two or three of them slept each night on top of a partly used haystack behind our barn. Dad decided to try to get one, as the fur was prime and worth a whole dollar, a lot of money in those days. So when Dad went one early morning to feed the cows and work horses, he took along the shotgun, loaded with buckshot. He didn't get a shot at a coyote, so he set the shotgun just inside the barn door. A day or two later, as he crossed the road between house and barn, he was charged by a big, bony red steer owned by the Two-Bar. The animal had been missed on the shove-down that fall and had hung around with our cows since, it being then near Christmas time.

This steer was an evil brute, goring the cows away from their hay, chasing us kids, and now giving Dad a narrow escape through the barn door. Determined to try to stop this nonsense by peppering the steer with shot, Dad grabbed the shotgun, and when the steer made another charge, let him have it. Dad had forgotten that he had taken out the light duck load and put in buckshot for the coyote. The steer came down, dead, almost at his feet.

After breakfast Dad hitched the team and dragged the steer down the road to near the bridge across Lay Creek, a distance of less than a quarter mile, but far enough so the odor would not bother us when warm weather came.

That same day, Sid Pugh, a Two-Bar employee and also a "stock detective," came along. He stopped and examined the steer. Usually Sid stopped at our house for a chat. This time he kept right on to the Two-Bar horse camp, two miles up Big Gulch. He probably knew that the Two-Bar foreman, Hi Bernard, was there.

In a few hours the big, soft-spoken Texan showed up at our house. After the usual greetings, he came to the point. "How about that dead Two-Bar steer down by the bridge, FitzPatrick?" he wanted to know. "Sid Pugh told me about it. Said he figgered maybe you might know something about it."

"Yes, I do," Dad said evenly. "I killed it."

"Y'mean you shot it?" Hi said in assumed surprise. He knew very well who had shot it.

"Yes. It was really an accident, as I had forgotten I had buckshot in the shotgun. But it would have been the same if I had known," Dad told him. "The steer has been a nuisance. He has our milk cows scarred by his attacks, he has chased the children, and this morning he chased me into the barn and again charged when I showed up. I intended to burn him and scare him but the buckshot was too much for him."

Bernard always talked out of the side of his mouth. Now, with his lip drawn down, he told Dad, "This is mighty serious business, FitzPatrick. Killin' a critter that don't belong to you is mighty serious."

Dad made no reply.

"A fellow could go to the pen fer a thing like that," Hi pursued.

Dad still said nothing. I'll bet he was doing some tall thinking, though.

Hi scratched the stubby red whiskers on his chin, shifted his feet, and was silent for a time. Mother and we kids held our breaths.

"Something's got to be done about that there dead steer," Hi finally said. "Haley just don't stand for cattle killin' by no ranchers. I hate to make y' trouble, FitzPatrick, we bein' friendly and all, but I got a job to think about and Haley's my boss. Maybe—I ain't saying so, but just maybe—he might stand fer y' just payin' fer the steer. I don't know. I guess maybe what I ought to do is jest go to the sheriff." He said this with some asperity, nettled at Dad's silence.

"What d' y' say, FitzPatrick? Y' want t' pay fer that there steer and t' settle it that way?"

"No, I don't think so," Dad replied evenly. "I think the thing to do is just wait until Mr. Haley comes and let him and me decide."

Hi nearly fell off his chair. It was a big thing to him, born and raised on cattle range and learning to despise cattle rustlers and those who killed the big outfits' cattle. To him Dad had just become one of them.

But he couldn't budge Dad, so after a lot of jangling he left without any definite decision.

"Good Lord, Tom," Mother said as soon as the door closed behind Hi. "Do you suppose that man will go to the sheriff?"

"I don't think so," Dad said calmly. "Hi knows that we don't rustle cattle. He knows as well as I do that I didn't try to hide the steer. Of course, he probably thinks I killed the steer on purpose—but he also knows that we and Haley are friendly. I don't think he's going to bother the sheriff."

It turned out that way, but better than we had expected. Early in the spring Haley showed up on one of his regular visits. After supper Dad told him about the steer. He also told him that Hi Bernard was quite properly concerned about the matter.

"I don't blame Mr. Bernard," Dad told Haley. "He is looking after your interests and naturally doesn't want people killing the cattle in his charge."

I wondered at Dad making excuses for Hi after the heated set-to they had had about the steer. At eleven I guess I was too young to understand about diplomacy and such things as "loving your enemies."

Haley was not at all put out by the matter. He knew quite well Dad was not stealing or butchering other people's cattle.

"It's unfortunate the animal bothered you and that the buckshot was in the gun," he remarked. "I'll speak to Bernard about it. I appreciate the way you have handled it."

That was the end of that. But it was not the last time Hi Bernard and Dad locked horns.

We had horses on the range and among them was a big white mare with a white colt. Riding out to check up on them, as we often did, I discovered, freshly imprinted on the cheek of the colt's rump, the "Heart" brand with which the Two-Bar marked their horses. The annual horse roundup was on. Probably some of the Two-Bar men had branded the colt by mistake.

The first time we saw the Two-Bar foreman passing our place Dad went out and hailed him. Hi stopped, turned his pony, and came back. Dad explained about the colt and asked Hi what he intended to do about it. Bernard tried his favorite tactic, a sort of mildly worded bluff.

"Now y' know what we'll do about it, FitzPatrick. Any horse with the Heart brand is Two-Bar property."

"But this colt is following its mother, our white mare," Dad objected.

"Well, now, y' and me know how colts are liable to foller any mare that will let 'em."

Dad looked at Bernard in amazement. That an experienced livestock man would voice such an idea was incredible. Even I knew better than that. I expected Dad to burst out in expostulation, but after a long silence he said quite calmly, "I don't think you and I can get anywhere talking about this. I'll just let it go until Mr. Haley comes."

What Hi might have said I don't know, for Dad just turned and went in the house. After a few moments Hi turned and galloped to catch up with the other cowpunchers.

I don't remember whether Dad and Haley talked about it or not. But at any rate, we kept the colt, it grew up, and was broken to work, and much later was traded for some other animal. I'm fairly sure, though, that it was the only horse wearing the "Heart" brand to be kept by anyone in the region. All the Heart horses were shipped to faraway markets, never sold locally.

So, I can say with authority that Ora Haley was a good man to meet, a pleasant guest, and fair in his dealings with us. But he liked money and would do almost anything to make, save, and keep it. So it was that he resisted paying taxes and paying fees for grazing his cattle on the National Forest. The confrontation that challenged him and changed his ways was at the Big Roundup.

★

The Crossing of the Burning Sands

George Davidson and I both were members of the local lodge of Woodmen of the World. Oliver Haughey was Consul Commander or Chief Officer of the lodge. Ol would permit no reading of parts but insisted on his staff officers learning their parts and charges. It made for a very impressive lodge. It made for a lot of mental perspiration, too. That is, to everybody but George Davidson. He memorized anything and everything and could reel it off like a tape recorder.

George and Leon Breeze and I did some hunting together, so we got to be cronies. This proved to be most fortunate on a most unusual occasion.

In the Woodmen Lodge you would hear from the older members a good bit of talk about the "Supreme Degree." This, you learned by inquiring, was a greatly advanced degree, awarded only to those who showed unusual devotion to the lodge, high intelligence, and a high degree of courage. It was all sort of mysterious, which piqued the curiosity of members who were not "on the inside." I had been in the lodge about a year but still knew but little about the Supreme Degree. I did not press the matter too much as I did not think I was qualified.

But from the way George Davidson learned his darts and from his perfect attendance and great interest in the lodge, some of us got the idea he might qualify for the "Supreme Degree." We mentioned this to Ol Haughey, chief officer.

"I don't have anything to do with that degree," Ol told us. "I just take care of the regular work. You can see Jay Paxman about that degree."

So we saw Jay Paxman. Jay was a butcher, weighed about 200, and was strong as a bull. He was also a good lodge man and an agreeable fellow to know.

"You just might be right," Jay told us. Leon Breeze, Ralph White, Dave Davis, and Joe Norvell and I had gone to Jay.

"I'll talk it over with some of the others who confer the Supreme Degree, talk to George, and let you know."

In a few days Jay told us George was elected to take the degree. But he also told us that before George could be introduced, Breeze and I would have to take the degree. That nearly floored us, as neither of us had the faintest idea we were qualified. But anyhow we took the degree, to our great amazement and discomfiture.

So came the night when George was to be exhalted to the high estate of the Supreme Degree. Breeze and I were to be the two "Supreme Conductors" to steer the victim through the rite. For victim he was, as Breeze and I well knew from our own harrowing experience.

For the fact was, the Supreme Degree had absolutely nothing to do with the work of the Woodmen Lodge. It was what is called a "side degree," cooked up to afford a lot of misery for the candidate and a lot of merriment for everybody else.

They had a hand-operated generator which was used to give electric shocks under many guises. For instance, the candidate was solemnly cautioned that "only the pure at heart and the clean in person can enter the sacred realm of the Supreme Degree." So, to be sure of physical cleanliness, the candidate must wash his hands in a tin basin presented by a member in the uniform of a priest. The moment the candidate's hands got in the water the fellow at the crank of the generator gave a turn and the shock almost sent the victim into a tailspin.

There was a "goat" to be ridden as part of the rite. This was a three-wheeled contrivance, with a wooden goat body, replete with horns. There was a handle like a lawn mower. The wheels were odd sizes, which gave the thing a lurching gait. With Jay Paxman on the handle, adding a few jerks on his own account, the thing was almost impossible to ride. Out of dozens I saw try it, only Johnny Bigtole, a bronco buster who had been with Wild West shows, and Joe Norvell rode it to a finish. Even at that, Joe pulled the "animal's" head off in the process.

And so it went, all deadly serious, but every step fraught with that kind of painful nonsense.

At length came the supreme test. That was called the "Crossing of the Burning Sands." To simulate burning sands, there was a strip of heavy canvas, about two feet wide and ten feet long. In it had been inserted carpet tacks until it was one mass of them.

"As you well know, the Supreme Degree is only for the one who can endure and not quail," Jay Paxman intoned, his face hidden by the cowl of the helmet of a Roman warrior's costume.

"You have proven of great fortitude and courage," he went on. "But what you have endured is only a mild preparation for the test to come. Open the hoodwink!" he commanded an aide.

The aide flipped back the lids that covered the goggles worn by the victim, so he could look at the tack-filled canvas.

"Do not fear," the solemn Jay went on. "All of those around you have crossed these burning sands into the land of knowledge, wisdom, and love. A doctor is waiting in the outer rooms. You will be guided and supported by two faithful brothers. It is very likely you will faint. Few make this passage without fainting. To spare you, we close the hoodwink so you do not have to see the torture inflicted on your naked soles."

At that, one of the helpers took off the candidate's shoes, another closed the lids on the goggles and two others, Breeze and I, propelled George forward.

During the few seconds while this was transpiring, two members had jerked the tack-filled canvas away and in its place laid down a similar strip of cloth, across which zigzagged from end to end a metal cord connected to the generator. The moment George's foot touched this the generator man began to turn the handle.

When I took this degree, I would have sworn I was walking on the tacks. I just *knew* that my feet would be a bleeding mass. I think if I *could* have fainted I would have. But I have never fainted or been knocked out in my life. But Breeze *had* come out of the ordeal in a half daze.

George went them one better, he *did* faint.

I was not too much concerned. I put my hand over his heart and found it beating, even though rapidly. He was breathing fairly evenly. But he lay without a twitch.

There was no doctor in the anteroom. One or two of the members pumped George's arms, half-heartedly. Jay Paxman disappeared.

Breeze and I knelt beside George and noting his breathing, expected him to come to and sit up. But he didn't. We looked around. The three of us were alone.

Breeze had always been a hand to do a lot of reading and to delve into anything that interested him. At the time, he had been reading a treatise on hypnotism. It flashed across his mind that George was hypnotized. He told me. I didn't know a thing about hypnosis, but agreed it might be the cause of George's somnolence.

Breeze got down close to George and began to talk soothingly to him. Finally he said, "You are now under my control, George," he told him in the way he had read in the book. "You are sleeping quietly and restfully. You are passing into my control. Before long I'm going to ask you to awaken. You are now getting ready to awaken. When I speak your name and command you to awaken, you will do so. All right, now be ready. George, awaken!"

It surprised me as much as it did Breeze when George yawned, drew up his legs, opened his eyes wide and rolling over, got up.

We sat and talked about the whole affair for an hour. Then we all went home.

Jay Paxman and some of the others told Breeze and I that they thought the three of us had cooked up a scheme for George to fake fainting, that we had told him all about the degree. So they just went on home. We didn't try to argue the case with them, but we did tell them we wanted no part of any more side degrees. I didn't know whether George would ever come out of his trance. That one scare was enough for me.

Oom Paul and the Bull

Sometimes you could get into difficulties so complicated they became ludicrous. One of the funniest such experiences I ever heard was related by my brother Art. At the time this happened Art was ranch and cattle manager for W. H. Rose, one of the first settlers in Bear (Yampa) River Valley. Art always referred to Rose as "the Old Man."

"Rose had a lot of bulls," Art relates, "and one of them had wandered off and showed up down at the Bogenschutz place. The Old Man heard about it and told me. So I told him I'd go and get it."

Rose was a civil engineer, although in later years he did little engineering work. But in his busy days he had built a snug little building as his office. Now, he had as a partner, occupying this office, a young engineer named Fred Kreuger. Kreuger was a small fellow, but sturdily built, and always eager to be doing something to make himself useful to his older associate. There was no great rush of surveying work so he had plenty of time to do other things, although he knew almost nothing of Western ways, having come here from back East.

Our Paul Krueger got his nickname from another Paul Krueger of greater fame. At that time most people well remembered the conflict between the South Africans and British, in what was known as "the Boer War."

In those days, Americans were nearly always on the side of the small people seeking freedom. We had not yet learned the political "wisdom" of siding with the side that was most likely to buy most from us. So all sympathy was with the Boers, fighting, mostly, to evict the British who had developed and largely taken over the gold and diamond mines.

Incidentally, the Boers lost this war.

The president of the Boer nation had been Paul Kreuger, although he was deceased by the time of this story. The Boers had affectionately called him "Oom" or "Father." The boys around town bestowed on our local Paul Kreuger the nickname of "Oom Paul."

So this day Art was going after Rose's bull.

"Mr. Kreuger is anxious to be doing something," Rose told Art, "so he might as well go with you and help. Bulls are sometimes hard to make go anywhere they don't want to go."

So, with Oom Paul along, mounted on a gentle mare, Art went to bring back the bull. They did not have too much difficulty cutting the big bovine out from the herd he had joined. In fact, everything was going well until they got into town. Although this was no wild range bull, but one that had been raised where people were around, he became a little skittish when he got in among the buildings and where a few people were moving.

There weren't 200 people in the town, but some of them were on the street and stopped to look curiously at the two riders and the bull.

All would have gone well but for Oom Paul Kreuger. Whether with a desire to be helpful or an urge to act like a cow-puncher, he spurred ahead and with the end of a lariat rope gave the bull a whack across the rump.

The insulted King of the Range let go an outraged bawl and with lowered head and flying tail, charged.

He didn't charge anything in particular. It happened they were right in front of the J. W. Hugus & Co. store and warehouse. The doors of both store and warehouse were open.

"The warehouse door was nearest, so he bolted through it," Art tells. "I was right at his tail, trying to turn him, so when he went into the door I went in after him."

It was a big building and filled front to rear with stacks and piles of merchandise the store sold.

"About two-thirds of the way to the back end, there was a pile of kids' bicycles and tricycles, reaching to the roof. When the bull caught sight of the projecting handlebars and pedals he must have thought them to be the horns of other challenging bulls. He tore into the shining pile and the bicycles came crashing down with a clatter to wake the dead. They scattered all over the place."

By this time El Toro was at the far end of the building. Raging like the Bull of Bashan he tore into a small mountain of sacked salt, bringing down a saline cascade that all but buried him.

"I was doing my best to get to him," Art said, "but my horse was tangled in the bicycles and I was having troubles of my own. I wished Oom Paul had been in Africa, or better still with his famous namesake, the late Oom Paul."

"The bull made a circle in the warehouse. By that time, Pete Howard, Martin Early, and some others from the store came tearing out and tried to herd the bull out of the warehouse. I thought he might charge them but by this time he decided to sulk. He backed into a corner and just stood."

"I thought maybe I could get a rope on him and drag him out. I got the rope on all right, but trying to drag an 1,800-pound bull with a 900-pound horse was no go. But I finally did get him to move, with the help of the other men, and after about an hour in the building, got him outside."

"By this time he was pretty mad and went just about anywhere he wanted to. Kreuger was tagging along but he was no help. Every time I'd give the bull a jerk with the rope and stop him, he'd get madder. He'd make a rush at my horse and at Oom Paul's, and both of them had pretty good digs in their bellies from his long old horns."

"Finally I tied him to a tree down by the river and went to get somebody who knew how to help me. When I got back he had busted the rope and when we followed him, he was right back in Bogenschutz's pasture where we first got him. I had the whole job to do over again. We got him to the ranch without trouble. But that time I didn't have the help of Oom Paul."

★
Don't Pull Leather

He was a big man, with a hawklike nose, a long sandy mustache, and eyes that looked at you and through you. I held him in dread, as I sat directly across the table from him and was under his scrutiny. This was my first job away from home. I had never spent a night away from my own family until that October day I arrived to become chore boy at the K Diamond Ranch on Bear River. I had never even seen before any of the people with whom I now would live. There was Ed Hodges, the ranch manager, his wife, Belle, her brother Clarence Barber, who was the foreman, the two Leonards, Art and Claude, two Baylor men who were cowpunchers, and John Campbell, a ranch hand. None of them impressed me much except Albert Gent, the man with the compelling eyes. Of him I was to know more later.

My job was to milk five cows twice daily, feed them and the saddle ponies and work horses, cut and carry into the house several armfuls of stove wood, several scuttles of coal for house and bunkhouse, and carry several buckets of water for household use from the river, nearly a quarter mile away. I also kept the corrals and barns clean.

Two days after the October day I went to work on my first job away from home everyone left. I don't remember why, if I ever knew. What I do remember acutely is that I was alone on that big ranch, at the foot of the slate bluff a mile or so up-river from Juniper Hot Springs.

To fill in time not devoted to the regular routine, the ranch manager assigned me the task of digging a couple of acres of sugar beets. I was also to dig pits in the ground, bury the beets in these and shovel over them two feet of earth. It was an experiment in which the beets were to be fed to selected cattle during the winter. It was all as new and puzzling to me as if I had suddenly been called on to walk.

The first day I dug a couple of tons of beets. The effort gave me a ripping appetite. I had been told to eat anything I wanted. In all my life I had never had quite enough canned tomatoes at one sitting. There were tomatoes on the supply shelves, and in the cool cellar were pans of milk with cream a half-inch thick. So what could be sweeter than all the tomatoes I could eat, with rich cream and sugar and a bit of bread? But how bitter the aftermath when in the dead of night I awoke with collywobbles wracking my insides and nausea flooding over me in waves.

I barely made it to the outer air before heaving up Jonah and all the whales. Then I crept back into the frigid house, lighted a kerosene lamp, and stirring up a fire in the cook stove, sat at the table, ready at an instant's notice to dash for the outside. As I sat in misery, feeling more alone and hopeless than ever in my life, I thought of my own home, the ready help in time of need, and realized I was on my own. What a way and a time to die!

On a shelf above the big dining table sat a huge book I had recognized at my first meal there as a duplicate of our "Family Doctor Book." Now my thoughts reverted to it. If ever I needed a doctor book, it was now. So I hoisted down the heavy volume and opened it at random.

My eye fastened onto a paragraph that began, "Symptoms: Darting pains in mid-stomach, audible sounds of internal convulsions, nausea, chills, dancing spots before eyes."

What could have been more accurate? What greater luck could I have had than for my eyes to alight on this very paragraph? Instantly I looked at the heading above. "Malaria!" The word lowered my temperature a few more notches. Malaria. I had heard my father describe its awful effects in India. Would it be as deadly to a boy in America? My head swam and I closed my eyes in dizziness. The pages of the big book slipped from under my fingers.

When again I could see the page before me I saw the symptoms of "Mercury poisoning." Strangely, as I read, it dawned on me that the symptoms were the *same*. Reading more closely, I found that the treatment for malaria and mercury poisoning were entirely similar. Thumbing through the book, I read various sets of symptoms. To my surprise, I found that many ailments had identical symptoms.

By this time the house was warmer, the wrenching of my innards had eased greatly, my head was clearer, and the nausea fading. So I crawled back in bed. When I awoke at daybreak, I felt pretty good. But I had no desire to breakfast on tomatoes-and-cream.

In a week the ranch people were all home. I was functioning like a crude piece of machinery, but getting all my work done and finding myself with some time on my hands to loiter in the October sunshine or do a bit of reading.

I knew how to work. I'd learned that from infancy. So as soon as I got into the swing of things, I did my work with time to spare. Right there I learned my first lesson in capital-and-labor relations. When the manager saw I didn't have my nose on the grindstone all the time, he told me I might help the Leonard boys feed cattle. So, rising earlier—an hour before daybreak instead of at daybreak—and working later, I put in almost a full day helping with tailing up weak cattle, chopping waterholes, loading and unloading hay, and rounding up the cattle to the feed ground.

Everybody else got $30 a month. I got $12 for the chores. I must have been doing the ten-hour cattle-feeding stint for free, I guess.

Along toward spring, when the snow went and cattle could graze a little, we fed them no longer. So Hodges assigned me to put in my "spare" time riding. We had to watch the cattle on the range, go to other ranches to get K Diamond animals they had picked up, or take to other ranchers strays we found.

To my dismay, my very first assignment on this actual "cow-punching" job was to ride with Albert Gent.

The first day didn't go so badly. Because most of the time I was not even *with* Albert, but anywhere from 50 feet to a mile behind him. Barber, the foreman, had given me Mrs. Hodges' private saddle horse to ride. Old Cap was a pacer, a lazy, fat roan, stupid and clumsy. So, my main job that day was to just keep Albert Gent in sight.

That evening, Albert told Hodges, "If that boy is supposed to help me, he's going to have to have a different kind of horse. That old pelter is no good in the hills."

Hodges didn't argue the point, although Mrs. Hodges flared at the disparagement of her steed.

"I don't know," Ed said. "The only pony he might be able to ride is Andy. And you know Andy might come uncorked. I don't want the kid hurt."

Albert turned to me. "Ever ride a bucking horse, son?"

I told him I'd ridden a good many colts, a lot of calves and cows, and sometimes didn't get thrown off.

"All right, give him Andy," Albert told the boss.

All went well for two days. Andy was a long-leg roan and I had no trouble keeping up with Albert. I even did a little good in handling the cattle. But coming in with a couple of strays the second evening, using the end of a lariat rope to urge them along, the rope got under Andy's tail and the show was on. He wasn't much of a bucker. But to be on the safe side I had a firm grip on the saddle horn. I finally got his head pulled up and we went on to the ranch.

I don't think Albert had spoken a dozen words to me during the two days. But that third morning, he seemed actually friendly. After a few general remarks, he told me, "You did all right with old Andy. You ain't a bad rider. But out here on the hills we don't pull leather. You got to forget about hanging on to that old saddle horn."

I didn't say much. It is hard for people nowadays to realize how bashful and timid a 12-year-old boy could be his first time away from home.

"There's a few tricks about this bronc riding a feller needs to know," Albert went on. "This old Andy is a good old skate to practice on. Thumb him up and I'll see what you do wrong."

I didn't quite understand, but he told me to just run my thumbs along the horse's neck. I never saw anything work so well. Before I could get leaned back in the saddle Andy threw me over his head. I was mad and not nearly so timid when I got up and dusted myself off.

"Try him again after a bit," Albert coached. "But first, let me tell you something. Don't ride stiff. Get limber all over except in your legs and grip with them like all hellsfire. But just give with the horse, but don't let your head get to flopping."

At his insistence, I again "thumbed up" old Andy and tried to do the way Albert told me. He'd yell instructions en route. So began my apprenticeship as a bronc buster. I came to respect, later to like, and eventually to greatly admire my teacher.

But it wasn't the riding instruction that meant so much in my life. It was something that happened one day Albert and I were riding across the flat on the way to Maudlin Canyon to get a couple of steers Zene and the boys had corralled. It was a cold morning, with a chilling drizzle of rain. Albert's horse put his foot in a badger hole and fell, throwing Albert into a muddy pool. He didn't say anything, but just got up and stood while I chased his horse and caught it and brought it back.

As we jogged along I told Albert, "A feller could get killed that way."

"Well, what of it?" he said grouchily.

"What of it?" I echoed. "Why a lot of it. When you get killed, why, that's all there is to it."

He didn't argue the point.

Presently I told him, "You know, I got a good notion to quit this cowpunching and get me a job herding sheep."

At that time, the spring of 1900, there were no sheep in this area. In fact they were not allowed to even pass through. Cattlemen and most cowboys hated the very name of sheep and looked down on a sheepherder as a pariah of the lowest order.

Al looked at me with those penetrating eyes. All he said was, "Go on."

"Well, I get 12 dollars a month, you get 30. But a sheepherder gets a hundred. I sleep in a room as cold as outdoors. Up before daylight and working after dark. A sheepherder lives in a nice warm sheep wagon, has anything he wants to eat, and doesn't get up until the sheep leave the bed ground."

Albert pulled his horse to a halt and got off.

"Get down," he commanded.

I saw anger in his eyes. I pulled my horse away from him. By now I was riding a good horse called Coal Oil Johnny, and I knew I could keep away from Albert.

"What for?" I ventured.

"So I can beat and stomp and tromp some sense into you," he said violently. "A boy raised on a cattle ranch, working for a cattle outfit, eating a cattleman's food, taking a cattleman's wages, and he talks about being a sheepherder. A dirty, filthy sheepherder."

At the time, I wasn't too sure but what he would do exactly as he said. Now I know better. But at that, he might have cuffed me around a bit, because he was pretty angry.

He finally swung back up and I kept my distance. We continued on up the trail, got the cattle at Maudlin's and were on our way back. Presently we came to an old road and were riding side-by-side.

"Are you still mad, Albert?" I asked him.

"Well, yes, as far as sheep go, I'm always mad. But not at you. You ain't bumped into this old world enough yet to know all about it. But about what I said about working for a cow outfit and talking in favor of sheep, I want to tell you how it is. Anyhow this is the way I *think* it should be."

"As long as you work for a man, say a cattleman, eat his grub, take his pay and so on, don't talk against him or his outfit. If you just feel that you can't abide his kind of work, why just quit."

It was a simple, honest way of saying how he felt. But it was a bit of profound philosophy, and I recognized it as such the moment he said it.

I've never forgotten.

"I don't figger on being a cowpuncher all my life myself," he went on.

"Course I'll always be around cattle I reckon. But I got a ranch up on Spring Creek, and when I get a stake laid up, I figger on being a cattleman myself and cowpunching for my own self."

"Why, I supposed you'd work for the K Diamond as long as you're able," I told him.

"No, I'll work for them and maybe other cow outfits to get the money to buy some of my own. I don't aim to steal from 'em to get a herd like some fellers do."

We rode for awhile in silence.

"It's alright to have ideas beyond what you're doing," Albert told me. "There's no law that says a man has got to stick to one line all his life. If you get big ideas, try 'em out. You may end up on your back but that ain't a disgrace if you try. But whatever you do, don't talk against the man or the business that is feeding and paying you."

And that was Albert Gent, who taught me the virtues of loyalty, ambition, daring, and honesty in a way I never forgot. He taught me some of the fine points of rough riding, too, another thing in which he was eminently qualified to act as instructor. Because Albert was a natural born horseman, one of the best men with a rope who ever tossed a loop, and a rider who dared to top off the worst of them.

Yes, Albert was a cattleman, through-and-through. But he was also an intelligent man and not one to let prejudice or bull-headedness lead him down the wrong trail. After sheep had come to the county, and Albert had seen and pondered the relative possibilities of cattle and sheep, he became also a sheepman. I never saw him after this, as I was out of the area during those years. I'd have liked to have talked with him about his entry into the sheep business. His reasons were sound. I'd have liked to hear them.

But anyhow, Albert was by nature and training a livestock man. He was born March 20, 1869, in Minnesota and arrived in Moffat County the fall of 1889. He had a love of the outdoors, a deep knowledge of the cattle business and of horses and horsemanship, and a keen business acumen.

I later worked for Albert and his brother Johnny on the Spring Creek ranch and found them to have good buildings, expansive meadows, and a good ranch setup. John later took land in Temple Canyon. While I was working there, I got to know Albert's wife, Ida, who showed me Albert's "letter of proposal." It was so much like that big, honest, modest man. Part of it ran, "As you know, I ain't any feller to make fancy speeches. You know about my way of getting along too. I don't have much but I got things going pretty well and am pretty sure I could support a wife pretty good. I just ain't got the gall to come right up and talk to you about this here, Ida. But I got to say it. What's the matter with me and you getting married?"

It wasn't a fancy letter. On November 14, 1897, Ida and Albert were married.

While I was working at the Spring Creek ranch, it came July 4. There was a big celebration at Meeker and all the Gents went for a week. I ran the ranch. Days I worked hard. Evenings were long and lonely. I had never before spent such lonely nights alone. One night, reading Teddy Roosevelt's book about his life in the West, I half-dozed as he told of hunts and cattle drives.

I had just come to the part where he told of a mountain lion hunt. There was a picture of a mountain lion, close up, with fangs showing. I knew about mountain lions, the biggest cowards in the mountains. I dozed and may have slept an hour. I awoke, chilly. As my eyes opened I was looking right into the face of a mountain lion. I rubbed my eyes to blot out the picture. But I suddenly realized that this *wasn't* a picture. A small lion stood, with its paws on the sill of the open window, looking me right in the eye. I must have "looked him down" for he slowly sank out of sight.

I was shaken. He *might* have just pounced on me and wound up my fashionable rancher career pronto. So, to settle my nerves, I made a fire in the cookstove and put some water to heat in a new, shiny saucepan to make some tea. Just then I heard a commotion among the milk cows in the corral. I grabbed Albert's rifle and headed for the corral.

There was no lion in evidence. A calf had gotten a leg over a fence wire and was making a lot of noise about it. I freed the calf, fired a couple of shots into the air just in case the lion had ideas about a veal supper, and went back to the house. Horrors! Ida's beautiful saucepan, the only new and shiny utensil she had, had boiled dry and was red hot. When it cooled it was a dirty red.

When Ida came home and saw it, she didn't say much, but I could see tears in her eyes. To a young wife it was a tragedy. To me it was a shock. If there had been a hole big enough handy, I'd have crawled into it and pulled it in after me. Later, she laughed about it.

Ida was, in her youth, acquainted with such noted characters as Tom Horn and Elza Lay and knew well Butch Cassidy and his family, the Parkers, of Circleville, Utah.

★
Riding with Butch Cassidy

Of the bad guys who were best known in our own region, the "Big Three" were Tom Horn, Harry Tracy, and Butch Cassidy. The names may be familiar to you.

In 1895, we were occupying what was known as the "Gregory place." This was located one-half mile north of the Lay post office, where the bridge crosses Lay Creek. It was owned by Ora Haley, whose brother-in-law, Charlie Gregory, had once lived on the place. It was at the crossing of the only north-and-south and east-and-west roads in this entire region. To our ranch house came all travelers who passed this way. Land-seekers, freighters, peddlers, other ranchers, cowboys, trappers, and even thieves and others trying to keep out of the clutches of the law. We fed them without discrimination and fed their horses. Some few were permitted to pay 25 cents for a meal and the same for feed for a horse, most though were treated as guests.

And so, as we shall see, came to our place at different times the three outlaw men whose names later were known worldwide. These three outlaws and others of their ilk, did, on many occasions, stick their feet under our dining table and swap ideas with our parents, while we kids with open mouths took it all in, and their horses hobnobbed with our nags and munched good bluestem hay.

George LeRoy Parker, the man later known as "Butch Cassidy" was born April 6, 1866, in Beaver, Utah, of parents who came of British stock and who took part in the "handcart migration" of Mormons. As soon as he was able to set a horse, young George first hobnobbed with and later worked for Mike Cassidy, a rancher who had accumulated quite a herd of cattle, supposedly by the quick loop method. Cassidy lived near what is now known as Bryce

Canyon. Its gorges, pinnacles, and torturous trails afforded good grazing for Mike's cattle, as few persons would venture into the place.

When George LeRoy Parker's dad bought the ranch Cassidy had been running, Mike stayed on as helper, so as to be near his own herd. It was here, no doubt, that George Parker learned the ways of the range, both orthodox and otherwise.

Cassidy's cattle herd got so big the lawmen began to notice. So he moved away up into the lacolithic eminence known as the Henry Mountains. Young Parker went along. In a couple of years Cassidy was again under the scrutiny of officers. So he disposed of most of his cattle, left a few with young Parker who took over the cabin, and herded some of the cattle south and into old Mexico. By this time George LeRoy Parker was known in the area only as George Cassidy.

George "Cassidy" didn't do too well with the outfit left him by Mike Cassidy. He extended his operations of mavericking into the area of equipment. Caught with a saddle that wasn't his, he did a couple of weeks in jail, being let out when Pearce, the owner of the saddle who now had it back, suggested Cassidy's release. It wasn't long until he was in another tight spot and, emulating the example set by his namesake, got rid of what he could of his holdings and headed for Colorado.

As young George was leaving the country, a couple of enterprising deputy sheriffs outwitted him, and snapping the bracelets on his wrists, headed with him for their home base. Came noon and the three stopped near a creek for dinner. While one man went for water the other started a fire. The green sagebrush didn't take fire easily so he stooped to blow it to life. As he bent over, young "Cassidy" snatched the gun from the officer's belt and drew a bead on his eye.

"Just tell that other feller to drop his gun and come on up here," the lad told the deputy. Soon the prisoner had collected the guns and horses and was on his way. He missed dinner, but the two deputies missed a ride. Afoot they started a 40-mile hike across the desert under a blazing summer sun. Luckily the ex-prisoner here displayed a trait that carried with him through life.

After going several miles and discovering that he had the officers' canteens tied to the saddles, he tied the two lead horses and took the water back to the plodding lawmen. Otherwise they could not have survived the trip. Rumor has it that this incident took place in or near what is now known as Capitol Reef National Park.

At Telluride, Colorado, George got a job with a pack outfit bringing high-grade gold ore off the mountain. In Telluride he met Matt Warner, whose real name was Willard Christensen. The two men came from Mormon families and though they had not met before, each knew of the other. Warner had come to the mining camp to stage a matched horse race, having a speedy nag he had bought or swapped from Charley Crouse. Warner knew Tom McCarty, an outlaw who had a sort of gang. Before long, the three planned and pulled off a robbery of the bank in Telluride. A younger brother of Cassidy (Parker) who had come to visit his brother, took part in the heist.

It must have been that Cassidy either had a desire to lie low for awhile after the robbery, or got dished out of his share of the loot, for he took a job on the Crist Ranch in the valley below Telluride and punched cows and did ranch work for awhile. During the next two years he had similar jobs in various parts of Colorado, Utah, and Wyoming. It has been suggested by some writers that he thus covered the country in order to "case" possible victims of future robberies. I do not think this is true. I think the bank robbery had given him a sort of shock when he contemplated its possible consequences and he just thought it might be a good idea to live and work like other young fellows.

Eventually Cassidy roamed into Rock Springs, Wyoming. It was late in the fall, cattle jobs were not plentiful, and those offered meant long hours feeding cattle.

The average cowpuncher worked a month, or several months under abominable conditions. The daylight hours were filled and crammed with work. His night-times might and likely would be broken by a time at night guard. The horse he rode was a risk and a threat, the ground over which he rode was thickly dotted with badger holes, prairie dog burrows, entangling sagebrush, rabbit weed, and grass that concealed the holes and narrow washes into which his horse might plunge one or both feet.

His work was either in heat and dust and the stench of cattle and horses, or in temperatures that defied the most clothing he could pile on. He slept on the hard, cold, bare ground in a bed from which he rose long before daybreak, ate crouched around the campfire in cold weather and farther back in warm, his food often salted with the dust and grit of a windstorm, his sight blurred by the glare of snow and the smoke of the campfire. And when at length he got fired or a break in the work came, he could draw his pay and head for the nearest town. There, clean, shaved, with hair cut and fresh clothes, he headed for the nearest saloon. A day, or two days, or maybe more if he had been away from town for several months, he would awake in a cheerless hotel room, sick, broke, and ready to "go back to the wagon."

This picture does not apply to *all* cowpunchers, but to the vast majority. "Westerns," whether stories, movies, or television programs, see the cowboy as a romantic chap, handsome, trailed by pretty girls, decked out in regalia no cowpuncher even dreamed of, plucking a guitar, and leading a crew of waddies singing through their noses about "Old Paint" or "Little Dogies."

Cassidy saw no such picture. Nor did I. Cassidy saw the picture the way it was. So he got a job in a butcher shop which at least offered regular hours, a minimum of risk to one's neck, sleep in a bed, and proximity and ready access to places where he might hoist a drink or play a hand of poker.

There was only one hitch in this! The wages of a butcher's helper didn't go far in sustaining the kind of life to which Cassidy wanted to become accustomed. This put him to thinking as he sliced off the round steaks, sawed through the loin roasts and tossed a bit of free liver in with the package of beef stew meat, a package that under his inept fingers always ended up with bones sticking out through the wrapping paper.

Every day he helped skin, quarter and cut into steaks, stews and roasts, beef that he knew for certain had been stolen. He knew that while he sweated for $2.50 a day the fellow who had sold the animal to the butcher shop had, in a few hours of time and a little quick work with a lariat and pistol, put into his pocket $20. (Stolen beef did not bring top price of probably $30, as the buyer knew it was stolen, and like any "fence," negotiated the seller down to bedrock.)

By this time, the fellows Cassidy knew around town had begun to call him "Butch" on account of his connection with butchering. Now this "Butch" was an intelligent fellow, an unusually intelligent one. He figured there was an even better way of making money than either butchering or selling stolen beef. A horse was easier to steal than a cow. You could lead it away or ride it away.

There was no killing, dressing, getting rid of the hide, and haggling with greedy butchers. Butch had already had a taste of horse stealing while with Mike Cassidy. He had probably been thinking this over for quite awhile. He was spurred to decision and action by a little set-to with the law people. A drunken freighter, when he sobered up, complained to the sheriff, that he had been "rolled" and all his money and a watch taken. Butch, who was seen in the vicinity, was thrown in jail charged with the theft. The charge didn't stick, but the affair made Butch so mad he told the court and all connected with it what he thought of accusing him of so mean a trick as robbing a drunk. Then he packed his duffle and, mounting his horse, headed for far places.

Observers might have figured that at last Butch Cassidy was going to settle down to the life of an honest ranchman. He filed on a homestead on the Popo Agie near Lander, Wyoming. There, before long he and another young fellow were in the "horse business." They did well as horse merchants. Neither of them were heavy drinkers, Butch being especially temperate in this line. He enjoyed social life, dances and general good time, but was not much of a ladies man. In short, he was the kind of guy who today might be expected to become an able executive.

This ideal existence might have gone on and on, but that some nosy law men observed that for a ranch that did not *raise* any horses, and for people who did not *buy* any horses, the Cassidy & Co. outfit had an awful lot of horses to sell. Result, Butch in jail for horse stealing. Again he pulled the "offender honest citizen" bit and backed it up with a bill of sale, signed by a well-known rancher, for the horses Butch and his pal had sold. It could have worked, too, excepting that by chance the well known rancher happened to come to town and seeing the horses tied around the courthouse, went over to see why all the excitement. He entered just about the time the bill-of-sale was being presented. The "bill of sale" was a forgery. Butch headed for two years in the Wyoming pen. The governor saw fit to favor this nice young man with a reduction to less than a year. The experience must have cured Butch of "jail fever" as he never spent another day in one.

By the time Butch had served his abbreviated time, Matt Warner had taken a ranch not far from Brown's Park (Hole) on the north part of Diamond Mountain on Crouse Creek. A sort of mysterious young man, William McGinnis, but who is better known as

"Elza Lay," had thrown in with Warner, or at least was a long-time visitor. Warner's other friends, mostly of his own kind, often visited the snug and well-stocked cabin he had. Into this congenial atmosphere came Butch Cassidy, recently a guest of the State of Wyoming.

This group of kindred spirits made frequent trips to Vernal, where Charley Crouse and Overholt had a saloon. It was the meeting place for the wild crew assembled at Matt Warner's hangout. And it was a wild crew, so wild in fact, that the saloon habitués, and then the citizenry generally, began to referring to their visits as "another raid by the wild bunch from Matt Warner's." A "wild bunch" in the language of that time and place usually meant a band of wild horses. So the name "Wild Bunch" fitted this band of rough-playing men.

Into this sweet place of milk and honey came a bit of curd and bitterroot. Matt Warner got in a fracas which ended with one man nicked, another's leg shot off, and a third permanently dead. From his jail cell Warner sneaked a note to Butch. It will be noted that it was Butch on whom Matt relied. That seasoned old renegade had already evaluated the intelligence and the dependability of the man who later would vindicate Warner's judgment by becoming leader of the Wild Bunch in its rosiest days.

Warner told Butch that money was needed to hire lawyers. So, Butch, Elza Lay, and a reformed cowpuncher named Bob Meek just about rode their horses down getting to Montpelier, Idaho, where they relieved a bank of $16,000. The money was enough to get the best legal talent, with the result that Matt got off on a simple manslaughter count with five years in the clink. While he lay there, brushing up on his techniques and hatching up new schemes for sharing the other fellows' wealth, Butch and his pals saw to it that Matt's wife in Salt Lake City was well cared for. The same combination of Cassidy-Lay rode into the mining camp of Castle Gate, Utah, and in daylight made off with the payroll of $7,839.40, taking the money out of the hands of messengers who were carrying it from the Express office to the mine office.

Butch's horse took off and left him running down the alley behind, until Lay caught the animal and stopped it. We didn't hear of the Castle Gate robbery for weeks after it occurred.

News traveled slowly in those days of no TV, no radio, no telegraph or telephone, and a newspaper that came once in two weeks. But we did know that in the spring of 1897 two youngish riders had dinner at our place. After dinner they visited for awhile, then rode on westward. I had to go look for a couple of horses in Sugar Loaf Basin, so saddled my mare and rode with them. We rode together only three or four miles, but far enough for me to say if I wished that "I rode with Butch Cassidy." Many a man *said* it who never saw Butch. But the joke was that I didn't know it was Butch Cassidy for a long time after.

When the two men and I parted, they went on west. Years later, comparing notes with Phil Shaver, I learned that they stayed at his ranch that night. Phil was one of the most famous of the "wild horse chasers" and also raised some good horses. His ranch was on the lower Snake River. Whenever we talked of the Castle Gate heist Phil would laugh loudly as he pictured Butch running down an alley with a sack of gold. I don't think Phil knew of the plan to lift the payroll, even though the two went from his place to Vernal by way of Elk Springs and the K Ranch, and from Vernal over the Wasatch range to Castle Gate.

Most of the haul was in gold, with $100 in silver, and a canvas bag the robbers took to be bills, but which proved to be checks. When Butch made the grab from the confused messengers, he tossed the bag of silver to Lay who fielded it handily, but it spooked Butch's horse, which Lay was holding by the bridle reins. Butch, standing over the bag of gold, now tossed the bag of paper to Lay. Butch's horse stepped forward just in time for the bag to brush its head as it went by. The horse jerked loose and trotted towards an alley. Lay whirled his horse and took after the big gray. The animal, which they had borrowed from Bob Meek, another outlaw, wasn't wild. But the alley was so narrow Lay couldn't get past the loose horse to head him. When they emerged from the alley both horses were running. Butch had grabbed the 40-pound sack of gold and, stumping along, impeded by the weight and by his high-heel boots, was not setting any speed records as he followed.

Passing a pile of mine ties, Lay dropped the sack of silver on the small hewn timbers, jerked down his lariat and soon had the gray caught. Cassidy caught up and scrambled aboard, still clutching the sack of gold. Lay was headed for open country and Butch raced behind him. By this time the steam whistle at the coal mine and the one of the locomotive on the sidetrack were splitting the air with their shrieks, drowning out the screeches of women and kids and the shouted orders of the local law men, as poker players upset tables and tore the batwing doors off their hinges in a dash for their horses tied at the hitch racks. In the excitement some small boys found the sack of silver.

The posse finally got going, but by that time, Cassidy and Lay with their better horses were well on their way down by Price, across the mountains and desert and finally to Robber's Roost. It was the one time they were really in a pickle, but after they got out of Castle Gate they were in no real danger. Cassidy had cased the situation and knew when the payroll would arrive and also the getaway route.

The stories and the movies tell a lot about the narrow escapes, with posses at their heels. This one time I know of, a posse did indeed follow them toward Robber's Roost. When they got fairly close, Butch took up a side gulch and let the posse go by. The other outlaw let loose a few shots over the heads of the posse from the top of a ridge, then rode quickly to another spot and shot some more. Butch did the same. The posse, imagining themselves to be surrounded, took the back trail fast.

This definitely put the two, and by inference the Wild Bunch, in the category of high-grade outlaws.

Outlaws, traditionally, must have a hideout. So, in the grand way, the Wild Bunch had three hideouts at least. One was Robber's Roost. Capitol Reef National Park is not far from Butch's old place where Mike Cassidy left him in the Henry Mountains. Near this is the town of Hanksville, Utah, where the Fremont River becomes the Dirty Devil River. The area the river runs through is as rough, inhospitable, and inaccessible as any strip of land on earth. Here was Robber's Roost.

Northward from this, the outlaws followed a general course leading to Brown's Park, through Irish Canyon, across the bad lands of the ancient lake bed and to Powder Wash and Powder Springs. At the lower spring Butch and his bunch contrived a dugout cabin, fixed a corral to hold their saddle ponies, and with plenty of cedar wood at hand and grazing for the horses they had a good hideout. Not that this place was inaccessible, though. It is in the wide open and any rider could, and many did, reach it.

And, in turn, the Wild Bunch could ride from this place to Baggs, Wyoming, where they could make wassail and shoot up the town without much chance of being bothered. They paid liberally for anything they needed.

The Outlaw Trail, beginning at Robber's Roost and leading to Powder Springs, continued on north over Cherokee rim and on into Johnson County, Wyoming, where was located the famous Hole-in-the-Wall rendezvous of cattle rustlers of the area and any other law-breakers who might come along.

The Wild Bunch was not the only organized band of outlaws in the country along the Outlaw Trail. Some of Matt Warner's friends did a lively business in stolen cattle and horses and an occasional robbery of store, saloon, or even a bank. An outlaw named Harvey Logan led a gang in the Hole-in-the-Wall country. The Tip Gault gang had been long gone but some lesser renegades operated singly or in bunches in the same territory.

Logan knew Cassidy and made his way with some of his gang to Butch's hideout. Butch probably wouldn't have chosen Logan as an associate, as the latter had nine notches on his gun handle and Butch would have considered him too quick on the trigger for his bunch. Butch was no killer and didn't counsel nor approve of itchy trigger fingers.

If Butch Cassidy had killed a few persons, he would have soon been lumped with the common run of outlaws and forgotten. The fact that he did *not* kill anybody, did not permit his men to do any reckless gun work, and robbed mostly banks and trains, made him and the Bunch outstanding, unique and–famous.

But anyhow, Logan arrived in Cassidy's camp, and with him brought Ben Kilpatrick, Flatnose George Curry, and Harry Longabaugh, who later became Cassidy's best friend and most trusted lieutenant and was known as "the Sundance Kid."

Up to this time, the Wild Bunch had been a rather loose organization. Members came and went. Ranch boys might go wrong and pull a few small capers and seek sanctuary with Cassidy's bunch. Wandering outlaws might drop in and stay overnight, stay for a few raids, or stay permanently. But with the coming of the high-class talent with Harvey Logan, the Wild Bunch took on a new complexion. The amateurs had become pros.

Logan was a strong-willed character and may have figured to become leader of the Wild Bunch. He had gotten his first outlaw training under the renegade Curry and in fact was known as "Kid Curry." He had taken post-graduate work under the infamous Big Nose George Parrott, so must have believed himself to be leader material. But Cassidy was just as strong-willed and a lot more intelligent. The experience with Tom McCarty, Warner, and the others in the Telluride bank robbery, in which Butch got experience but very little money, had shown him the advantages of being the boss. He was a diplomat, too, or he couldn't have led and controlled a pack of men, most of whom were bigger and meaner than he. By a man we will come to know later, I was told that Cassidy let Logan know who was boss, and also impressed on the killer that gun play didn't go in *this* bunch excepting as a last resort to save the gunner's or a mate's life.

To those who would like to follow the Outlaw Trail and to vicariously take part in the many robberies of banks, trains, payrolls, and individuals perpetrated by Butch Cassidy and his Wild Bunch, the libraries of the land are groaning under printed matter dealing with the subject. So we will not attempt to recapitulate here. Rather, we will discuss some phases of the outlaw gang that are either known to us alone, or are controversial points on which we know the real facts.

It was about 1900, at the very height of the activities of the Wild Bunch, that there came to our ranch house two young men who were evidently cowpunchers, but whom we did not know.

In those days, people *told* you what they wanted you to know. You did not *ask* strangers their names, their business, nor their reasons for being where they were. So, when these two young men came to ask if Mother could feed them, they were invited in, given seats, shown where to wash the dust of travel from their faces, and made comfortable until Mother had prepared a hasty meal. While this was being done, they chatted amiably, while we kids watched every move and listened to every syllable, as was our custom.

While they were eating, the taller man had little to say, but the other praised Mother's cooking and was particularly interested in one food on the table. This we called "Dutch cheese." It was the schmearkase of the Germans who first made it. Today we call it "cottage cheese."

The men offered to pay for their meal and when Mother refused the money were going to leave it anyhow, but she put it back into their hands. They both thanked her warmly and bidding us all good-bye got on their ponies and headed west. It was a year or so later that one of the men and another came again. This time our father was home, too. Talk of the outlaws was a staple topic. Everybody knew about the Wild Bunch and their leader, Butch Cassidy.

Our family agreed then, and still agrees, that Butch Cassidy was a well-behaved, pleasant, well-mannered young man. I knew it at the times he visited our home. I still think so.

Butch Cassidy was well liked by the many ranchers and others who knew him well. He was liked and admired by the men of his own Wild Bunch. I have the word of two of them to that effect and their acceptance and retention of his leadership to the end testifies to it. Yes, he was a well-liked and respected man in his circle. His home influence and training had started him off on a different track. But like many a youngster from a good home today, he chose the wrong fork when the road of life divided. I think it was the way the nameless rider told Lew Caldwell and I, by a campfire at the edge of Irish Lake.

"Tain't hard to figger why a feller like Butch would foller the kind of life he did. If you'd knowed him you couldn't imagine a feller like him sticking to a hum-drum job of punchin' cows, cuttin' meat or any regular job, nor settlin' down on a homestead with a flea-bit team, haywire harness, cow, plow, wagon, and maybe a frumpy wife and a raft of kids. Maybe in 40 years a feller like that gets to be worth $5,000, too late to get any fun out of it. Butch bein' like he was, it was jest natural he'd figger out a quicker and more excitin' way. He knew the risks and the dangers all right, but he was willin' to gamble. That one hitch he done in the Wyoming pen taught him a lot. He used what he learned there to steer clear of jails from then on. Yeah, his bein' an outlaw was no accident. He took it up just like some other feller maybe figgers out he wants to be a doctor, or a storekeeper, or a preacher, and studies up on it and then sticks with it."

This lone rider, with three horses following, one of them bridled, one of them bearing his bed and camping effects, rode into our camp late in the evening. He was a cowpuncher I knew well. He was the better type of cowpuncher and usually held one of the better jobs.

We were glad to see another human and he was glad to have company, rather than a lonely camp. We all joined in getting supper and doing the camp chores. Then we threw a log on the fire, as even in July the evenings were cool, and sitting on our feet fell into the kind of talk you might expect. We talked first about what was going on in town and in the outside world. Then, being Westerners, and being in a country the world knew as the hangout of outlaws, our talk turned to outlaws. Soon we were discussing Butch Cassidy and the Wild Bunch.

In later years, looking back on that meeting and on the free-and-easy camp talk of three congenial men in the heart of what had been outlaw country, I formed an opinion. This opinion was based on remarks, facts, and associations that I have been able to piece together from that campside talk. That opinion is that our chance visitor had ridden with the Wild Bunch. He may not have been a regular member, but certain it is that he was on some of their forays. He readily admitted knowing most of the gang. That alone was not unusual. Many ranchers and cowpunchers knew one or more of the members of the Wild Bunch. But this man knew more. Much more.

So, feeling as I do, that he certainly had taken part in some of the raids and robberies of the Wild Bunch, I am going to repeat some of the things he told us. This may help to clear up some of the many questions that persist in regard to this famous band of outlaws. It may also refute some of the myriad untruths, half-truths, and downright fairy tales told over the years about Butch Cassidy and the Wild Bunch. Because what we heard was told in the mellow light of a sagebrush fire, in a situation and at a time when men of the outdoors, will, if ever, speak what is in their hearts. As we talked, the fire sank to a bed of ruddy coals, the soft summer night-breeze could be heard sighing in the pinyons on the mountain almost near enough to touch its base, the zoom of an occasional bullbat or the cry of a cuckoo accented sentences, and the wail of a lonely coyote furnished "background music" for our quiet conversation.

We didn't ask the cowpuncher, whom we shall call Bert, a most unlikely name for a cowpuncher, where he was headed or why. You didn't ask that kind of question at that time and under those conditions. We knew he wasn't headed for any roundup in the middle of July, nor were there any summer-ranging cattle anywhere near. They were all in the high country far to the east, unless it might be those of Charlie Sparks, and his rider wouldn't be camping so near the home ranch. When the talk drifted to the outlaws, we did ask some questions.

"Do you think Butch and the Wild Bunch ever buried a lot of gold coins in Irish Lake, like people say they did?" Lew asked Bert.

"Yeah, I've heard that yarn too," Bert answered. "How a cow brought out a twenty-dollar gold piece in the crack between her toes. Sounds fishy to me. Besides that, the boys were always well mounted, they didn't let their selves got ketched without a change of horses, so no posse was liable to crowd 'em too close. Besides that, I never heard of no posse gettin' started in time to crowd 'em. Even that one time the bunch was supposed to bury a lot of gold bars near Powder Springs, the posse was at least two hours behind. Besides, they wouldn't hide stuff that way."

"What would *you* do if you was on the run and a posse at your tail and you had a lot of gold or such stuff?" I asked him.

"Jest like what *you* would," Bert replied. "I wouldn't stop and make no hole and leave a lot of horse and man tracks to tip off the posse. I'd pick me a clump of brush or a gully, and toss the gold into it as I passed. That way you don't leave any sign of having left it. And you can easy go back and find it if you got a lick of sense about hidin' anything."

"How about that $40,000 in gold the Bunch stole off the Union Pacific train?" Lew wanted to know. "Wouldn't that be an awful load?"

"I've heard a lot of fellers talk about that," Bert told us. "Charlie Ayers is mighty good at figgers and he says it would weigh just about what a good-size man would weigh. About 160 pounds. On a pack horse that wouldn't be much of a load. But the Bunch probably divided it up among five or six of 'em, so nobody had much weight to carry. None of the Bunch was awful big men so they could carry some extra weight without hurtin' a horse. Another thing, if they did cache any gold or stuff they come back and got it. They'd all know where it was for sure."

Of course we were not firing these questions at Bert as given here. A great deal of other conversation was mixed in, so the conversation did not take the form of a third degree. We were not at that time trying to prove anything nor to straighten out history. What we were just talking about was things we had heard.

"Butch liked women jest like he liked likker. He'd take on a little jest for the hell of it. But nobody ever saw Butch Cassidy likkered up enough but what he knew every move he was making. He was a real boss, that feller. He would have done good runnin' some big company. So, he was all business and no monkey business.

134 × The Arbuckle Cafe

Oh sure, he didn't lord it over the Bunch. All the others had their say and some of 'em, like the ones I jest mentioned, had a lot to say in makin' plans. But everybody knowed all the time who was boss."

One of us asked what Bert thought about the report that Butch Cassidy was *not* killed in South America, but had come back alive to his old haunts.

"You'd probably know if he did come back around here, wouldn't you?" Lew asked.

"Yes, I reckon I *would* have knowed if Butch showed up around this country. Course I was no bosom friend of his'n, but we were pretty good friends and a good many times had some drinks together in Baggs or around the country. Yes, I'd know if Butch come back. But I sure ain't seen him around here have you?"

"But suppose he did come back alive and didn't come to his old haunts," Lew suggested.

"That's something I wouldn't know anything about," Bert said positively, and added, thoughtfully, "And if I did I prob'ly wouldn't be tellin' about it."

That was all we could get out of him. But later, I heard others talk on the same subject.

Those who would like to read of not only the Wild Bunch, but all the outlaws of the West can read Charles Kelly's "Outlaw Trail." Kelly did a good job of research. It is regrettable that he went to great lengths to blacken Brown's Park and its people as the habitat and colleagues of the outlaws. Kelly lived in the Park while gathering his material. It became known that he intended to portray park residents as outlaws themselves, hand-in-glove with the Wild Bunch. This didn't set well with the settlers so they clammed up on Kelly. Not only that, but he was invited by some of them to leave the Park. The only place he remained welcome was the cabin of Albert Williams, "the Speckled Negro." Knowing why Kelly had this prejudice, and making allowance for the fact he published his book nearly 30 years after the events occurred, the book is highly entertaining.

Another fascinating book is Larry Pointer's "In Search of Butch Cassidy." This book makes a very good case that Butch returned to the United States and lived to be an old man. It also contains photos of Butch in his older years that make the case even more convincing.

But back to our conversation around the campfire with "Bert."

"Did the boys do much reading, have books or magazines, card-playing or have much music in their camps?" was my question.

"Not many of 'em *could* read good enough to get much entertainment out of it," he told me. "Once in awhile you might see an old, thumb-marked, greasy trashy novel around. Newspapers they read in towns, after holdups, to see how the people took it. They didn't take 'em into camp much. They done a little gamblin' but not too serious. Fellers throwed together so close as they was who play too much cards are bound to get into rows and have hard feelin's. The most gamblin' they done was on runnin' horses. Everybody knowed about the race track at Powder Springs. It wasn't much. Just a narrow strip from which they had removed the scrub brush by using lariat and horse to jerk it out. It was just a straightaway 'bout a short half-mile long. They didn't bet big. Just enough to make it exciting. They'd rather *keep* their money and blow it on a high old time in some town."

"You asked about music. I guess Elzie Lay did a little singin' to hisself and maybe if he drunk a little too much he might sing some songs out loud. Nobody much savvied his kind of singing. He was an educated feller, you know."

"Did any of the Wild Bunch go in much for having love affairs with ranch girls and other decent women?" I asked him.

"Not that I ever knowed about. 'Course Elzie Lay married a Vernal girl but the way I got it she did most of the sparking."

"Do you think the reputation and deeds of the Wild Bunch caused many young fellows to go wrong and become outlaws?"

"I s'pose some. Small ranch life was so danged monotonous maybe some fellers would rather be outlaws. But mighty few did. It was older fellers that joined up. The Bunch didn't want to run no school for infants."

I would have asked him, "What did they do if they got sick or wounded?" but I already knew the answer.

The Butch Cassidy literature has a story about one of the Bunch being wounded in a gun battle and of how a doctor was kidnapped and taken to their camp to treat the outlaw. It is related that one of the outlaws asked the doctor about the latter's wife, whom the outlaw had seen when he went to get the doctor.

"Mighty nice lady, that wife of yours, Doc," the renegade said.

The doctor agreed.

"I reckon you think a lot of her," the outlaw observed. Again the doctor mumbled his assent while concentrating on the work at hand.

"Well Doc," the other told him, "you do the best you can for this here feller. You got to make him live. If he makes it all right, you'll see your wife pretty soon in your house. But if he dies, the next time you're goin' to see your wife is in heaven."

I don't know about that story, or rather the last part. But I *do* know about the "kidnapping" of the doctor. Because he was *my* doctor, too.

We lived in Aspen for a time, and there our family doctor was Dr. J. M. Downs. In the early spring of 1893 I had the measles. Along with the speckled pest I developed pneumonia. Came a day when Dr. Downs doubted my chances of pulling through. So two other doctors were called in consultation. Dr. Robinson and Dr. Skully looked me over, held a short confab with Downs, and left. Dr. Downs relayed their decision to mother, and also left. No sooner had the door closed than mother ran the bathtub half full of hot water, gathered my emaciated seven-year old form in her arms and doused me into the tub. She kept adding hotter water. Presently, nicely parboiled, I was plucked out like a scalded chicken, wrapped in two or three heavy wool blankets and put back in bed. I had been so weak I couldn't even lift a hand to scratch. But in two days I was feeding myself and am still alive, I think.

In 1902, after my father's death in a horse accident, mother and we three boys stayed on the ranch. Later, in 1905, we all moved to town. There, we again met Dr. Downs. He took up where he had left off as our doctor. He was an agreeable man and always had some good stories on tap. One of these was his account of how he was virtually abducted by a cowpuncher and taken to Butch's camp to treat a sick man.

"The fellow wasn't all shot up like some of the stories go," Downs said. "His horse stepped in a badger hole, fell, rolled over the man and crushed him badly. But I'm ahead of my story. Here's how I happened to have this patient."

"One day about noon, a cowpuncher came to my house and told me he wanted me to come along and treat a man who was in bad shape. I supposed it was another cowpuncher."

"So I hitched up my team to the buggy, took my cases, and followed the fellow north. Sometimes he rode in the buggy with me. We gassed along and finally got to Fourmile creek. There we met two other men. One of 'em took my team and they had a saddle horse for me. They explained that the rest of the way was off the road. The three of us rode down Fourmile to where it empties into the Snake River. There, one of the men told me he hated to ask it of me, but would I mind if they put a blindfold on me. I began to get the drift and realized what I was into. I didn't see any use in arguing, so they tied my eyes so I couldn't see a thing and we rode on."

The doctor was no stranger to a saddle horse. Those were the days when a country town doctor made house calls, day or night, and most of the time he rode many miles on horseback. Those doctors really earned their fees. The only hitch was, country doctors, including Downs, seldom collected more than half their fees. Lots of people were very poor, or forgetful and ungrateful.

"The men took me quite a way. From the wind direction I knew we were heading generally speaking to the northwest. From the time taken, and the gait of our horses, I figured we went about 20 miles. When they finally took off the blindfold, I was in a dugout, with only one window in front and a coal oil lantern giving most of the light."

"I went to work. The man was in bad shape and semi-conscious. Two of the men, a medium-size, sort of pleasant fellow, and a taller younger-seeming fellow who spoke mighty good English, helped me, getting hot water, fixing up some "bitch" lights made of some deer tallow in a dish with a wick made from a strip off a white rag, and whatever I asked them to do. There were several men there. All were quiet and solemn."

"We had food and about all there was to do was to wait and see what took place. During the night I told the men there was no chance for the fellow. He didn't last long. So they bundled me up again and we rode on back. It was daylight when we got back to Fourmile. My team was there, as they had brought them back from Baggs where they fed them in the livery barn."

"The men thanked me a lot, and before I left, one of them put in my hand five twenty-dollar gold pieces."

The old dugout hangout of the Bunch is still visible, though caved and desolated. The race track, which was little more than a strip with the sagebrush cleared from it, was visible for years but is now brush covered. This and other places like it were the only homes the outlaws knew. True, they were welcome to a meal and even a bed at many ranches. They dared not tarry long, for the danger of betrayal was always present. They were welcome at the saloons and in the redlight houses so long as their money lasted. But even there, the danger of an ambush was not to be ruled out.

So these men, always on the dodge, sleeping uneasily no matter where they went, must have regretted many a time that they had set their feet on the outlaw trail. They produced nothing, lived on what other men had produced and when they passed left few to mourn.

They may not have feared the local lawmen, but the Pinkertons—the FBI of that day—were a real threat. And rewards might tempt some rancher, or even one of the gang, to turn informer. For the leader of this gang, there was always a greater risk. When the time came that large rewards were offered for his capture, dead or alive, there was always the chance that some of his own men might turn him in—dead.

The knowledge of the killing of Jesse James by his own "friend" Bob Ford, was fresh in the minds of these men. Viewing the old Powder Springs hangout, we wonder whether the spirit of the man who died there and perhaps the wraiths of his companions still linger there in mournful vigil.

★
Frontier Entertainment

People often ask me what we did for entertainment those days.

Entertainment? An oldtimer wouldn't understand what they are talking about. Who needed entertainment? Most of the things you just did normally were entertaining. And how!

In drama we were taught that for a play to be rated as well-written and well-played, it must combine and alternate the serious and the comic. If that is true, some of our experiences on the ranch would qualify.

I recall especially one hunting trip which included a runaway. We had runaways as often as one-a-week. Most of our horses were half-broken, treacherous beasts, bent, it would seem, on doing away with those responsible for their bondage.

Our brother Arthur was just about four months old in the summer of 1902. Mother had never taken him on any kind of trip, so this morning she was to go with Dad on the biweekly hunt for antelope. My sister Eva was to stay at the ranch to take care of the chores and to have supper ready when we came back in the evening. My other sister Oney went along to help care for the baby and to do most of the cooking of the noonday meal on a campfire.

Old lunkheads Mike and Nell were the team. They plodded along quite amiably, switching their tails to drive away the mosquitoes and deer flies, and occasionally snorting, swinging their heads and rubbing their jowls against their legs to ward off the hateful bott flies. These pests, looking somewhat like a dark-colored honey bee, lay their tiny, yellow eggs on the tips of the hairs on the horses front legs. Never anywhere else. They then sting the animals' legs, setting up a burning and itching. To relieve this, the horses use their teeth to scratch the itching places.

Nell lowered her head to scratch an itching place. The cheek of her bridle hooked over the end of the neckyoke. She jerked her head up, terrified, and broke into a run. Mike didn't have any enthusiasm in the race, but when the whiffletrees banged him on the hocks he threw up his tail and joined in. That throwing up of his tail was our Waterloo. Dad was sawing on the lines with all his might, trying to control the team. He had them slowed almost to a halt when one of the lines went under Mike's tail, who then clamped his tail on the line and sprang forward. Nell, still anxious to run, bolted forward, but not before Mother, terrified, had grabbed Arthur and jumped from the wagon.

Away we went, Dad with feet braced against the top of the jockey box, hauling on the lines. The one under Mike's tail was clamped as if in a vise, so had no effect on the team. The strain on the other line pulled them to the right and in a wide circle.

When Dad saw the futility of his efforts he pushed the lines into my hands and yelled, "Hold the lines."

I thought he too was going to jump out. I saw myself perched on the wagon seat, pitting my puny strength against that of the two racing horses.

But Dad was not abandoning ship. Instead, he dropped off the wagon seat, lay on the bottom of the wagon box and reaching out at risk of falling from the wagon, got hold of Mike's tail. I knew then he was going to try to free the line.

All this while Oney was clinging for dear life to the back of the wagon seat, standing right behind me. Suddenly she screamed in my ear, "The gulch! The gulch! The gulch ahead!"

I shot a glance ahead and saw that we were headed for the deep-cut channel of Jackrabbit Gulch. I could hear Oney's voice fading as she continued to yell "the gulch" while she bailed out. She must have rolled a dozen turns when she hit the ground. I didn't know, for at that moment we hit the bank of the gulch.

It was about a four-foot drop. We sailed out like a bird. When we hit bottom, the kingbolt must have jumped out, as the front wheels and gear of the wagon separated from the rear, and there I sat, while Dad, clinging to the bolsters of the running gear and clutching Mike's tail, went careening up the sandy bed of Jackrabbit Gulch. I just sat watching, fascinated by the strange spectacle. I saw the team head for the opposite bank as they veered. The next thing

I saw was a cloud of dust, as the wheels of the front gear hit the two-foot bank, the doubletrees broke, Dad was catapulted about 20 feet, and the team, free of the vehicle, went racing across the cactus flat to disappear toward Antelope Springs.

For a moment I didn't know what to do. I feared that maybe the baby had been killed or Mother injured in their wild leap from the wagon. I was sure Oney would be crippled or killed as she had quit the race when it was at top speed. I couldn't see anything of Dad, and thought maybe too he was killed. All I knew to do was to go and try to find him, as I knew he was the key to our problem.

It didn't take me long to run to where I could see the wagon tongue sticking up like the mast of a herring boat. But no Dad, either alive or dead. I circled and found the tracks of the horses and on them Dad's tracks. He was following the team. I knew he wouldn't be running and I could overtake him.

I'd lost my hat and the sun was merciless on my head. But watching ahead as I ran, I saw the team come into sight, more than a mile away, and come circling back. I quit the tracks and cut across through the scrub sagebrush to try to head them off. I got in ahead of them all right, but I might as well have tried to stop a snowslide. They would have run over me if I hadn't leaped aside nimbly at the last moment. They left me like a dog leaving a hornet's nest.

So I hustled back across the flat, a half mile, to try to pick up Dad's tracks and catch up with him. I followed the tracks for not more than a couple of hundred yards when they turned abruptly to the right. I soon lost them in the brush and weeds. I knew then that he had sighted the team, just as I had, and probably cut across to try to head them off as I had. I wondered that I hadn't seen him, but concluded there must have been a low ridge between us.

I started back toward where Oney and Mother were, but had only gone a few yards when I saw small human footprints in the sand, headed the other way. I knew instantly that Oney had followed the wagon and had passed while I was over on the flat trying to stop the team. I was only six, but all my life had been in this environment and its ways and customs had become a part of me.

So now I turned around again and took off on a trot on the small, barefoot tracks I knew were Oney's. But luck wasn't with me that day. I had gone no more than a quarter mile when her tracks, just as had Dad's, turned to the right, and I soon lost them in the harder ground and grass and small growth. She had seen the team coming back and had run across the flat to try to intercept them and to keep them from going on back to the ranch.

But where was she now? I scanned the flat, but nary a human could I see. I began to feel very much alone. So I decided to back-track and help mother get back to the ranch with the baby. That is, if they weren't both killed. I took off on a high run.

It was no trouble to find the place where mother had quit the wagon. Her hat had fallen off and I found it at once. But not a trace of her or Arthur. I "coo-eed" as Dad would call it, but no sound answered my yells. So once more, with a good second wind, I broke into a long trot and headed for the ranch, two miles away.

While all this was happening to me, Dad had done as I thought. He had cut across the flat and met the team but with the same results I had. They would have run him down if he hadn't side-stepped in time. So then, he headed back toward where the front gear of the wagon had hit the bank.

There he saw the small barefoot tracks and also my tracks headed north, away from the ranch. By this time he was pretty well fagged, but nevertheless he took off on those tracks, finally losing them just as I had done. So then he headed back for where mother had quit the expedition. About the time he got there and had spent a few minutes trying to puzzle out Mother's tracks and to determine which way she had gone, Oney showed up, having given up trying to find Dad and headed back toward the ranch.

They held a quick confab and decided Mother and little Art were headed for the ranch, or at least for Emersons, the neighbors. So at a good stiff walk they took off in the same direction. They had gone only a short distance when Dad had a better thought.

"We've got to find Sonny, too," he told Oney. "Oney, would you be afraid to stay here and look for him?"

"No, sir, I wouldn't mind," Oney said in her quiet way, although actually she was scared stiff. But she stayed anyhow, and began to search for me, although she had no clear idea as to where I might be. Actually, I was on my way to the ranch. Dad now headed in the same direction.

It was only a little more than a mile to Emersons, so he knew Mother would head for there. He did likewise. But when he got there, he really became alarmed. Mother had not shown up there at all.

Emerson had only one saddle horse at the barn, so he told Dad, "Colonel, you go on to your place and get a saddle horse. I'll saddle Banty and go back and start to hunt for them."

This they did.

When Dad got to our ranch and told Eva of the situation, she ran like a deer to bring up the other horses. Dad threw a saddle on Johnny and left the ranch at a gallop. Eva, slipping off her shoes the better to travel, lit out in his dust.

Meantime, I had taken the short cut from Emerson's reservoir over the hill and to our ranch. When I got there, not even Eva was there. I fooled around a while, drank a couple of dippers of water, and headed for Emersons.

Mrs. Emerson was no hand to leave the house. But this was something unusual. So slipping on a hat and taking little Allie, who was about my age, she trudged up past their cliff and to the top of the hill, where she could scan the country toward Jackrabbit Springs, where the action was. Their hired man, John Board, was fixing fence up on his place. So when I got to Emersons, it too, like our place, was deserted. I began to wonder if I'd ever see people again.

I monkeyed around a little while, not knowing what to do, but finally decided to head back toward where the rear wheels and box of our wagon was. I was pretty sure that if anybody was still alive around there they'd eventually go to the same place. By that time I was getting pretty tired so kept to just a walk.

When Dad left our ranch horseback, he took the shortcut across to Emerson's reservoir. Mrs. Emerson, who was on the hilltop, saw him and yelled, but he was a little hard of hearing and didn't hear her.

While all this was transpiring, Mother was pegging along at first toward Emersons. But as she drew near, she realized that her face was scratched, her dress torn, and she must be a sight. Mother thought the sight of her, all torn and bloody, might upset Mrs. Emerson. So, instead of coming by Emersons, she took the short cut. But about half way up the hill she glimpsed a small herd of wild cattle. She knew that to wild cattle a human afoot is something to be attacked, so she swung up a draw lined with chokecherry bushes, keeping out of sight of the cattle but slowly edging toward our ranch. She stopped frequently to rest, as the fall from the wagon had shaken her up pretty badly and she felt her strength ebbing.

So it was that when Dad came loping along the cutoff trail, she saw him and shouted and waved wildly. But he, intent on getting back to where this thing had started, did not see her. So, still on her own resources, she headed for the ranch, while Dad kept on up toward Jackrabbit. When Mother finally got to the ranch, she too found it deserted, not even Eva being there. But with nothing else to do, Mother philosophically went about getting things ready for a meal when and if anybody else ever showed up. Though by now, she wasn't at all sure that might ever happen.

When Emerson left his ranch to join in the search, he swung up onto the mesa above his coal mine, so as to have a view of most of the Jackrabbit Springs flat. From that point he saw no sign of life, but he finally glimpsed the rear part of the wagon. He rode to it and there found Oney, who was making short sorties in various directions trying to find somebody or anybody.

He took her up behind him on his horse, who resented this double load and nearly bucked them both off.

Emerson began to circle. He had made about one circle when Dad showed up, the sweat pouring from the horse. Dad and Emerson and Oney compared notes and made a decision. They knew that I was on the flat somewhere if I hadn't gone back to the ranch. So they made a couple of quick circles, yelling bloody murder to try to attract my attention. When they came together, Dad told Emerson, "I don't think the boy is in much danger if he isn't seen by wild cattle. He knows enough to watch for snakes. So I think the most danger is to Kate and the baby."

"You're right," Emerson agreed. "We'd better spread out and head toward the ranches." This they did.

Emerson had come up the road and Dad the cutoff, so they headed back the same two ways. When Emerson got to his ranch, he was shocked to find it deserted.

Meanwhile, Mother had peeled potatoes, sliced meat, and after washing her face, putting on some salve on the scratched places and changing her dress, and still no one showed up, she went the back way to Emersons. She was drawing near it when she saw Emerson come riding in, make a quick survey and go galloping toward our ranch. Mother was debating whether to go on to Emersons or return to our own place when she glimpsed Mrs. Emerson and Allie coming down off the high hill.

Mother went ahead and soon the women were together, comparing notes, one as much at sea as the other.

Dad had arrived at our ranch shortly after mother left by the back road and of course found the ranch deserted. He galloped to Emersons, meeting Emerson half way. They hastily compared notes.

Both ranches deserted, two women and three children missing and night fast coming on.

There was no help to be had. There were no telephones, no neighbors nearer than Lay, an hour's ride away. So whirling their horses, they hurried back to Emersons ranch. There, to their unspeakable relief, they found both women and two of the missing children. Only Sonny was now missing.

And where was Sonny? Well, I was headed back to the rear part of the wagon. I was down in the gulch getting a drink when Emerson passed me within a hundred yards. By the time I could scramble up the bank and yell at him in my squeaky voice he was too far gone. So I went on to the wagon.

There I stayed for what seemed an eternity. I perched on the projecting rear end of the wagon box, keeping an eye peeled for a glimpse of anybody. It did not matter much who, just so it was some human. I could see the forbidding cliffs above Jackrabbit Spring, hear the desolate moan of the hoot owl that had his perch there, and noted the dark maw of Emerson's coal mine. But more important, I noted the shadow of the hill as it crept across the flat. I had studied and understood the shadows of hills as far back as I could remember. To my father, working in the field, the shadows were timepieces. When the shadow of our cliff reached a certain clump of bushes, it was time to quit.

So now, watching the shadows, I knew that when that shadow had crossed the narrow flat, climbed the low hill opposite and reached its top, it would be twilight. And twilight to me was a deadline. All my life, I've been like a chicken. The moment it begins to get dusk, I begin to lose my keen sense of vision. I'm just about as helpless in the dark as an owl is in the daylight. I knew this, even at the age of six. I knew that if I was going to get to the ranch, I'd better be on my way. And the thought of spending a night on the upended box of that wagon, with that owl moaning from the frowning brow of that bluff, and with the cold creeping into my bones, was even worse than the thought of again finding both ranches deserted and myself all alone in this vast world. But at least going to the ranch meant action, and I took off at a swift trot.

I had gone nearly a mile, came up over that little rise and came within an ace of getting trampled by the horses of Dad and Emerson as they came loping, for one last chance to find me before night descended. All were now accounted for.

Yes, indeed, we did not lack for entertainment, I guess.

And how about the authors of all this confusion? We found them next morning, at the lower end of our place where they had spent the night trying to get their heads down to the water, an effort defeated by the checkreins that held their heads too high to drink.

When I thought of my blistered feet and all the trouble we had been to, I didn't feel terribly sorry for the two rogues.

★
The Pantomime

In 1870, the Wilson brothers, Crane and Dummy, made a horseback-and-packhorse tour of the country, having a look at the Timberlake Gulch country and eventually reaching Brown's Park. There they squatted on a piece of land and put up a cabin. This is still known as "Dummy Bottom." During the autumn and winter the Wilsons explored the valley and even went into Lodore Canyon, riding as far as they could and then walking as far as they could on the ice.

The next spring, the Wilsons made the long trip to Rock Springs for a supply of groceries and other needs. The railroad had arrived there two years before. They arrived in the Wyoming coal town just in time for an event of national importance. That day, May 22, 1871, Major John Wesley Powell and his party embarked from Rock Springs on the second trip through the Grand Canyon of the Colorado. F. S. Dellenbaugh, who wrote the history of that trip, had this to say concerning the day they made ready to launch the three boats:

"The only unpleasant circumstance was the persistent repetition by a deaf-mute of a pantomimic representation of the disaster he believed would overtake us. "Dummy" as we called him, showed that we would be upset, unable to scale the cliffs and would surely all be drowned. This picture, as vividly presented as possible, seemed to give him and his brother great satisfaction. Other wise men of the town predicted that we would never see Brown's Hole at the end of Red Canyon."

They had good reason for their fears, for Mayor Hook of the town had perished on just such a boat trip, and Dummy and Crane Wilson had had a close look at the Canyon of Lodore, Ashley had found the canyons highly dangerous, and Powell himself had lost a boat at "Disaster Falls" in Lodore Canyon on his first trip.

We who knew Dummy Wilson intimately knew how well he could make his grim forecast in pantomime. Fortunately, it did not come true.

About 1881 the Rawlins-to-Meeker road by way of Lay was the superhighway of the region. Along it plodded or sped soldiers, freighters, prospectors, trappers, Indians and outlaws. In that year the Wilson brothers located a ranch at "Timberlake" spring, northwest of Craig about 30 or 35 miles.

When we made our first trip over that road we kids expected momentarily to catch sight of the "timber" that surely must surround "timberlake." We saw neither timber nor lake, for neither was there.

W. E. Timberlake, who in 1875 was running big herds of cattle on Snake River, built a cabin and corral at the spring that came to be known as "Timberlake Spring." The gulch took the same name. The government road ran through the front yard of the house the Wilson brothers later erected at the spring.

W. H. Wilson, oldest of the two, was 6' 6" tall, straight and serious. His neck was noticeably long, so in that land where nicknames were more the rule than the exception, he was dubbed "Crane Neck." Some shortened this to "Craney," or "Crane." To us he was "Mr. Crane Wilson." In those days, children did not forget the "Mister."

The younger brother was known as "Dummy Wilson." He had been a deaf mute from birth.

Crane was a courtly, dignified man, with the manners of a Chesterfield, the culture of a savant, and musical taste and skill of high order.

Dummy was a six-footer, sturdy, jolly, and with natural skill in mechanics and taxidermy. He was also a cook with a magic touch and adept at drawing. As soon as their house was ready they went into business. They put in a stock of liquors and Crane became the merchant. Dummy opened an eating house, using any spare time he had when not cooking or serving to mount wild animals and birds, which helped boost his income.

By the time we got to know them, about 1887, the flow of freighters, soldiers, and others along that road had slowed to a trickle. The White River Camp of the military had been closed and the telegraph line dismantled and the wire poles sold to ranchers and others. Dad and Emerson each had some and donated enough to build the first schoolhouse in that part of the state a few years later.

Wilson's saloon and roadhouse had been phased out and only occasional cowpunchers and ranchers with a sprinkling of trappers, prospectors, and outlaws visited the Wilsons. But by this time they had built up a fair herd of excellent work horses, and Dummy still had considerable taxidermy work to do. Besides those activities, each spring while the runoff of snow water was on they did gold placer mining. With team and scraper and huge sluice boxes they labored early and late to wash out a modest stake of gold.

The Wilsons enjoyed company and welcomed all who came. One of the pleasures to which our family looked forward was our annual trip to Snake River to buy such vegetables as we did not grow ourselves. The Sheehans and others around Dixon raised scads of vegetables. We usually arrived at Wilson's about five, after a grueling 28-mile day from our ranch. We met with a royal welcome. Crane, who spoke in a deep-throated voice, always greeted each of us with a grave handclasp and words of kindness. With a deep bow from the waist he bent over Mother's hand. Dummy's handshake was vigorous and his welcome positively bubbling. He could make only one sound, a sort of loud and guttural "Ah-h-h." It won instant attention. With that sound he greeted friends, called guests to meals, roused Crane in the morning, warned of danger, praised, condemned, and even controlled and "cussed out" their horses. Coupled with a wide grin, a gentle smile or frown or by nods or shakes of his head it could speak volubly.

It was not long before we kids could carry on a conversation with Dummy almost as well as if he had been able to speak and to hear. His pantomime was eloquent. But if a point was obscure, he would seize pencil and paper and with words and pictures clarify it. His freehand drawing was the equal of many highly talented cartoonists and illustrators I have known. How I wish I had his skill.

Never to be forgotten is a story he told us of the visit of a bear to their watermelon patch. By pantomime and pictures he told how the bear was sighted, how he thought to throw rocks at it but thought better when the bear halted and stood erect. Dummy's race to the house for the rifle, trailing the bear, but finally losing him. Then the anger of the narrator when he came back to the garden to find that besides destroying most of the melons, bruin had dug up most of the potato vines and even clawed out beets and carrots.

Then, tapping his chest with a finger and doing a bit of a dance, he explained that he liked to dance. Drawing a picture of himself arrayed in his best clothes, he began by drawing the brim of his hat first. In after years, at my suggestion, both Paul Gregg and "Doc Bird" Finch, *Denver Post* artists, tried to do it that way and couldn't.

Dummy delighted in going to dances. Although he could not have heard the discharge of a big Bertha, he could sense the vibration of music in some way and in a quadrille go through the "changes" without error. At intermission in the dance, if the fiddler would play a lively hoedown, Dummy would jig with grace, precision and great enjoyment.

Crane had a music box. It played from a cylinder about the size of an Edison phonograph record of early design. Pins in this cylinder plucked reeds. The resulting music was soft, sweet, and plaintive. The selections he had were of the world's finest music. Our favorite was "The Carnival of Venice," with all manner of variations. Crane also played violin.

The music and the stories did not come until after supper. That was an event in itself. The moment greetings were over, and our horses stabled, Dummy was among the skillets. He welcomed Mother's assistance. Together they created a meal fit for kings and better things. Venison, sage chicken or some other meat, mountains of mashed potatoes made with plenty of butter and cream from the Wilson's cow, a couple of kinds of cooked vegetables and also lettuce, radishes, and onions. But no watermelon. Sarvisberry or chokecherry or buffaloberry preserves and cake which Mother would have brought, with milk for us kids and tea for the adults. The Wilsons were English Canadians and like Mother, enjoyed tea.

Finest of all, the matchless conviviality, the solicitude with which both Wilsons saw to it that each and all of us were served and regaled. All this in a spotless kitchen and a dining room that might have been in a mansion, instead of in a cabin of stone, logs, and adobe.

While dishes were being done, Dad and Crane would fill and light their pipes and sitting before the fireplace, enjoy conversation. We kids huddled on the animal skin rugs before the fire. Crane was always anxious for any word of the outside world. They'd discuss current events—current in this case meaning what might be gleaned from the newspaper that came a week late to our home every two weeks, the *Denver Republican*. This, and the *Omaha Bee* the Emersons received, were probably the only papers received in an area of 5,000 square miles! The talk might veer to mining, philosophy, politics, or anything else.

Then came a little routine that meant delight, yet torture to us youngsters and even to our parents. After Crane had played a few selections on the music box, he would bring forth his dulcimer. This was a square, flat boxlike instrument with many strings. It was played by tapping the strings with two small mallets. Its soft music was entrancing.

We could hardly wait for Crane to begin. Yet, what an ordeal.

With the dulcimer in place on a small table, Crane drew up his chair and was seated. He took his stance. Sitting bolt upright, austere, head unmoving and long neck seeming to be extended, he followed the motion of the little hammers with movements of his face. He'd frown, raise his eyebrows, twist his mouth, open and close his eyes, while the most heavenly music poured from beneath his finger tips, as he tinkled away at the dulcimer, an instrument invented at the dawn of civilization and actually the progenitor of the modern piano.

Just when we were absorbed in enjoying this musical came the moment for which we had hoped and yet dreaded. Dummy would come from the kitchen, approaching Crane from the rear without being detected. Standing behind Crane's chair, Dummy would assume the same stance as Crane, mimicking every posture, grimace and motion, tapping away at an imaginary dulcimer.

We kids, caught in the glare of the light from the fireplace, in full view of all, were torn inside by spasms of mirth as we watched the pantomime of Dummy. We dared not even smile, much less laugh. To have burst out laughing would have been akin to ridiculing the Almighty. So, clamping our jaws and biting our lips, with our "innards" typing themselves into double bow knots, we managed to make it through the ordeal without giving even an inkling of the screams of laughter that were struggling to burst forth.

Crane Wilson died in 1901 and is buried on the hill above their house. Dummy went back to his birthplace in Canada. Crane was only 57 years of age at the time of his death. He seemed much older to us.

Years later, as a surveyor on the Elk River Irrigation Co. project which was to take water from Elk and Snake Rivers and with it irrigate the Iron Springs Divide country, we stayed for weeks at the old Wilson place, then abandoned.

Sometimes, in the evening, I could in imagination feel the presence of those two remarkable men, hear the tinkling of the dulcimer, sense the glow of the fireplace fire and even see the pantomime of Dummy, standing behind the chair of his brother. It all came back, even to the long-drawn "Ah-h-h-h" of Dummy.

★
Buzzards Don't Talk

I eyed the old woman with deep misgivings and a tinge of dread. To listen enthralled to her stirring stories when she visited here at our ranch was one thing. But to go with her to spend a month at her lonely ranch near Cross Mountain, where she and I would be alone, was a different matter.

"It'll be good fer yuh, young feller," she told me, as I stood, twisting uncomfortably and digging my bare toes into the sand. "Good fer any young chap to get away from his maw's apron strings once in awhile. I'll fatten you up some. I c'n cook. Good as yer maw. I got hosses, dogs, cattle, and chickens, and yuh got a hull outdoors to roam over. What do yuh say, huh?"

The craggy, seamed old face reminded me of the pictures I'd seen of witches. Toothless, the chin and nose almost met. But the sharp eyes that seemed to bore right into me like a gimlet were not unkindly, and a half-smile twitched at the corners of the grim lips. My parents stood silent.

I knew the decision would be mine to make. It was a decision of vast importance to a nine-year-old who had never spent a night apart from his family. I was sure that if my parents felt disapproval of the idea, they would have spoken up immediately. The fact they hadn't left it in my lap.

"I guess maybe I have to help Papa with the dam," I temporized.

"The dam c'n wait. Yer paw 'nd you been buildin' that dam in the crick ever since you was big enuf to drive a team. 'Taint goin' to hurt none to let it rest fer a month. Well, I ain't got ferever to monkey around. Yuh got to make up yer mind. Say, that's fine. That's the way fer a man t' be. Make up his mind right now. All right, grab a clean pair of socks and we'll be rollin.'"

I hadn't even opened my mouth, much less given assent to the idea of going with her. I looked at my parents in desperation. Mother smiled and nodded her head. I knew I was trapped. I had utmost confidence in the wisdom of my parents. But the suspicion was in my mind that this time they might have slipped.

So, I found myself on the wagon seat with Maggie Mills, headed for her ranch, a long day's trip distant. It was a long drag, but so far the time had passed quickly and the miles down Lay Creek and across Sugar Loaf Basin had not seemed very long as the old ranchwoman had an endless fund of stories of her experiences. She had too a way of drawing out others to talk of themselves. It was not so bad, after all, I congratulated myself.

The team was a young one and full of life. There was a buggy whip in the socket at the driver's right. But no need to use a whip on the grays. All she needed to do to remind them to quicken their gait was to drag her hobnailed shoe across the edge of the dashboard. The sound stirred the team to a faster walk.

At the bend of Bear River where Sand Creek joined it, we made camp for lunch. While I led the team to the river to water them and to fetch a pail of water for cooking, Maggie started a sagebrush fire and went about preparing food.

Every action was deliberate, prompt, and performed with the precision born of long practice. Maggie was a child of such environment. Hers had been a life of action, most of it in rough surroundings. Although she told of many of her own experiences, she seldom talked of her life before she had become Mrs. Mills. Rumor had it that she'd been resident of one of the gaudy houses of the night on Second Avenue in Leadville. Jim Mills had been a miner in the famous camp and there met and married Maggie. He brought her to his mountain ranch at the foot of Cross Mountain, in northwest Colorado.

The mountain which towered above their log dwelling cast early shadows which made even summer afternoons cool and bearable. Cross Mountain is the easternmost extension of the Uintah range, the only east-and-west major mountain range in North America.

My family had met Maggie soon after their arrival in this country in 1886. At that time the country lying west of the Continental Divide in northwest Colorado was truly the last frontier. Cut off by lack of communication by wire, rail, or mail, with ingress by an almost impassable road, the country was still the abode of roaming Indians, trappers, cowboys, and the few homesteaders who had settled here and there where springs furnished water for themselves and their livestock.

"Mighty fine folks you got," Maggie remarked as we sat in the shade of the wagon eating our dinner. "You're lucky to have 'em. 'Tain't many younguns in this country got eddicated folks that c'n teach 'em like what your folks do."

I agreed. I hadn't given the matter much thought but took it for granted. But it was true. None of the few other children of whom I knew had any schooling. But my parents held regular school all during the winter months, using regular school textbooks.

"Me, I never had much schooling," Maggie told me. "Had to hustle to work when I was still little. When I finly got to makin' m' own money I had other ideas 'sides school." She smiled wryly. "Oh I got a lot of schoolin' but it was the rough-and-tumble kind and didn't come t' me in no school house. Well, we better sand out these plates and get them grays to headin' west," she concluded.

The days passed quickly at Maggie's. I was delighted with the ranch and its neat log house. I'd been in the cabins of some of the bachelor homesteaders. A few were well kept, but most were not very clean and reeked of the odors of bacon, sour dough, cooking odors, and the barnyard. Maggie's house was clean as my own mother's, and the ranch showed the results of hard work and knowledge. "You sure have a nice ranch, Mrs. Mills," I told her. I didn't call her Maggie. My parents had always impressed on us youngsters respect for our elders.

"Oh, so you don't think it's so bad," she chuckled. "Now ain't yuh glad I kidnapped yuh? That was a dirty trick the way I worked it," She chuckled again.

"Oh I'm glad I did come. I'm glad you did—well, I kind of figured on coming anyhow."

Maggie didn't answer that. I knew I didn't have her fooled.

"Well, I wouldn' a blamed yuh if yuh hadn't come," she confided. "Tain't many boys want t' go traipsin' off with an old woman like me. I know I ain't no great shakes to look at. But one thing you'll find out lad, the longer you live. All the people that are good and kind and not skeered of their own shadders ain't purty ner handsome."

I was willing to swear to this. I'd had my eyes opened during the week at this ranch. When the old woman spoke of people who were "kind and good and not skeered" she could be thinking of herself. She was all those things, I was ready to agree. I had to admit too that she no longer looked as much like a witch as I'd thought before.

Every day was a new adventure. One day we didn't do any ranch work, but instead climbed Cross Mountain, looked into a huge crack in the rocks that almost divided the mountain and with chills chasing each other up and down their spines, gazed down into the awesome maw of the deep canyon through which roared the Bear River. We saw deer fawns hiding among the pinyons and cedars and viewed the vast panorama of mountains, plains, and canons to the west and to the east.

Another day we hitched the team of old mares to the wagon and drove ten miles to Snake River. There we shot some young sage hens, picked enough black currents to make two pies, and gathered some greasewood stumps to be taken to the ranch and used to make a smokeless fire for broiling the venison we hoped to get later.

We got back from this trip late in the evening. Maggie went at once to the house to start supper, while I unhitched the old mares, rubbed them down with curry comb and brush and watered them. I turned them into the big pasture to join the young grays. As I walked to the house, I saw the dust made by a wagon as it turned off the main road and into the side road that led to the ranch.

Arrived at the gate, the strangers tied their team and walked up to the house. Maggie and I had ceased operations and stood at the door, watching the approach of the two men. Strangers in this country were rare as angels visits.

The men walked single file. The one in front was a tall black-bearded fellow who walked with a shambling gait, long arms swinging at his sides. The other was short, stocky, and wore a straggly red beard and what seemed to be a perpetual grin. Both were covered with the dust of travel. Even under the dust neither appeared to be very clean. This was not to be wondered at nor condemned in this land of few accommodations and scarce water.

"How do you do, madam," the tall fellow greeted, coming to a halt a few feet from the threshold.

"Yuh know me?" Maggie asked sharply.

"No madam, can't say as I do. Why?"

"Oh nothing," she returned. "What c'n we do fer yuh?"

"We come a long way today, madam," the man explained. "Looks like a long way more to that river valley. Our team's pretty well tuckered out. Could we make camp here and maybe get a little water fer us 'nd the hosses?"

"Yuh sure can, mister," Maggie assured him. "We never turn nobody away. Better pull yer wagon inside the gate er the range stock'll bother yuh out there. Turn yer hosses loose in that little pasture. Plenty of grass. Don't open the gate to the big pasture. I got a couple of teams of mighty fine hosses in the big pasture. I don't want 'em gettin' in no fight with no strange hosses. Plenty of good cedar wood in the woodpile there. Yuh c'n use what yuh need."

The men did as told. Maggie went about getting the evening meal, while I carried in wood from the woodpile and water from the spring. Sagehen breasts were sizzling on the wood stove and the table spread when the men finished.

"Wonder what them fellers are doin' in this country," Maggie said as we attacked the victuals. "Mighty uncommon to see anything but a roundup wagon out this way. Good lookin' outfit they got. I hope they come by it honest."

She then launched into a lecture on honesty and the evils to be expected from being otherwise.

"I bet you think I'm suspicious," she told me. "Guess I am. Yuh get that way livin' the kind of life I have. We was always poor when I was your age. Mostly 'coz my father never suspicioned nobody and let every slick rogue bamboozle him out of his money. Even his own friends took him in sometimes. I don't aim to be hard, but I don't aim to let nobody get more'n what's hizzen."

I agreed that this was a good policy. I knew of a few times when my own father had been the victim of some supposed-to-be friends.

"I worked hard for what little I got," she declared positively. "Course I didn't have nothin' when I married Jim Mills. But I had two willin' hands and a strong back. Him 'nd me worked like dogs buildin' up this ranch. Yuh got to work to get ahead. You'll find that out. But when yuh get it, hang onto it and take care of it."

The meal finished, I dried the dishes while Maggie washed them, keeping up a running fire of conversation that fell like music on my willing ears.

We'd just finished and were relaxing in the big deerskin-lined chairs when a knock sounded on the door. Maggie nodded to me to open the door. The two strangers came into the fitful light of the kerosene lamp.

"Come right in, men," Maggie invited. "Shove them two chairs over this way in the light."

The men were seated, their eyes taking in the interior of the comfortable cabin.

"Thought we might come over and see yuh 'fore yuh went to bed and get some information 'bout the road," the big man said. "Yer man around?"

"I ain't got no man," Maggie confessed. "Died some time back. Don't need no man. This young feller is a good man his own self. 'Course he ain't goin' to stay long. But I'm man enough myself when there ain't nobody else nigh."

The men looked her over. They saw a tall bony frame, inured to hard work, strong, sinewy hands and the witch-like face, crowned by a wisp of hair pulled severely back and tied in a knot. The eyes were as clean and as bright as the calico wrapper she wore.

"Looks like you'd need to have a hired hand to run the ranch," the black-bearded man opined. "Seems like yuh got quite a bit of hay ground. Put up some hay?"

"Some. 'Bout 30 ton. But me 'nd this young feller aim to put it in the stack. Take our time. Ain't no men nearer than the river anyway."

"Ain't it a bit dangerous livin' alone?" It was the first time the smaller man had spoken. His voice was almost a squeak. Maggie and I regarded him with surprise.

"Not a bit of it. Nobody goin' to bother me. The ranchers all know me. The cowpunchers ain't goin' to bother no old woman. If any outlaws come along I'd feed 'em jest like I would anyone else. I c'n shoot good as they can. I got the stuff t' do it with too." With a motion of her hand she indicated the guns in the deerhorn rack.

After getting directions as to the road leading west, the men got up to leave.

"You men jest as well come over fer breakfast," Maggie told them. "No use burnin' two fires when one'll do the job. If you c'n stand sowbelly, corn meal mush, 'nd sourdough flapjacks, er maybe I'll have biscuits, that's what we'll have."

They told her they would be on hand for breakfast.

"Ordinary we ain't early birds," Maggie told them. "But I reckon you boys want to get on the road in the cool of the day, so how about five-thirty fer breakfast?"

The men signified that the hour was agreeable and left.

"Kind of dirty, ain't they?" Maggie remarked to me. "Guess men can't be blamed fer that, though Jim Mills never was no feller t' be dirty. He never seen the time but what he could find water enough t' keep clean. He'd say, 'Yuh may have t' be ragged, but yuh ain't got t' be dirty.'"

"That's what my folks say," I agreed.

"Good folks, them of yourn," Maggie told him. "Well, son, I allow we better turn in. Goin' to get up a mite early t' get them fellers off while it's still cool."

I wondered, as I prepared for bed, why she was concerned about the two strangers. I didn't like the looks of either of them. The big fellow wasn't so bad, but the smaller man had a shifty look about him.

I had hardly touched the pillow, when I was roused by the shrill voice of Maggie, raised in anger.

"Come out of it, boy," she was shouting. "Come out of it. We got no time to waste. Come on!"

I heard the front door slam as I shot from the bed and pulled on my shirt and overalls. Maggie was in the yard, her eyes glued to a pair of field glasses, pointed to the northwest.

She was talking to herself as I reached her side.

"The skunks, the damn ongrateful skunks," she gritted. "T' think I had it in mind to treat 'em good 'nd they rob me. An old woman like me," she barked, whirling to me. "Grab two of them halters hangin' on the corral gate and run down in the pasture and see if we got any horses left. I c'n see by the tracks where they took four hosses out. Maybe they left the old mares."

I didn't stop to find out more. I was accustomed to obeying without question. Grabbing two halters I started on a trot for the pasture below the house. On the first rise I glimpsed the two old mares, but no sign of the team of gray geldings that were Maggie's pride and joy.

I caught the mares with some difficulty and mounting one, led the other on a long trot, knowing there was need for hurry.

As I pulled up to the corral, Maggie met me and told me to give the mares a feed of oats.

"They'll need the extra strength," she counseled. "And get a gunny sack and put some extra in it. I'll take it along for 'em. Put my saddle on the stockin'-foot mare and the other saddle you've been usin' on the other mare."

I did as told. I had not quite finished when Maggie called me to breakfast. When I hurried in she motioned me to the table.

"Got to eat for strength for th' job afore us," she said wisely "I'm gettin' that team back, lad. I'll beat the tails offen them old mares and ride 'em 'till they drop dead if I got to. I hate to abuse 'em, but by God no damn coyotes are goin' to make off with my hosses and me not chase 'em. God knows if they stole anything else 'nd I ain't got time to look t' find out."

"What will we do if we do catch them?" I asked. "They have the best horses don't they? How are we going to catch them?"

"No we ain't goin' t' try," she explained "Me, I'm goin' t' be the one to catch 'em. It's my job. You're goin' t' stay with the ranch. Somebody's got to stay here and tend to things."

"Can't I go with you and help?" I begged.

"I don't need no help and I don't want nobody 'round in m'way when I catch them bastards," she said, her voice rising.

"You just hang on there. Feed the chickens and them cats, milk the cows, and keep yerself fed up. I don't know how long I'll be gone. But I ain't comin' back until I get m' hosses. You know where stuff is to eat. If yuh can't cook just eat what yuh c'n find that don't need no cooking."

I reflected that she might never come back. In imagination I could see her overtaking the big man and the shifty-eyed little coyote-man.

Maggie threw together such food as would suffice for a fly trip. From the gun rack she selected a weapon. Not the new Winchester 45-90, but a long-barreled singleshot Ballard of 40-65 caliber. She threw a handful of cartridges into the grub sack along with a brass-mounted Colts revolver.

"Jim's suggins," she explained, as she tossed a rod of blankets onto the led mare and tied it on. "I don't figure on sleepin' much but might grab a wink while the old mares eat and rest. Got to let 'em."

There were a thousand questions I would have liked to ask, but she gave me no time nor encouragement.

"I'm dependin' on yuh to keep things," Maggie told me. "If any more strangers come along shut the gate and tell 'em to go on down th' road. Nothin' left t' steal but the cows and chickens but some damn renegade might do that. Take care of yerself. I'll be back 'fore long."

Maggie mounted the stocking-foot mare. With the long-barreled rifle slung at an angle across the pommel of the saddle, grim-lipped, the blue calico sunbonnet drawn tightly around her face, she looked more like a crusader of old than a grandmotherly old ranch-woman. She clucked to the mares, swung through the gate which I threw wide for her to pass, and jogged down the road, turning to wave to me only when she reached the top of the rise that soon hid her from sight.

I walked slowly to the house, loneliness already settling on me. I knew I should have gone with her, but I didn't know how to argue the matter and anyhow now it was too late.

South of the house was the dark bulk of Cross Mountain. To the north stretched the somber sagebrush flats of Peck Mesa. Westward, the way Maggie had gone, lay the gray-white hills beyond Snake River, the way to Brown's Park and beyond that to Utah. It was toward this point, in the hours that ensued that my eyes were most often turned. I imagined a thousand times that I saw dust rising where I conceived the Browns Park road to lie. But each figment dissolved into nothing. Neither that day nor the next did Maggie return.

I did everything I could devise to drive away the loneliness. Walked to the surrounding hills, cleaned the house several times, weeded the garden, and other small chores. It was toward evening of the third day when I at last described what I knew this time to be dust on the road. When this turned in at the side road to the ranch, a weight lifted from my spirit. I started a fire in the old charter oak stove and put on the filled teakettle. By that time the ranchwoman and her equipage came over the rise, I swung wide the gate and let them in.

Instead of the one team of old mares with which she had left, the grim old woman now had the young gray team hitched to the wagon, which I recognized as that of the strangers'. Tied by their halter ropes to the rear of the wagon were the old mares, while tied to the old mare's tails and bringing up the rear was still another team.

The moment she hauled the team to a stop, Maggie began giving orders to me, while she headed for the house.

"Feed 'em all. I'll get to burnin' grease."

I did as directed. Finished, I went to the house burning with curiosity as to what had happened. But not even when we were at the table did Maggie give me any chance to question her.

"Now let's roll in," she cut me off when I would have put a question. "I'm dead beat. No more talk until morning."

With chores to do and planning the day's work during breakfast, it was not until we stood in the yard after breakfast, waiting for the horses to drink, that I started to ask a question about the happenings on the west road.

"Mrs. Mills, what did you do to those . . . "I began.

At the moment she was kneeling, removing a bit of tangled string from the leg of a tiny chick. She held up a hand for silence. Giving the little chicken a kindly pat, she stood up.

"I know yer just fairly bustin' to know what happened," she told me. "Well, the main thing is for you to know to never let no man impose on you nor do yuh dirt 'thout hittin' a lick back. 'Member that. As to what happened. Well, see them birds circlin' up there?"

I followed her pointing finger. So high as to be almost invisible, I saw the tiny black dots. Vultures, I knew. The buzzards that are the scavengers of the desert.

I lowered my gaze from the circling buzzards to look inquiringly at Maggie.

"There's some things I know," she said quietly, "and will be buried with my bones. If you want to know, ask them," she pointed upward.

I understood. Vultures tell no tales.

Buzzards don't talk.

All the names and places in the story are factual, except "Maggie Mills." I should add that 14 years later, when we had moved to Craig, "Maggie" was a good and valued neighbor, in the same block.

Horseplay

It wasn't in the *real* old times, but later in 1908, during the time Bill Patton was foreman of the Two-Bar, that a bunch was using the horse camp for base of operations one spring. Bill Patton's nephew came out from the East to become a cowboy. He was about 16, a likable chap, but very gullible, believing everything he was told. Link McGowan was cook and at about the first meal he asked the young fellow if he wanted any of the mixture of prunes, apricots, and raisins that were for dessert.

"I sure do, thank you," the embryo cow waddie replied.

"Well, you see, it's this way," Link told him. "Fruit comes extra. The regular chuck goes with your wages but fruit's extra."

This, of course, was pure fabrication. But the neophyte inspected his bank roll and said he'd take fruit anyhow during that week, as he thought he had enough money. The arrangement was strictly adhered to, the lad digging up his quarter at each meal. About that time Patton came to camp and at dinner the victim forked over his two-bits as usual. Patton wanted to know why, and the gag ended in a good laugh by everybody, including the boy, who got his money back. Patton wasn't too well pleased, we thought, but he probably realized that the nephew had to learn the hard way. He was eager to learn, so the punchers were cooperative. They did indeed try to teach him the things a rider should know, but added a few extras. One such extra was a "snipe hunt."

After several days of casual allusions to the delights of snipe hunting and the excellence of baked snipe, the "hunt" was organized. Since the boy was not conversant with the techniques of snipe hunting, he was naturally given the easiest job. That was to crouch on the trail at an assigned spot holding the gunny sack wide open on the trail. A lighted candle was held near the sack to attract the snipe. When the snipe, following the trail, ran into and filled the sack, he was to clamp it shut.

Ike Patterson went with the young fellow to locate him, promising to return in a half-hour or so. The "station" was about two miles from the ranch beyond some hills, in dense sagebrush. It was reached by a circuitous route covering about four miles and calculated to confuse the victim and make him lose all sense of direction. After he was posted, Ike departed, taking both horses, since the presence of a horse would frighten away the snipe. All the cowpunchers then returned to the horse camp and went to bed.

It was about three o'clock when the victim of the joke finally reached the ranch. He had stuck to his post until he realized he had been made the victim of a gag. By good luck he had found the ranch house without much difficulty, and without tumbling into a washout or walking off of a bank. But he was mad and waking all hands told them off in no uncertain terms. This only added to their merriment. They finally calmed him by telling him that *all* newcomers went through the same trial. His chance would come when another new hand came to camp.

The old Haley house at this same horse camp was supposed to be haunted, although most of us knew the apparition to be nothing more than the occasional phosphorescence given off by the "hot" cow manure in the old building, where cattle sheltered. But it is likely that some of the waddies at the horse camp this spring *believed* this was indeed a spook. At any rate, the budding young cowhand soon learned of the ghost.

The imaginative Ike Patterson and Charlie Bates, neither of whom believed in ghosts, embellished the story quite a bit. Not only was there a ghost in camp, but it *walked,* according to their version. It had even been known, a long time before, to enter the bunkhouse at dead of night.

This sort of talk went on for days. They never overdid it, but made it casual enough to be credible. But all the time the plan was being formulated. Came the night when the big episode was to be staged.

Bed time was usually before nine. This night, Ike, Charlie, and Bill Ford, who was visiting and knew all the plans, stayed awake until sure the victim was sound asleep. Then they arose stealthily. From the kitchen they brought all the dishpans, kettles, and tin plates they could lay hands on. These were quietly stacked near the head of the lad's bunk.

Next, a yellow slicker was laid outside the window on the stone flagstones and to it a lariat was tied, the rope being passed through the window and to Ford's bed. Incidentally, this same Bill Ford had been "initiated" in like manner a few months before, he being a green hand from Pennsylvania at the time, but now a homesteader not far from the horse camp.

When all was still, Charlie Bates, outside the window, let go with a moan. Some of the men awoke. All were in on the gag, so lay expectantly. Again Charlie groaned, a little more loudly. After a couple more heartrending moans, the young fellow stirred. They could hear the catch in his breath as Charlie emitted a quavering groan ending in a whiffling sigh. All were awake by now, but their heavy breathing and snoring went on as usual. Charlie was exceeding himself in his dramatic presentation of the "ghost." Even the scoffers were not too sure it was Charlie.

"Link! Link, what's that?" the victim asked in a hoarse whisper. Link McGowan had been kindest of all to the newcomer and to him he now turned. But Link kept mum. Finally Boston Shedden, the horse wrangler, whispered, "I reckon it's that there ghost, kid."

The byplay went on for as long as the men could hold back their laughter. Then, as Charlie outside let loose with a shriek that would have curdled the blood of a dead man, Bill hauled on the rope and in the bright moonlight all could see the "ghost," the old yellow slicker, come sailing in through the window. At the same instant, Ike, near the pile of tinware, gave a shove and a kick and the thing came down with a crashing and banging, the washtub that crowned the pile rolling across the bed where the victim lay.

With a yell that drowned out all other sound, the youth sprang from his bunk. In three jumps he was in the kitchen, had the door open, and clutching his drawers to keep them from falling and hobbling him, darted out into the sagebrush, rabbit weed, and prickly pears, not halting until he came up against the fence two hundred yards from the buildings.

It took persuasion, explanation, and confession to induce the chap to return to the bunkhouse. It had been a bitter lesson, but it was a productive one for him. He took the joke good-naturedly after it was explained. From then on, he was one of the boys and no longer the butt of their jokes. It is likely he entered with zest into the initiation of the next green hand who came along.

John Ledford, a rancher at Lay, sometimes indulged in a practical joke. But John was no addict, and his jokes were harmless. On one occasion, following a trail from his Big Gulch ranch to Craig, accompanied by a lad of about 15, John stopped his horse, dismounted, and reaching down, came up with a shiny silver dollar. In about a mile, the performance was repeated. This went on until the boy was fairly frantic. There he was, riding in the lead, and failing to glimpse all these shiny dollars. Of course it was the same dollar that John was palming and seeming to find. For days, the lad went every day to that trail to try to see if *he* could find a dollar.

It might be thought that cowpunchers devoted a lot of time to such "monkey business." The opposite is true. During roundup times they had no time nor energy for horseplay. At the main ranches it would not have been tolerated. The horse camp was the one place where such shenanigans might be had, as the men there worked shorter hours and the boss was seldom at the camp.

★
The Wild Horse Man

Of all the men I've ever known, Engle Edinger was at the head of the list.

I suppose the reason I had so much affection for Engle was because he treated me as an equal. When Engle was 30, I was 11. Yet, we hunted together, worked together, chased wild horses, and rode for cattle as equals. Where other men treated me as the child I was, correcting, instructing, patronizing, Engle acted as if he expected me to make a hand, offering suggestions if any in a quiet, offhand way.

Engle was as homely as a mud fence. His hair was rather scant and his face always red. He was a rather big and strong man, but his shoulders sloped. He was bow-legged and had a double chin. That was what you saw on the outside. But when you knew Engle, and came to know him *inside*, he had all the charm and handsomeness and charisma, if you will, of the most personable and noble.

Engle came to this area in 1888, two years after we came. He was born near Stuttgart, Germany, in October, 1867. When he was four, his family came to America. Engle grew up on a ranch near Denver. As soon as he reached age 21 he struck out for himself, heading west and arriving eventually in Moffat County. He was a rider and having but little money, went to work for the cattle company that dominated the ranges of the region, the Two-Bar. Engle was a worker, and got along well with the other cowpunchers and with his neighbors.

Ora Haley, owner of the mammoth Two-Bar, was a man of imagination and resourcefulness. He played the game of getting rich from all angles. One angle was this:

To any of his regular cowpunchers he made an offer, that if they would file a homestead entry on a piece of land with a good spring of water, fulfill the five-year residence requirement in the way a good many homesteaders did by building a cabin and by sleeping on the place now and then, he would give them employment, and at the end of the term, give them $100 in cash in exchange for a bill of sale to the place.

Many of them accepted this deal. It assured them a job for at least five years. Few of them wanted to be ranchers so were glad enough to turn the place for the cash fee. Engle was one who accepted this proposition. He filed a homestead claim on Big Gulch. There was a good-size natural hay meadow and a good stream of water on the place.

But after Engle thought the matter over and became more acquainted with the country, he decided he'd like to remain permanently and that he wanted the homestead for himself. He mentioned this to Johnny Slates, another cowpuncher who had filed on the land around Sand Springs on the same kind of deal. Slates, and the other riders, told Engle, "You'd better get that idea out of your noodle. Old Man Haley ain't goin' to like it."

"Oh, I think I can get him to see my side," Engle told them.

"You don't know Haley," one of the old hands explained. "That's slapping him on the pocketbook. He *wants* that place. It's a good one. You even hint that you're going to keep it for yourself and you'll not only have him land on you with both feet, but you'll never ride for the Two-Bar no more."

Engle didn't argue. But when Haley came along a few weeks later, and stopped at the horse camp where the men were working, Engle broached the subject.

"I've been thinking about that place I homesteaded on, Mr. Haley," he told the owner. "I like this country so well I think I want to stay. So I'll need a ranch if I'm going to do any good."

They discussed the matter a little, and Haley told him, "I think you're making a mistake, Engle. Getting a start on a ranch without money is mighty uphill business. First, you know you have to have a cabin and some fencing and tools and things to work with. How are you going to manage that?"

Engle said he believed he could. As they talked, Haley was doing some of his chain-lightning thinking. He was no fool. He knew Engle for a reliable and capable cowhand. He no doubt admired any man who showed enough imagination and ambition to want to amount to something. He told Engle, "Well, you're a good man, Engle. You may make it all right. I suppose you are going to stay on this job until fall, anyhow?"

"Well I sure would like to, Mr. Haley," Engle admitted. "This winter I can put up a cabin and get some fencing ready and do some other things. I've saved a little money."

"All right, Engle," Haley told him. "You go right ahead until after the shovedown. Do you want to work for me next year?"

Engle, somewhat surprised, told the cattleman he would be glad of the job.

"Well, in case I don't think about it," Haley told him, "when time comes for the spring roundup you see Heck (the foreman) and go to work. If you need to do some of your ranch work, at least stay on until after the shoveup is over. And I'd sure like to have you for the horse roundup."

It was agreed. Relationship between the old Cattle King and the earnest young German was always amicable. For years Engle worked for the Two-Bar a month or more each season. It was a good situation for both sides. Besides that, Haley drew a bonus that neither had mentioned. He knew quite well that a man with the integrity of Engle would not be stealing his calves and butchering his beef and that Engle would take no part in such shenanigans.

So Engle got his homestead and kept his job and he and Haley remained friends. Few could have accomplished this, but though Engle was a mild and kindly man, he did not lack for courage, either physical or moral. In fact, the only trouble we ever knew Engle to have was with John Richardson.

Being near neighbors, Engle and John were "swapping work" one summer in the hay field. They were working at Engle's. As usual, John disputed something Engle said. Soon an argument was going between the stubborn Welchman and the equally stubborn German. The argument led to John calling Engle a vile name. Engle proceeded to chase John right off the ranch with a warning to never come back. John never again ventured on the property of "the Dutchman" as he sneeringly referred to Engle. Engle seldom mentioned the matter. When others did, Engle only smiled. His smile was as individual as most other things about him. It was mostly in his eyes and the lines near them, but it was a smile to warm the beholder's heart.

There was a patch of several acres of natural hay meadow on Engle's place. By grubbing sagebrush at every opportunity Engle soon had doubled this meadow in size. So almost from the start he had plenty of hay for the horse herd he began to build. A hard worker, he soon had a comfortable log house and barn and a good fence around his hay land.

Just as our father used his skill as a miner to get a job in wintertime to get cash to build up his ranch, Engle used his skill as a rider and stockman, working for the Two-Bar.

We saw Engle only about once a year until in 1894, when we lived on the Gregory place owned by Ora Haley near Lay. Engle came almost every week for his mail and always stopped for a chat or a meal. We visited him more often too, so got to know him well.

The folks sometimes let me stay for a day or two with Engle and we hunted antelope, chased wild horses, and enjoyed good meals and his good stories. Every other man I had ever been with, alone, had sooner or later brought up subjects of which I knew nothing, such as stories of drinking and fighting. Engle never did.

"Wild horse chasing," like big game hunting, was both a sport and a business. There were many "wild bunches" scattered over the country, particularly in the Big Hole and Bald Mountain areas. On the "horse roundup" each year about May, cowpunchers and ranchers chased these wild bunches to try to recover their own domesticated horses that had gone with the wild bunch. Geldings joined the wild ones on a voluntary basis, but tame mares were often literally kidnapped, or "marenapped," by wild stallions and added to the harem.

Professional wild horse men, like Wild Horse Brown, Phil Shaver, and a few more tried to capture entire wild bunches, to be culled for the very few that might be broken and used, and the many that were sold for use on farms. Engle's brother Adolph, who had a ranch on Snake River near where the road to Powder Wash now crosses, caught wild horses and at one time had 40 head broken to ride.

The wild horse business continued for many years. Even as late as the 1930s men still chased wild bunches. At one time Elmer Mack and others were known as "the wild horse catchers of '29."

I rode a good deal with Engle, but the one incident concerning horses that stands out in memory was the time we captured Aspen. "Aspen" was the name of a handsome bay gelding. Our sister

Eva, with a romantic turn of mind, usually was the one to name our animals. As a result we had Aspen, Glenwood, Lucky, Venus, Con, and other names like that for cattle and horses.

Aspen was the son of our impulsive Molly. He was a high-spirited horse and wasn't handled much, so when he got to be three years old and Dad decided to break him, he was full of fire and resistance. He wanted no truck with such things as halters, bridles, saddle, or harness. He wasn't vicious as were many broncs, but true to his Cleveland Bay breeding resisted being tamed fiercely, but without resort to kicking or biting.

I was 11, so Dad did not let me take much part in the handling of unbroken horses. I did loiter around the corral though, suffering untold fears that Dad would be hurt. He was 67 years of age, and although strong, active and alert, he still was an old man and I realized it. I could not forget that Uncle Jack Williams had been killed by a horse in this same corral.

After a few days of handling the colt, putting on first the halter, then the blind bridle and finally the harness, Dad had the idea that it was time for the horse to become accustomed to something moving behind him, as preparation for eventually being hitched to the wagon.

We carried a pole to the corral, wired a singletree to it, and hitched the tugs of the harness to the log. While Dad did this, I held the lines to curb the efforts of the restless, high strung horse to move. When the hitching up was complete, Dad took the lines and clucked to the horse to get him started. What happened in the next few seconds was a blur.

The horse lunged forward with a tremendous leap, jerking the lines from Dad's hands. Like a red streak he circled the corral twice. I stood petrified in the middle near the snubbing post. The second time he came to the bar gate he went over it like a bird. He cleared the six-foot barrier but the dragging log hit it and splintered the rails. At a speed that amazed us, the horse raced down the road. At the old John Ledford stage station he quit the road and headed across the flat, across Big Gulch and towards Horse Gulch.

Even before Dad told me I was leading my saddle mare Daisy into the barn and throwing on the saddle.

"I think he'll stop before long," Dad told me. "He can't keep up that pace long. He'll be winded. Don't try to unhitch him. He might kick you. Just unhook the hame-strap and the harness will pull off. Then you can lead him back."

I was already in motion before he finished. Daisy was well-fed and lazy but I sent her skimming along the track of the log in snow nearly a foot deep. This was late in February.

I finally had to slow to a trot and then a fast walk. The sun was sinking and the purple frost ring in the east predicted a bitter night. Dad had told me not to follow after night, so when I could no longer see distinctly the single track in the snow I turned back.

When the sun rose the next morning I was five miles from the ranch, following the trail, that like the trail of a mouse, had a single line with hoof marks on the sides. I don't think I averaged more than three miles an hour, as in the foot-deep snow it was necessary to let the mare stop frequently to rest and recover her breath. When darkness again settled I had covered much of the country on Horse Gulch, Fuhr Gulch, and the Sand Springs country. I was much nearer Engle Edinger's than home, so headed for his place.

Engle was just finishing chores when I pulled in, and soon we were in his snug house and antelope steak was sizzling on the stove while I put the plates and cutlery on the table. As we ate, washed dishes, and sat, we regaled each other with accounts of our doings since our most recent meeting. I hated to stop this to go to bed, but Engle reminded me that we had a horse to find the next day and it might be a long one.

We left the ranch at sunrise next morning. Engle was mounted on his rangy, long-legged bay, Swallow, a horse famous in that country. On this animal Engle hunted wild game and wilder horses. He claimed, and I'm sure truthfully, that the horse had never fallen with him. In a land where badger holes, pup holes, sagebrush, greasewood, washouts, and hummocks endangered every step, this was almost a miracle. He had raised the horse from a colt, broken it himself, and trained it well.

We took the log trail where I had left it. But we had gone no more than a half-mile when we found the log. Its front end had been driven into a cleft in a low ledge of rock and the wire holding the singletree had broken. Taking the trail, we soon found the singletree.

Aspen had kept northward, crossing Big Gulch and continuing in the same direction.

"There's some of my horses on the range up here," Engle told me. "Probably your horse will get in with them. They're about half wild so probably won't like a horse with a harness on and tugs dragging."

His surmise was correct. A few miles north of Engle's we spotted the bunch. They were on the run. With the field glasses we could see that close behind the fleeing bunch came Aspen. Without a word we spurred our horses into a run and headed across a narrow valley to gain a ridge and to cut in front of the bunch. After a breathtaking race of nearly a mile the bunch was thundering down another small valley. Without even giving our mounts time to catch their breath we raced to cut in between the bunch and Aspen. The latter was impeded by the harness, the flapping tugs and the blind bridle which had his head reined up so he could not lower his head. For all the time since he took to the hills he had had neither food nor water. Yet, true to his Cleveland Bay ancestors he was nearly keeping up with the herd.

As we sped down the steep incline I firmly expected Daisy to stick her foot in a badger hole, hidden under the snow, and turn a flip-flop. I only hoped I'd not be underneath. As we came out of a narrow gulch and onto the flat the bunch swept past us. Engle had his rope down and as Aspen came abreast, raced him neck-and-neck and dropped his loop over the bay gelding's head. Engle slowed Swallow and let the tension on the rope come slowly. When Aspen felt the rope tighten, he reacted with a suddenness and ferocity that neither of us expected. It takes minutes to tell. It took seconds to happen. Brought to a stop he whirled and with mouth wide and teeth gleaming came at Engle. Engle's horse tried to avoid the rush but could hardly get started before the charger hit him.

For the first time in his life Swallow fell. He fell for 40 feet, wildly trying to keep his feet until he went down rolling. Engle had been thrown clear and sprang up and started toward the struggling Swallow.

I had gotten my rope down before we reached the herd and it was lucky I had. Glimpsing Engle afoot, Aspen charged. As he did so I rode in at an angle and made a desperate throw of my noose. Again luck was with me and the noose fell true. Even before it landed I had swerved Daisy and dug in the spurs. She came to the end of the rope when Aspen was within 10 feet of Engle.

Daisy was no rope horse. Never before had she felt the terrific impact of a "run on the rope." It jerked her sidewise and off her feet. She left me perched on thin air, and when I hit the ground it knocked the wind from me and sent me rolling. As I scrambled to my feet, dashing the snow from my eyes to try to see what was happening I heard Aspen scream.

If you have never heard a horse scream, you cannot conceive of the wild savagery of the sound. It would chill the blood even though you might be a distance away. But when you are afoot and right in the middle of the action, it freezes it.

Aspen was coming with ears laid back, neck extended and his wide, red mouth showed the flashing teeth. I turned and ran, though I knew it was useless. But I had forgotten Engle's rope. Like mine, it was tied hard and fast to the saddle horn. Swallow was now on his feet and with the skill of a trained rope horse had those feet planted to receive the shock. When that shock came, Aspen was within inches of me, I think. At any rate, as I raced through the foot of snow with every ounce of energy I possessed, I heard the scream checked in the gelding's throat, and snapped a quick glance over my shoulder to see him upended, his head in the snow and his flailing hind feet coming to me. But by the time they came down I wasn't there.

Daisy was now on her feet and I ran to her, even as I saw Engle darting toward old Swallow. In seconds we were ahorse and in a few more instants we were spread out, with shortened ropes, and with Aspen stymied between us. We scooped up our hats without dismounting and turning toward the ranch, led the unwilling gelding between us. After a mile or so he gentled down a bit and Engle rode alongside, and picked up the tugs and threw them across the gelding's back. Another mile, and gradually shortening our ropes, we were close alongside, and jogging along as if nothing had happened. It was then that either of us spoke for the first time since our sighting the herd.

"I'm glad I've got that kettle of beans and pork cooked," Engle remarked. "I feel like I could use some of it. How about you?"

I took my first full breath in quite awhile and heartily agreed. And we made good our threat, after the horses were stabled and fed and we had skimmed some thick cream for the coffee we soon had boiling.

After dinner we chatted awhile, used some baling wire to tie the harness up snug so it wouldn't bother the horse, and I headed for the ranch. A Chinook wind had risen while we ate and by now the snow was sinking and water was running everywhere.

The sequel of all this commotion was that Dad finally did get Aspen broken. But the animal was always nervous, started and shuddered at the slightest sound or movement, and while gentle and of a kind disposition, could not be trusted. So the folks decided to sell him. That summer Dad and I made a trip to Rawlins. We led Aspen behind the wagon. In Rawlins we usually did most of our trading with a store owned by Mr. Rendle. The moment Rendle saw Aspen he wanted him.

"Is that horse for sale?" he wanted to know.

Dad said that was the reason he had brought the gelding along.

"I've looked everywhere for just such a horse," Rendle said," He's the most beautiful animal I've ever seen. My wife will adore him. It is for her I want him. She has a handsome single buggy and what a sight it will be when we hitch that horse in the shafts."

"I'm afraid not, Mr. Rendle," Dad objected. "He's certainly good looking, but through my own fault he was so badly spooked when I was breaking him that I guess it shattered his nerves. He might run away and hurt your wife badly."

"I'll take that chance," Rendle laughed. "I'm a horseman, you see. Born among 'em. My wife is an expert with horses too. We won't have any difficulty. How much do you want for him?"

"Well, I shouldn't, I know," Dad told him. "But if you feel sure you can handle him, I'll take 90 dollars for him."

The price was very high for a horse at that time when a good cowpony could be had for 30 dollars. But Rendle paid it without quibble.

Sure enough, the next day while we were loading our supplies, Mrs. Rendle drove up beside our wagon with Aspen, accoutered in a handsome silver-mounted harness and hitched to a handsome single buggy. Dad and I surveyed the equipage and patted Aspen's neck before she drove off. Afterward Dad told me he was not surprised. He realized he was no horseman and blamed himself for the spoiling of the gelding.

The next year, when we again visited the Rendle store, we learned the sequel. Three days after we left, as Mrs. Rendle drove toward home, Aspen had suddenly bolted. He ran into the brush and rocks north of town, wrecking the buggy, injuring the driver, and running so far that it took two men a week to find him. When he was brought back, Rendle sold him to the Army at Fort Steele. As a cavalry saddle horse, he was ridden with pride by one of the officers, who, incidentally had been a cowpuncher and horse-breaker for the Army before getting his commission.

But how about Engle? Well, all those years, with his industry and German shrewdness, he was building up and accumulating. When the bad years of the Depression came, Engle had plenty of money in the bank to share with his friends who had none, and usually such loans were made at trifling interest. He had broken up more land and put it to alfalfa, and sensing that the automobile would supplant the horse, had worked into the cattle business. He had built a bigger house and equipped it with electric lights and many other conveniences.

Then, tardily but wisely, he married. His mate was Mrs. Mefort, a widow who also had a ranch, just a short distance west of Craig. She too was industrious and shrewd. Their pooled resources of property, good sense, and companionability were ideal and productive. They lived the good life that both richly deserved.

★
Teton Jackson

Somebody had stolen our shovel.

This was in the early 1890s.

Two simple facts, taken separately. But connected, they could spell disaster. Today it is hard to realize the importance of a man's shovel. It was the main working tool of his profession. Then, a rancher's existence might depend on it. It was his basic tool for earth-moving. There were no bulldozers, backhoes, front loaders nor any of the earth-moving tools we have now. The shovel was used in making roads, ditches, small dams, and irrigation laterals. With it you dug your dwelling, dug postholes, mined, covered your house or barn, removed snow and ice, cleaned out springs, dug wells. And when at last the owner laid the shovel down for the final time, somebody else used it to dig the grave.

So our shovel was gone. We did not know it at the time, but its disappearance was tied in with the activities of the greatest thief of them all. A thief who commanded a gang of thieves guilty of depredations that made the raid of Butch Cassidy's Wild Bunch, Tip Gault's gang, the Ketchum brothers, and all the rest of the Western outlaws seem like kid stuff. This master thief was intelligent and a good organizer. He was given the name of a famous mountain range and in turn gave his name to a famous mountain paradise. He was Teton Jackson, of Jackson's Hole, Wyoming.

The mysterious disappearance of our shovel occurred at the Gregory place, owned by Ora Haley. We rented the place from Haley to add to our hay land and to have the big house at the crossroads.

Our father had been doing some digging, filling in a big hole where the road crossed the creek. In the evening, he sent us kids to bring in the tools, the shovel, a pick, and crowbar. Hortense and I found the pick and bar, but no shovel. It had disappeared while we were at supper.

"Did you children look thoroughly?" Dad asked us.

We assured him we had.

"Do you suppose somebody we know came along and had to fix that hole in the road and used the shovel and didn't put it back in the place they found it?" Mother asked.

We were sure this hadn't happened as we had looked all around.

Besides that we all knew that if a neighbor had passed we would have noticed it and anyhow he would have stopped and talked. A cowpuncher wouldn't take a shovel or any other tool that meant manual work. If anybody had gone along the road past the house, old Bummer the dog would have barked. But anyhow, the shovel had disappeared.

Next morning when Dad started down to the crossing he took the pick and bar and an old square-nosed shovel with a short handle. It wasn't much of a tool but was all he had. When he got to the crossing, to his amazement the good shovel was sticking in the pile of earth right where he had left it.

Quite a to-do about a mere shovel. But to understand its significance you need to know about subsequent events. And you need to know about Teton Jackson.

In 1852, our mother was born in England. The same year a boy was born into a family named Jackson on a Missouri rock-land farm. Although alike in the time of their birth, there all similarity ended. Mother could have walked under my extended arm without touching it. I could have walked under the arm of this Jackson boy when he had grown up without knocking off my hat. He was a giant. He stood six-feet-four and weighed more than 300 pounds.

No doubt the parents of this Jackson boy instructed him in the precepts, morals, and dogma of the Baptist faith. If Jackson had heeded such instruction, he might have grown up to be of great value to the human race. As it was, he became a menace and a scourge to society. The life he led was rough and dangerous, but he must have liked it. Asked by a law officer one time whether he would choose such a life if he had it all to do over again, Jackson told him, "Why not? I eat good, sleep good, have scads of good friends, plenty of work, and never lack for money. Do y' know anybody doin' any better?"

In early teen years Jackson learned to dance and loved it. He seldom missed any of the dances or parties held at community log houses or farms in the Missouri woods. This wasn't in line with the principles of his straight-laced family. Nor was drinking and fighting. Jackson liked both. With his size and strength, only the tougher and bolder ever tackled him. Even on the toughest of them Jackson did not exert his full power. He didn't need to. A mild smack by one of his big paws was enough to send even a 200-pounder rolling. A partly-pulled punch put even big burlies to sleep.

Jackson got a lot of fun out of slapping bullies and would-be tough boys around. But one unlucky night he over-reached a bit and put more steam behind a punch than he intended. It left his adversary stiff and unmoving. His condition and appearance were a good enough facsimile of death to impel Jackson to grab a few extra clothes, his shaving kit, and the first freight train out of the country. He headed west.

By the time he was 24, Jackson had become westernized enough to be a scout for none other than General Crook, probably the greatest Indian fighter of them all. He was the general who effected the capture of Geronimo, "the Scourge of the Southwest." Jackson was not with Crook on that occasion, but he was with him in a campaign that covered the area surrounding the spectacular Teton Mountains in Wyoming. By the time the campaign was concluded, Jackson knew every peak, ridge, and valley of the area, and every trail that wound through its gorges and forests.

Because of his knowledge of this region he was known later as "Teton Jackson."

The 300-pound giant had a brain that matched his body and an eye that missed nothing. That eye told him that opportunity for him lay in the green bowl surrounded by the Tetons on one side, the range through which Togotwee Pass leads, and in the center of which spreads the great lake that would get its name from Jackson. Here in this isolated and sequestered land of broad, lush meadows lay opportunity for fun and for profits beyond calculation. We cannot quarrel with the accuracy of his estimate, much as we may deplore his method of implementing his dream of wealth and well-being. Because Teton Jackson decided and determined to become a cattle and horse rustler on a grandiose scale!

At first, it might be said, he ran his business by hand and alone.

Cautious sorties into the surrounding country enabled him to perfect his technique. When he felt that he knew the ropes he took in helpers. The method was to go quite a distance westward into Idaho, where cattle or horses were stolen and herded to the hidden valley. Like other enclosed valleys of the West, this was called a "hole." So, with Teton Jackson its king, it was "Jackson's Hole."

After awhile, fattened on the good feed in Jackson's Hole, the animals would be trailed eastward, usually to the mining camps of Wyoming, there to be sold. Title, in those days and for long after, was no great problem. Any man who could scribble a crude "Bill of Sale" could sell any animal he offered.

Having gotten off the "lone wolf trail," Jackson steadily enlarged his operation. More than 300 men, dodging the law, were scattered over portions of Wyoming, Colorado, Idaho, and Montana. Jackson knew some of them and through them soon knew many others. And at one time or another most of them funneled stolen livestock into Jackson's Hole. He had a "general manager," and his own trained crew did the selling, while every Tom, Dick, and Harry among the outlaws helped by stealing horses and cattle and watching the trails on behalf of "the syndicate."

Westerns, whether in print or on screen, usually depict the stealing of great herds of cattle. While generally speaking this was rare, in the case of Teton Jackson and his cohorts it was routine. But they did not disdain to steal single animals either.

In 1887, a brief interlude occurred in Jackson's activities. Angry lawmen, sick and tired of being badgered by livestock owners about Jackson's depredations, united to stop him. Frank Canton, sheriff of Johnson County, Wyoming, led a posse that sneaked up on a cabin near Paint Rock, in which Jackson and some of his gang were spending the night. Some men were playing draw poker in one corner of the cabin while Jackson rested in another corner, with all their guns near him to forestall trouble if a loser in the game got nasty. When Canton jerked the door open and showed the boys a pretty pearl-handled six gun they gave up.

Teton Jackson, as grand sachem of the rustlers, drew a heavy jolt. He was in the clink for three years before he got a chance to terrify and nick one of the guards with a hunting knife somebody had sneaked in to him. He went back to Jackson's Hole. But he found that most of the gang had high-tailed it when he had gone to jail. Only about 20, either too brave or too stupid to run, remained. But no quitter, Jackson was soon back in high gear, but specializing mostly in horse stealing. He found it easier to make away with a bunch of fast horses than with a herd of plodding cattle. His henchmen ranged far and wide in search of choice horse flesh. The farther and wider they ranged the less was the chance of being caught.

Their ranging brought them at length into our country of northwest Colorado. Here they spirited away some of the choicest nags to be found, slipping them across the state line in dead of night and disposing of them in the booming mining towns of Idaho.

Believing, it would seem, in the Law of Compensation, the rogues not only removed horses from our county—they brought horses *into* the county. We knew of several ranchers who unwittingly bought such horses.

One of the victims of Jackson's missionaries was our own family. We had a good brown saddle gelding called Jeff. With a few other horses, Jeff had ranged around Jackrabbit Springs and on Lower Board Gulch. One late September day Art, Vern, and I walked up Board Gulch to try to get a deer or antelope. We saw the nine horses, including Jeff. We mentioned it to our folks that night. Dad suggested that since deer hunting was coming up, we had better bring Jeff in and get him on better feed and ready for packing in deer. So, next day I rode another horse to bring Jeff in.

I couldn't find the gelding. Six head of the small herd were still on the range where they had been all summer. But Jeff and two more of the horses were gone. I rode most of three days, covering a wide area. We never saw Jeff again. It is not surprising. We didn't look in the right place. We should have hunted for him in Idaho. For we are sure as sure can be that Jeff was one of Teton Jackson gang's pickups.

Shortly after the incident of the loss and return of our shovel, two boys were riding in Sugar Loaf Basin and came upon a saddle. It was a good saddle and with it were bridle and blankets. It was rolled over on its side with bridle and blankets on top in the way any range man would leave his saddle. The boys reported the find but as far as we ever knew nothing was done about it. It was years later that our brother Art learned the solution of the mystery of the abandoned saddle. The explanation came from one who undoubtedly knew.

"Yeah, a lot of folks like your people lost horses. One here and one there. But there was some fellers that lost several head. Mostly one at a time, but all told quite a few. They pretty well knowed which way their horses was goin' but no use to try follerin' them."

"Yeah, they sure did. Idaho and Montana probably. Anyhow the fellers got pretty sick of raisin' and breakin' good horses and havin' them stole. So a bunch of 'em got together. Now I jest *heered* about this, of course. Anyhow they talked it over. The upshot was a plan to ketch these horse stealers."

"They lined up the men so about three would be in the hills all the time. Taking turns. They just camped out. They was along the Wyoming line. One feller I knowed was on Powder Rim. They all had good field glasses."

"Well sure enough," he continued, "Twasn't too long 'til about a half dozen riders showed up from the north, along toward evening one day."

"The watcher give the signal to the other two. The strangers camped on Snake River but the watchers high-tailed it for—well, over this way. The bunch got together and was ready by daylight. That afternoon they closed in on some fellers with a pretty good size herd an'—well got their horses back."

So we know that the ranchers spotted the thieves, and the ranchers, alerted by the watchers, "came down like the wolves on the fold." How many of the thieves fell is not known.

Maybe only the one whose saddle bore mute witness to his taking off. But however they fared, our shovel was used to bury the dead and to smooth and disguise the unmarked grave so even other thieves could never find it. After that year, about 1899, our county suffered no more from the Jackson Hole thieves. The gang was breaking up. Jackson had died and without his leadership the gang evolved into just a number of thieves acting singly or in twos or threes, without organization and without the capacity for big action. Teton Jackson had passed and his era too.

Jackson was a thief and a scoundrel. But those who knew him maintain that he was an agreeable man, a man who paid his debts and settled with fellow thieves with the honesty and care of a big businessman, which he was. He had an Indian woman for a wife and treated her kindly and with respect. He might have settled down to enjoy the fruits of his nefarious efforts, but in 1893, he again fell into the hands of the lawmen. He was jailed in Boise, Idaho. While making another try to escape, he was shot and killed. So ended the career of a man who might have done much in an honest occupation, but chose to cast his lot with other thieves. He was the greatest thief of them all.

This country had horsethieves after the Teton Jackson era. But they were small fry, bunglers, lacking the capacity, cunning, and courage of the "old maestro." Typical of their petty depredations was the theft of Elmer (Whitey) Hindman's work team from his ranch north of Craig. Elmer told me of this. It happened in 1918.

It was right in the middle of spring work, when loss of a man's team might mean loss of the summer's crops. Value of a work team was at the peak at such time. So work teams were choice pickings for the thieves.

Whitey Hindman knew the country and its people far and wide. As a cowpuncher he had ridden every hill and valley. He knew too, who the local lads were who were not adverse to snatching a neighbor's horses.

That Saturday night, as usual, Whitey went to the community dance. Everybody who danced was there. Among them was the chap whom Whitey felt pretty sure knew about the missing team. He was one of the bunch of would-be Teton Jacksons. In a friendly, confidential way, Whitey drew the young neighbor aside and told him, "You know, some so-and-so got away with my best work team. And me right in the middle of my spring work. You know, I don't get mad easy, but I'm mad clean through. I pretty well know the jaspers that got my team. So tomorrow I'm going on me a horse thief hunt. And that old hog leg on my flank ain't goin' to be fer shootin' prairie dogs. I'm goin' lookin' fer me a horse thief. Dirty bugger, to take a man's team that he has got to make his livin' with. Do you blame me?"

Oh, no, the neighbor didn't blame Whitey at all.

Usually all the dance bunch stayed until daylight came. But the sympathetic neighbor left early. And strangely enough, next morning when Hindman glanced out the west window of his house on the ranch on Fortification, there was his work team, just where they should have been all the time.

To Teton Jackson and Tip Gault must go the "honors" for volume horse stealing. Butch Cassidy tried to follow in their footsteps, but after a jolt in jail took up less hazardous and more profitable ways of making thievery pay. Since then, up to the present day, there has been horse stealing, but only by small-fry, unimaginative, and inept novices. They had but little success or luck, unless it was the good luck not to be strung up to dry.

★
Dirty Cattle Thieves

John had an intense dislike for the cattle people. As with many like him, he envied Haley and the other big cattlemen because they were successful. But even so, John didn't butcher Two-Bar cattle nor rustle.

One day two Two-Bar men came by John's place with a small gather of cattle they had gotten on North Fork. Among the cattle were two or three of John's. His small herd ranged that area. John saw his cattle and ran out to the fence, hailing the men.

"Where are you Two-Bar thieves going with my cattle?"

One of the riders, Sid Pugh, explained that John's cattle had gotten in with the others and would be cut out when they worked the herd where the wagon was camped at Sand Springs.

"You dirty cattle thieves, you'll cut them out now," John blustered. "I ain't goin' to let Haley's cattle thieves steal right under my nose."

"We ain't stealin' your cattle," Sid told him. "Get your horse an' come with us and you can bring 'em back when we cut 'em out."

John uttered a few vulgar epithets and when the men made as if to ride on, he went through the fence and tried to drag Sid from his saddle. We think the other man was Bill Flannagan (when we later asked him, he just grinned). But anyhow, as John reached for Sid, a much smaller man, the second rider unholstered his gun and stuck it almost in John's face.

"Get back through that fence," he commanded. "If you don't I'll put a couple of holes in your hide. Git!"

John got.

But in telling us about it, John had a different version.

Using, as he usually did, words of which he did not know the meaning, he explained, "Them two thieves, them toadies of Haley's were out to rob and steal and clean me out. Pauperate me, yes indeed, pauperate me. But I soon convicted them that they wasn't goin' to make a pauper of me. Yes indeed, I convicted them. They turned tail and got over the hills."

"Did you get your steers back all right?" we asked.

"Yes indeed, yes indeed," and he laughed loudly. "They was mighty careful to cut out my cattle. They knew what I'd do. The dirty thieves. After a little I rode over and got my cattle. I'll hate and despise Haley and his cattle thieves to the end of my destination."

It was a year or so later that one day John took team and wagon to the hills north of his place to get a load of wood. After the wagon was loaded, and he was passing under a big dead cedar, a heavy snag caught under the collar of the handsome buckskin coat he wore.

John was scraped from the top of the load of wood and held suspended "twixt earth and sky." The lines slipped through his fingers but he was able to grasp them by the very ends. But with his arms pulled backward by the coat, he could neither pull on the lines to back the load in under him, nor could he unbutton the coat to release himself. He realized he was in a desperate situation. After struggling vainly until almost exhausted, he finally emitted a yell.

It was nothing short of a miracle that in those lonely hills where no man might pass in a year Sid Pugh happened to be riding. In moments he had swung the wagon back under John and helped him from his precarious perch.

From then on, John had only good things to say about "that Sid Pugh," where before he had been a dirty cattle thief and scoundrel. John was grateful. He should have been. Without Sid's appearance John would have met his end.

★
Whispering Green

Robert H. Green was born March 27, 1855, near Springfield, Missouri. Most of his education was gained, as he said, "in the school of hard knocks." He came to Colorado in 1875, and in 1885, in company with C. E. Baker, Green came afoot over the Continental Divide to this country.

Green located a homestead in 1885, eight miles east of Craig, on the Yampa River. Twenty-two years later I worked with Green in the hayfields of that ranch, by then a productive spread owned by Green's son Irvin.

Father and son were both tireless workers.

I worked a lot for both Irvin and R. H. The latter had a ranch at the west boundaries of Craig. It is now part of the city of Craig. Green was county commissioner, justice of the peace, and a member of the board of education during his later years. He was tall, raw-boned and powerful, but even his great physical power was dwarfed by the power of his voice. "Whispering Green" was known far and wide for his vocal might.

"Irvin, I'm goin' to town. I'll be back in the morning and bring the new sections for the mower."

A routine and uninteresting statement, except for the fact that Green was at Irvin's ranch house and Irvin was down in the hayfield, at least 2,000 feet distant. Irvin heard the information perfectly.

One Halloween night a bunch from town went out to Green's, and with a dozen pulling and pushing, brought one of Green's wagons up town and left it with several others in the middle of the street. The same night, the revelers carried all the small outhouses they could find and arranged them in the form of a little "town" on the main street. They took the signs off business places and put them on the privies. The fury of the backhouse owners was ample reward for the anonymous town-builders.

The next Halloween day, Whispering Green was up town as usual. At Coulter's drug store he made an announcement. "By doggies, I want to have you fellers spread the word that it won't be any use for the Halloween bunch comin' to my place tonight. I've got my wagons chained and padlocked. Thought I'd better let it be known to save somebody a lot of trouble comin' out there for nothing."

Borden Coulter, the druggist, and Harmon Coulter, the store owner, promised to spread the word, as did others who were in the store.

That night, about 30 men and a few women crept like Indians along the fence of the Green place. Scouts found that the wagons were indeed secure, with heavy log chains woven through the wheels and padlocked. They had anticipated as much.

Silently, stealthily, smothering chuckles and giggles, they crept into the yard, surrounded one of the wagons, picked it up bodily, and carried it to the road. Resting often, they finally got to town and with *another* chain, padlocked the wagon to the big pole near the telephone office. Next day, they waited, and not without trepidation, for the appearance of Green. When he showed up, near noon, the usual bunch was around the drug store, looking as innocent as the lamb that ate the fellow's wig.

"By doggies, I'll tell you, I didn't think you had it in you," Green told them. "Now I'll tell you what I'm goin' to do. I'll unlock *my* chain. Then I'm goin' on home. You fellers unlock the other chain and bring my wagon on back and when you get back up town here you'll all have a treat coming. Borden, you see that all of 'em who help bring the wagon back get a set-em-up. I'll pay the bill next time I'm up town."

Whispering Green was a dyed-in-the-wool Republican, even though from Democratic Missouri. One summer he was in Rawlins for a load of supplies. After loading at the grocery store, he walked over to a harness shop and bought a horse collar. He paid for it and slung it over his shoulder. As he made his way back to the wagon he heard a tremendous cheering and yelling down toward the railroad depot.

"What's all the yellin' about?" he asked a fellow who hurried past him.

"It's Teddy," the fellow flung back. "He's going to make a speech from the car platform."

The information prodded Green like an electric shock. "Teddy," Theodore Roosevelt, was his idea of a perfect president. Rough and ready like Green himself, Teddy got things done. Besides, he was a Republican president running for re-election. Green headed for the depot, taking steps four feet long.

Roosevelt made his speech, in his usual direct, sincere way. Although stocky and barrel-chested, he spoke in a high-pitched voice. When he finished, and before the applause died down, Green stepped forward.

"Mr. Roosevelt, Mr. President, I'm R. H. Green from over on Bear River. I'm just an old farmer from Missouri, but I'd sure admire to shake your hand!"

The President stepped to the edge of the platform, shot out a big hand and grasped the calloused one of Green.

"It's an honor to shake the hand of a rancher from Bear River, Mr. Green," he said heartily. "All we need to win this election is enough good old Missouri farmers with horse collars around their necks."

Green nearly sank into the earth. He had forgotten the horse collar.

I worked for R. H. on his Craig ranch. At the time, Halley's comet dominated the evening sky for months. Green was intensely interested in the fiery visitor from outer space. He was interested in everything.

Later, I took part in a number of plays in which his daughter, Alice, had parts. In one such play, Alice and I had a scene together, eating at a table. She and I each had parts in *other* plays being given by other organizations. Inadvertantly, I gave Alice a wrong cue, a line from another play. Confused, she followed with the correct line, but from the *other* play.

We gave the audience an unintentional "preview" of the other play for a minute or two. Then we simply adlibbed until we got back on the right play. By that time, I was perspiring like a wind-broken horse climbing Pikes Peak.

I was wearing, as part of the character I was supposed to be portraying, one of those white shirts with a stiff bosom, and a high, stiff collar that made you look like a mule looking over a white-washed fence. As we floundered with our lines, I thought I could feel that "boiled front" working up and my shirt tail pulling out from my trousers.

Desperately hiding the action as much as I could, I reached down and tucked the cloth back in. I knew my part called for me to stand up in just a minute or two, so worked fast, ramming the loose cloth down in and straightening the stiff front. Then I stood up.

When I did, the tablecloth and dishes came clanging around me. I had tucked the tablecloth into my trousers. When I pulled the tablecloth toward me as I stood up, the weight of the dishes in the slack between me and the table pulled the rest of the cloth across the table. The scene ended with the dishes in a pile at my feet and me standing like a ninny, with the tablecloth draped from my middle. Alice had bolted at the first crash and I was left alone in my glory, to stand transfixed until somebody mercifully drew the curtain.

It took a long time to live that one down.

★
Frontier Firewood

You may think that the one, single thing that enabled people to live in the West was running water. This would not be correct, for when no stream was found, rain was utilized, or snow was melted. You might answer that wild game meat was the great sustainer, or that that the horse alone made it possible. But people have survived without meat, as the vegetarians among the pioneers did. And many reached, occupied, and survived on the frontier afoot.

Maybe you'll think it was the trusty old muzzle-loading rifle, or the Colt's revolver, or the Bowie knife, or sourdough bread. It was none of these.

The single thing that did most to preserve the lives of the Mountain Men and those who followed them was sagebrush! Common unlovely, simple, unobtrusive, homely sagebrush.

Probably once covering more acres of land than any other single plant on earth, sagebrush stretches from the Canal Zone to upper Canada, from the Rockies to the Pacific. The gray-green of its foliage is almost as familiar to Westerners as the blue of the sky.

Sagebrush was the firewood of the West. And without fire, people would have starved and frozen to death. It was just that simple. Even with all the abundance of wild game, people and particularly white people, could not have long subsisted on raw meat. Nor could they have prepared the simple fare of bread, beans, and coffee. Without fire, the winters would have been unendurable.

The objection might be made that in a country of pine, spruce, and fir, why depend on sagebrush? Where pinyon, juniper (cedar), mahogany, cottonwood, willow, buckbrush, cherry, sarvis, alder, tamarack, greasewood, and many other woods grew profusely, why isolate sagebrush for such an important role? The answer is simple.

Have you ever built a campfire in a drizzling, all-day rain or snow from any of the woods just named? If you have, you performed a miracle!

There are three things from which you can start a fire in very wet weather—the tiny twigs under the limbs of forest trees such as pine and spruce, the inner bark of a juniper on its "dry side," and sagebrush. The chance of being near forest trees or junipers was about 10 to one. The chance of finding enough dry wood to *keep* the fire going after it started was another 10 to one. But how different with sagebrush. Never was rain so long or snow deep but dry sagebrush could be found. And found easily. Break a good-size sagebrush trunk over your knee and inside you'll find layer after layer of wood, each layer protecting that under it until the inner part is dry and easily ignited.

With a plentiful supply of this inner, dry wood, it is no trick at all to pile on wet wood which will soon be dried and burning. With the bed of coals that soon forms, you need worry no more about fire for cooking or for keeping warm. And it will be a fire the smoke from which will not blind you, the odor of which will regale your nostrils, and from which no sparks will pop to set fire to the surrounding grass and growth in dry weather.

When I was 15, in company with two other riders, we were holding a bunch of about 300 cattle, while waiting for the roundup to come by. We held the herd on the North Fork of Big Gulch. We took turns riding into the Two-Bar horse camp where we prepared our meals. Ike Patterson was a good cook so he usually went in with Charlie Hurlburt and got dinner. Then Charlie would hold the cattle herd while I went in to eat and help Ike with the dishes and other camp chores.

Charlie had been complaining of feeling sick. This day he became violently ill so Ike helped him stay on his horse as they rode to camp. Ike took Charlie in a buckboard we had at camp to Craig to Dr. Nichol's hospital. Ike told me he'd try to get back in time to go on night guard.

Night came and no Ike. Worse, I hadn't had anything to eat all day and rain began to fall. I should have ridden in and got some grub while it was still daylight. But I didn't, so, when night closed in I fixed to hold the herd alone.

I circled them a good many times, singing to them while they bedded down. They were full of good grass and didn't act as if they wanted to wander, although new to the range.

With the herd quiet, I pulled up a few sagebrush and broke into them for dry wood. I had matches in a 45-90 empty shell with a cork in it. I soon had a fire roaring. Then I snaked in a pile of sagebrush wood. I piled plenty on the fire. I had a slicker, so kept dry, excepting my feet. They were soaked.

By the time the fire died down to a glowing bed of coals, I had dried out a couple of big sticks of sagebrush. Using these to sit on, I crouched by the fire, the slicker taken off and pulled up over my head, my feet extended to the fire to dry out my boots.

The rain came down in a gentle drizzle all night. I dozed by the fire. In breaks in the rain I circled the herd and brought up more wood. After dawn, when I had the herd scattered and they all seemed intent on filling their bellies, I rode hard to the ranch, made and gulped a hot but hasty breakfast of hotcakes swimming in bacon grease, some rice we had cooked and black coffee. I took with me some hotcakes and bacon for lunch.

My fire had died to a bed of red embers when I got back to the herd. I built it up and kept it going all day. By noon the herd had grazed their fill, taken on water from the gulch, and were full of life and eager to go just anywhere to be going, and each with a different idea. It kept me busy and nearly wore out my horse keeping them from scattering in every direction. I had little time to wonder about Ike. But knowing his conviviality and easy-going ways, I figured he was probably with some kindred souls, telling big jacksons and taking big drinks. Later I learned that was the case.

I stuck with the herd from Tuesday noon when Ike and Charley left until Friday when Ike showed up about sunup, fairly sober, and full of sorrow for having treated me so badly. He proceeded immediately to treat me somewhat better—from a quart of Old Crow he had brought along unopened.

During the time I kept lone watch over the cattle I did not once suffer from the chill of the rain which lasted until Thursday evening. I had long before learned about sagebrush and its characteristics. One of the first things my folks learned when they arrived on Lay Creek with me along in 1886, was the value of sagebrush as fuel. We burned it in the small cookstove winter and summer. In winter we had coal and cedar wood, but the ever-present pile of sagebrush wood was where we got kindling and fuel for a quick meal, for baking, and to boil the water for the weekly washing and bath.

All pioneers did the same. Even though they might be near big timber, they found sagebrush in the open parks and used it to start fires when nothing else would burn. In a way, their lives depended on and revolved around a sagebrush fire. They may have learned this from the Indians, who follow the same custom.

Sagebrush served the pioneers in many ways other than as firewood. Wherever it grew in abundance there was good soil. Its leaves are shed each year, and combining with the other soil, produce a loam that is rich in everything needed by plant life.

Brush often grew to great size for a bush, some of it as high as the waist of a man on horseback. It afforded excellent shelter during storms for both wild animals and domestic livestock. Sharing the land with the sagebrush, bluestem grass grew profusely. This grass, unique to the western country, had the same strengthening and fattening properties for livestock as a combination of hay and grain.

Our father discovered that sagebrush leaves, dried in the oven of the cookstove, made an excellent substitute for tobacco. In fact he liked it so well he smoked it in his pipe exclusively. One of my chores as a kid was to gather and dry his "smoking sage." Its aroma in the house was pleasant, it had none of the sickening and offensive odor of cigarettes, and did not leave the stink so characteristic of "dead" cigars. Dad had asthma, and sagebrush smoke did much to relieve it. Eventually, a good many asthma sufferers used it. But perhaps the most important by-product of sagebrush was as a medicine.

"Mountain fever" was an acute illness that afflicted most persons coming from the low altitudes to the high. Ordinary home remedies did little to alleviate it. Left to run its course it might keep the victim feverish, nauseated, and without appetite for as much as two or three weeks. But, with liberal doses of "sage tea," the fever would be broken in a couple of days and the sufferer well in one or two more. In any other kind of fever it was very effective, too. It, and a tea made from Oregon grape root, were effective in livening up a sluggish liver.

Wild horse hunters used sagebrush effectively for building brush barricades to turn the bands of wild horses. Piled loosely it caused the herd to veer away. Two long "wings" of brush, funnel-shaped and with the small end leading into a camouflaged corral, made an effective trap.

Sagebrush was also useful for building dams when combined with rock and earth. In that day, when bridges and culverts were unknown, sagebrush tramped into the bottom of a gully made it possible to cross with teams and wagons, or the mounts of cavalry.

A sagebrush fire meant the difference between being alive and being dead. We should treasure our last remaining stands of the old "big sage."

★
The Wolf Man

Wolves were in this county for many years. In 1910, when our survey party on the Great Northern Irrigation project was camped at the Dummy Wilson ranch on Timberlake, we heard the cries and saw the tracks of wolves at intervals of 16 days all summer and fall. There were seven of them.

We'd hear their moaning cry in early morning faintly to the west. That night they'd be howling directly south where deer might be found in the buckbrush on the top of Iron Springs Divide. The next morning the sound was only a quavering cry far to the east, at about the elbow of Fortification Creek. Then they were gone. As nearly as we could guess, they moved about 20 miles a day. Their circle must have been about 300 miles.

Wolves were the most difficult of all predatory animals in the region to kill. Trappers had little luck with them, as they seldom returned to a kill or ate anything they did not kill. So poison was of no use, either.

Their eyesight, hearing, and sense of smell are superior, so few were approached for a shot. The $20 reward offered for a wolf scalp was seldom collected. When a bounty was collected it was usually the $10 paid for the scalps of wolf pups.

People today know very little about wolves. In his native habitat and unmolested by man the wolf did little harm. Instances of wolves attacking humans are very, very rare.

This highly intelligent animal is of the same genus as dogs. A big wolf is about four feet long and nearly three feet tall and will weigh 80 pounds or more. His long sharp canine teeth and both pre-molar and molar teeth are made exactly right for seizing, holding, tearing, and grinding the flesh of other animals. Their tails are short for an animal of the canidae or dog family, coming only to the hocks. The eyes are yellow and slanted and the fur of the gray wolf such as we knew is a dark gray.

The animals mate for life and the male helps care for the young. If a wolf loses his mate, he may live with another pair, helping with the hunting and with the care of the pups. Sometimes the pups remain with the family even when grown and with pups of their own.

Speaking of wolves, I should tell of "the Wolf Man."

He came to our home at the Gregory place one September evening. He was tall, rawboned, and dressed in the customary clothing. But we noticed at once that he was "different." He spoke good English in a well-modulated voice.

We kids couldn't guess what his business might be. He didn't have any picks or shovels, he didn't have a gold pan, and no traps dangled from the pack saddles on the two burros he led behind the one he rode. So he wasn't either a prospector or a trapper.

The folks invited him in for supper, although he assured them that he had food and camping equipment. During the meal, he and Father talked of many things. We could see that Father was enjoying it, as he delighted to visit with intelligent people, and especially those who had traveled and could talk on many subjects.

During the evening the visitor told us he was on his way to Wyoming to hunt wolves. He didn't look like a trapper, so we were all puzzled as to why he should be headed for the state to the north to try to capture some of the most elusive and intelligent animals known. Of course some other people we knew didn't look exactly fitted to the work they were doing, so I suppose we concluded the Wolf Man might be another whose looks were misleading.

Dad didn't express his thoughts, but observed, "So you intend to hunt them for sport, or—"

"No, it's my business," the man interrupted. "I've been a wolfer for years. Wyoming seems to have more wolves than anywhere I've seen. I see lots of them there."

"We have a few around here," Dad told him. "We go across southern Wyoming about once a year on our way to Rawlins, but I don't remember seeing any wolves. What part of Wyoming do you live in?"

"I've never been in Wyoming," the stranger said.

"But I think you said you had seen wolves there."

"Yes, I have. That may seem strange to you. But you see, I am a clairvoyant. I can see any place and any thing I want to."

We were all flabbergasted. Our faces must have shown it. The man smiled.

"You see, sir," he explained to Dad, "it is a power few have. You and I talked of places in Australia, in Africa, Canada, and other parts of the world. I have never been to any of those places."

"But—but, why you know Melbourne as well as I do. And I spent quite some time there."

"I have probably seen *more* of it than you have. But in my mind's eyes. Not my physical eyes."

The talk went on and we became more mithered. I think our parents did, too. In Dad's strict Catholic training he had come to believe that such things as fortune-telling, hypnotism, second sight, and the like were "works of the Devil." They were infringements on God's prerogatives. But the man was so matter-of-fact about the matter, and seemed so sure of himself that they pursued the subject to some length, to the complete mystification of the rest of us.

Before he went to his camp, the stranger was urged by our parents to come to breakfast. This he did. Afterward, he insisted on paying for the meals, but the folks firmly refused. Turning to Hortense and I who were standing near, he told us, "If you youngsters will bring in my jacks, I'll give you each a dollar."

"Yes, sir," Hortense said respectfully. "We'll bring them in and you don't have to pay us. But we may have to hunt quite awhile to find them."

"Oh, I'll tell you exactly where they are," he smiled. "They are in that little gulch just over that hill," pointing to the ridge on which Uncle Jack's grave could be seen. "The big blue burro I ride is standing about fifty feet up the west fork of the gulch. The small gray one is lying on the bank a few feet higher up and the old jenny is lying in the dense sagebrush between the two forks."

We set off at a trot, eager to see if this man who could "see" things far away was just fooling us. Winded, we reached the top of Uncle Jack's ridge. We could see the gulch beyond. The gray donkey lay right where the Wolf Man had said he was. When we got to the gulch, we found the other two exactly as he had said. We were pretty sure the man had never been beyond the ridge.

It was something none of us understood, nor did our parents try to explain, deny nor affirm it. We talked about it a great deal, referring to the stranger as "the Wolf Man."

I still don't quite understand it. It is like water witching. I don't know enough about it to deny it, yet I don't quite believe it.

★
Before the Hello Box

When telephones first came into use, some people referred to them as "hello boxes." But the incident I'll relate came even before the "hello box" had come to this region. Nor was there telegraph or daily mail. To outlying places, the mail, such as it was, went no oftener than once a week.

So, it was lack of the hello-box or any other prompt communication that got a young fellow named Raftner in trouble, and might have gotten him shot. Sometimes men *were* shot for running from a lawman, and Raftner might have run when the lawman stopped him, because Raftner was desperate to be on his way.

It all began when Raftner, who was working for Gray Shaw, a rancher on the east fork of the Williams Fork, came to Craig on an errand for Shaw, riding one of Shaw's best saddle horses.

In the way coincidences have of happening, when Raftner had attended to the errand, he went to the post office to get the mail to take back to the Shaw ranch. In the mail was a letter to himself, telling him of the serious illness of his father in Saratoga, Wyoming.

After thinking the matter over for a few minutes, he returned Shaw's mail to the post office. He had seen one of Shaw's neighbors, Bren Sullivan, in town. He knew Bren was staying out at the Ranney place in the west end of town. So he rode out to the Ranney place and found Bren, who agreed to take the Shaw horse back to its owner when he went home.

"How are you going to get to Saratoga?" Bren asked the young ranch hand.

"I'm goin' to start walkin' and keep hopin' somebody comes along and gives me a lift. I'd take the stage to Rawlins but I don't have enough money for a ticket."

Frank Ranney was standing nearby and now spoke up, "I know a way to beat that," Frank told him. "That is if you don't mind walking twenty miles in the wrong direction."

Raftner was interested.

"Well, you see, I just came in yesterday from Lily Park. That man Lowell who runs the Lily Park outfit for Wells Fargo, told me he and his boy are going to Saratoga tomorrow. They drive good horses and have a light spring wagon. I know they'd give you a ride. Lowell is a good feller."

And that was the way Raftner decided. So he took off at once afoot, headed for Lay, where Lowell always stopped. When he got to Lay, he told the Wallihans that he was going to walk on up the road.

"That way," he explained, "in case this Lowell doesn't come, I'll still be further on my way to Saratoga."

Meanwhile, when Raftner didn't show up back at the ranch, Shaw became uneasy. So he mounted another horse and came into Craig. There he found neither Raftner nor his horse. Inquiring around town, he learned that the young fellow had been seen riding westward.

So Shaw hunted out E. A. Farnham, the sheriff who gained fame when he captured the outlaws Harry Tracy, Dave Lant, and Pat Johnstone. Shaw swore out a warrant for Raftner and with it in his pocket, Farnham rode westward in pursuit of Raftner and Shaw's horse.

Dad and Farnham were long-time friends, so when the sheriff got to our place on Lay creek he stopped for a chat and to ask if we had seen a man on a good-looking gray horse pass that way.

Yes, we had seen a man, but no horse. The man was afoot. It had not been long since he passed. Farnham went on up the road and overtook Raftner at the Emerson place, a half-mile north of our ranch. Raftner explained as well as he could, but since Farnham had a warrant for his arrest he had to take him back to Craig.

Red Renfro had come to town to get some barb wire for Charlie Egryl and had heard of the "theft" of the Shaw horse by their hired man. When he got back on "the Forks" and passed the Shaw ranch, he told Mrs. Shaw about it, and gave her a message from Shaw. Meanwhile Bren Sullivan had taken the show horse home.

Mrs. Shaw was in a quandry. There was her husband, waiting in town for the arrest of a man he thought had stolen his horse, and

here was the horse safe and sound in their own corral. So, she saddled another horse, her private pacer, and took off for Craig. Just
about the time she arrived, Farnham was back with Raftner.

The sheriff, his prisoner, the complaining witness, and the
latter's wife all went into a quick huddle. By that time it was night.
So when the huddle was over, Shaw paid for supper, bed and breakfast for Raftner and gave him enough money to buy a ticket on the
stage to Rawlins and fare from there to Saratoga.

"All's well that ends well," so Raftner's father recovered,
Raftner came back to work for Shaw. None of them "lived happily
forever after," but they did live for quite awhile and we will hope,
happily.

Tom Horn

Everybody in the country was scared.

It's one thing to be scared of something you can see and face up to and fight. It's something else when you're scared of something that *nobody* has seen. If that something is out to take your life—well, who wouldn't be scared?

The first inkling we had came from Tom Emerson. Passing on his way to Lay to get his mail, Tom told our parents, "You know, I heard something mighty curious yesterday. Al Hurd was at our place and he told us there is supposed to be some feller in the country to wipe out the settlers."

I should repeat what I've said a good many times before, that this was in a country where there was no way to communicate except to walk or ride. So news and information traveled slowly, if at all. Despite this, it wasn't long before news about the killer spread. In a couple of weeks just about everybody in the country knew that there was supposed to be a man hired, presumably by the big cattle companies, to run out or wipe out the settlers who had ranches that the cattlemen coveted, because the water and grass were good.

As in any case where positive, definite information is lacking, people vied with others in claiming sure knowledge of this killer. Some even claimed to have seen him. Everybody got into the act. But beneath all the rumor and claims and counter claims ran an undercurrent of real fear and dread, the terror of the unknown.

Almost overnight the thinking and habits of an entire population changed. Men who for years had freely ridden the range alone now went in twos and threes and armed. Those who had enjoyed evenings around the family dining table under the light of a kerosene lamp now ate early and in daylight and no lamps were lighted. Before this thing was to end, some of those warned did leave the country while others so warned stayed.

It was weeks before the killer was given a name. When at length somebody first whispered that name, it was to shock and amaze those who heard it, for the name was of a man of whom most people knew, a man who had distinguished himself as an Army scout, an Indian fighter, an expert cowpuncher, and a trusted employee of the Pinkerton Detective Agency, the FBI of its day. The man was Tom Horn.

That Tom Horn could be the one assigned to evict or kill peaceable, hard-working, honest ranchers seemed beyond belief. If the assignment had been to wipe out those rustlers who preyed on the herds of the big companies, it would have been understandable.

This was in fact the case, but it was months before this truth emerged. The rustlers, those who stole and butchered Two-Bar and other big company beef, kept alive the belief that *all* ranchers were due for sudden death. When the truth did emerge, the ranchers who did not rustle breathed easier and again the lights might be seen in their homes at night. But the cattle stealers trembled in their boots. Some of them disappeared, leaving the country.

During the months all this was transpiring, our home at the Gregory place near Lay had the usual run of callers and passers-by. Among the callers was a cowpuncher who told us his name was Hicks. I think that from the first our folks may have suspected that James Hicks was Tom Horn. True, he stayed at the Two-Bar horse camp and rode a horse with the Heart, the horse brand of the Two-Bar. He looked like a cowpuncher. He talked the language of the range. He volunteered his name but no other information, and of course our folks didn't ask.

Only a very few of the cowpunchers we knew could, or did, show any desire to talk about anything but cattle and horses, but Hicks did. He usually got down and had quite a confab with Dad. On the occasions when he came in for a meal, he entered into the conversation on almost any subject.

It was evening one time when Hicks came by. Chatting in front of the house, Dad remarked on the field glass case tied to the pommel of Hicks' saddle. Most ranchers had field glasses. Few cowpunchers did. Hicks took the glasses from the case and handed them to Dad. Dad remarked on the fine quality of the glasses and on how in the semi-darkness he could see plainly back under the shade of trees. We kids noticed that Hicks had a carbine in a scabbard slung under the right stirrup skirt.

"Tom Horn the hired killer." That was the way he was classified then, and that is the way history portrays him. "He killed Matt Rash and Isom Dart in Moffat County, Colorado, and killed a mere boy, Willie Nickell, in Wyoming, a crime for which he was hanged." That is history's verdict and that is the way people talked then and writers have written ever since. To say, or even hint, that Tom Horn was *not* the hired killer for the big cattle companies, or to say that he did *not* kill Willie Nickell, is hearsay.

That Tom Horn killed men there is no doubt. In line of duty, on the side of the law, he pursued and caught some of the most desperate, wily, and resourceful along the Mexican border. Possibly he killed Isom Dart in our own country. But that he killed either Matt Rash or Willie Nickell is highly unlikely.

Tom Horn was born in Missouri, in 1860. He ran away from home in 1874. He eventually got a job driving team for an outfit headed for Santa Fe. As a stage driver and shotgun on stages, he quickly got more education of the Western kind. Sent with a herd of horses into the Apache country around Camp Verde, Arizona, he got his first impressions of the fiercest Indian tribe. After he and the others delivered the horses, Horn went over to an Army post not far away and helped herd horses for the military.

At our place, Horn did not talk much about anything beyond this point. He was a ready talker, but knew how to be silent and listen. He did tell, though, that while at this fort he learned to speak Spanish pretty well. This accomplishment led to him being noticed by Al Sieber, chief of civilian scouts for the Army in Arizona.

Al Sieber was the greatest of the Indian Scouts. He and Horn went from Fort Whipple more than 200 miles to San Carlos, where Horn was official interpreter. Horn learned Apache, as well as the sign language which all Indians understood. After Geronimo was conquered, Horn became a miner not far from Camp Grant.

The local sheriff, Bucky O'Neill, prevailed on Horn to act as mediator and peacemaker between cattlemen arrayed against each other in a cattlemen's war, much like the contest between the Brown's Park small cattlemen and the Middlesex and later the Haley Two-Bar. Horn spent the summer at this job then went back to his mine, but the next spring another county sheriff, Glenn Reynolds, first sheriff of Gila County, deputized Horn in 1888.

Horn sold his mine near Aravaipa and came to Denver, where the big talk on the streets was a recent train robbery by Watson, known as "Pegleg," and Curtis. The law seemed to be stymied. Tom did some inquiring and found that an outfit called "the Pinkertons," were getting into the play. With what information he could get he tackled the Pinkertons for a job. He got it instantly. And before long he got the two holdup men too.

Horn made some firm friends while with the Pinkertons. But he still was curious about "what was on the other side of that hill," and moved on into Wyoming, sort of riding the chuckline and stopping mostly at cattle ranches.

This was 1898 and the war with Spain broke out. Horn joined the Army, where his experience and knowledge of Spanish made him invaluable.

The cattle rustlers had for years plagued the ranchers in the Iron Mountain area of Wyoming. They took advantage of war conditions. The ranchers and bigger cattlemen were short of cowpunchers, most of whom were in the war. The rustlers' inroads on the cattle herds were devastating. What more natural, then, that when the "Rough Riders" and other riders came back from war, Tom Horn among them, than the cattlemen should hire him to help make another kind of war—on the rustlers. The reputation of Horn had gone before him and carried a lot of weight.

I think Tom Horn had probably worked out a technique in his dealing with the rustlers in Wyoming, whereby rumor and warnings were the most effective weapons. Anyhow, that was the way it worked in our country. Rumors flew thick and fast. There were rumors of men being killed from ambush all over three or four Colorado counties and over into Wyoming. Sometimes names were given, but we did not recognize any. Actually, *nobody* had fallen to the bullets of the fabled killer up to that time.

After a time, "Mr. Hicks" left the horse camp and moved westward. In Brown's Park he stayed at various ranches and got to know most of the people. We never saw him again, but we know from others that he helped whomever he happened to be staying with.

★
Queen Ann Bassett

Up to about 1906, the words "Brown's Park" were heard more often than the names of all other places in northwest Colorado. And, since then, many words have been written about Brown's Park, the Wild Bunch, Queen Ann Bassett, Butch Cassidy, Lant and Tracy, Tom Horn, and a few more.

Two residents of the Park I knew well—Ann Bassett and J. S. Hoy. Both were well educated, even by today's standards. Both were highly intelligent, observant, and skillful writers. And both were independent.

In the early days the trappers and explorers called any valley enclosed by high mountains a "hole." Such were Jackson's Hole, Pat's Hole, Harding's Hole, and numerous other "holes." So this valley on the Green River, with the towering heights of the Uinta Mountains on one side and Cold Spring Mountain on the other, was a "hole."

One of the very earliest who tarried in this hole awhile was a French-Canadian trapper, Baptiste Braune. To the other trappers, he was "Baptisty Brown." These other trappers coming into the "hole" and finding Brown already there, secure in his cedar-post cabin, called the place "Brown's Hole." It remained Brown's Hole until the arrival of the Herbert Bassett family in 1871. Mrs. Bassett, on getting her first view of the beautiful valley, suggested that "hole" was not a fitting description for a so lovely valley. She christened it "Brown's Park."

The story of "Queen Ann" Bassett has been told scores of times. But a personality such as Ann Bassett offers great temptation for authors to let their imaginations run riot. Even though the facts are sufficiently startling, some writers have had a field day in competing with each other in "gilding the lily." They have attributed to

Ann deeds of which even she never dreamed. One of the fictitious roles in which she has been cast was as "Queen of the Outlaws." True, outlaws visited the Bassett ranch, ate at the Bassett table, fed their horses Bassett hay, and no doubt admired and dreamed of this beautiful girl. Some or maybe all of the same outlaws visited *our* ranch, ate at our table, fed our hay, and no doubt admired and dreamed of my sisters. But neither our family nor the Bassett family took any part in making the plans nor in the performances or profits of thieves and killers.

I first met the Bassett boys, Eb and George, at dances at Maybell. Our folk had known the family long before. Ab Hughes played the fiddle and called the squares, excepting when Pete Farrel was on hand for the calling. Ab could get more tone out of a fiddle than anyone I ever heard. But even so, Pete could drown him out. Pete's "calling" voice was high-pitched. As he warmed to his work the pitch rose. To a total stranger, approaching the long, low, dance hall, windowless and wrapped in darkness, the wailing of Ab's fiddle, the shrieking of Pete, and the low hum of the dancer voices and shuffling feet would have led to the belief that the population of Maybell was being tortured by Indians.

Through Eb and George I got to know their sisters, Ann and Josephine. Josie I never got to know well, but Ann and I became good friends over the years. She was a remarkable person. She could top off a bronc, throw an accurate loop or a salty word in a roundup, or wear the clothes and speak the cultured language of the best society.

I got to know something of Brown's Park even before I saw it. The Bassetts told me about their ranch, cattle, and of other places in the park. I met other cowpunchers and a few ladies too. One cowpuncher named Anderson, whom everybody called "Antelope" on account of a wild story he told about roping an antelope, proved to be a third champion of mine. One evening when a couple of riders insisted on me drinking some whisky, Antelope told them, "Aw, let that kid alone. Just because you're a pair of whisky guzzlers, don't try to make him one of him."

He smiled when he said it but the two got the message.

Ann Bassett was eight years older than I, but she was one of those ageless persons who know nothing of generation gaps. I wondered for a long time how the name "Queen Ann" originated. In recent years I've heard many versions: that she was so dubbed by the outlaws, that she was chosen queen in college, that the name was conceived by a reporter during her trial for rustling. The truth is, Ann herself did not know for certain how the title "Queen Ann" came into being. But she did know the story that was told her:

"I first heard about it at a dance at our ranch. The dance was given to celebrate the finish of a roundup. The night before the dance the cowpunchers were camped on Beaver Creek. I had left the roundup the day before to come in to help get ready for the dance. The boys at camp were of course talking about the coming dance. Of course there was about five boys to every girl in the country. So the biggest thing at a dance was for a boy to have a girl to eat supper with him."

"I guess Jing Malone told the other men that he was going to ask me to be his partner at supper. The dance always stopped at midnight for that."

"'What, her eat supper with you?' Matt Morelock asked him. 'Why you whopper-jawed, sawed-off-and-hammered-down imitation of a bronc peeler, she probably won't even dance with yuh, to say nothin' of eatin' 'longside of yuh.'"

"'Well, you don't have t' rub it in,' Jing complained. 'I know I ain't no great shakes fer looks and I don't dance so good. But c'n eat good as anybody. And anyways, th' cat c'n look at th' queen can't it?'"

"'No siree. No thirty-dollar-a-month cow waddie cat c'n look at our Queen Ann.'"

"The next evening when they came in they pulled the Queen Ann gag all evening. So that's where it started. Later when newspaper reporters wrote about me at the trial, they played up that Queen Ann title to the limit."

By 1875, Ann's parents' ranch had been improved by the building of a commodious ranch house. It had for quite awhile been the center of community activities. With a big house and accommodations for wayfarers and their animals, it was the stopping place for ranchers, hunters, cowpunchers, and even outlaws. The big gate was always swung wide for any who wanted to enter, and the latch-string hung on the outside.

In this and other ranch homes, the rough edges of the Old West were being rounded off. These settlers were from more civilized places. They made plans and implemented them, to have a good life with social gatherings, church services, and schools. Life was becoming milder in Brown's Park, but by no means did these people have the West "tamed."

At this time little Ann was five. Children of that age began to learn the rudiments of riding. The method was simple but effective. Each evening, in summertime, neighbors gathered and surrounded a space that had been smoothed off and covered with hay. The young men acted as the "horses." On all-fours they bucked, reared, sunfished, and did all the tricks and twists known to broncos, trying their best to unseat the young riders, boys and girls, clinging to their backs.

Ann soon became an adept "bronc peeler," but nearly lost her reputation when, at the sly suggestion of a sheepherder in the crowd, she put on a pair of sharp spurs and roweled the surprised "horse" she bestrode. Ann later wrote, "I had the privilege of living in a bronco West and began life as a hand at the mature age of six."

She did indeed ride the range as a working "cowboy," holding up her end in any part of the work at an age when most girls are playing with dolls. It was her mother's hope that her girls should become "ladies," in the way the word "lady" was interpreted in the East from which the Bassetts came. Ann became a lady all right, as we who knew her can testify, but she proved in her own way that a woman can be a lady and still wear chaps, brand and castrate calves, top off a bronco, and take part in the cowboys' activities, conversations, and pastimes.

There were very few ordinary or average people on this last frontier in those days. They were unusual or they wouldn't have been there. The first wild game refuge in the *entire* West was in the basin of which Brown's Park is the center.

Jack Rife was a big man in body, mind, and soul. He came to Brown's Park in the early 1870s. Unlike most of those who came, he did not try to acquire much land or livestock. He preferred to live simply and as close to nature as he could get. On the north slope of Douglas Mountain, so named by Rife, at a spring just off a narrow valley, Jack established himself. Before long, he had effected an agreement with the Indians that there would be no hunting nor shooting in the confines of an area laid out by Jack with the approval of the Utes.

Into this area, over the years, Jack enticed animals of every kind to be found in the country. Rife brought into the country two tamed buffalo, "Sampson" and "Delilah." It was because of his tame buffalo driving team that Rife came to be known far and wide as "Buffalo Jack."

When the giant Middlesex Cattle Company moved their herds into the region, covering every hill and valley, many small ranchers saw that they could not survive. The people in the park hoped that the bulwark of the Unita Range on the south, the dense juniper and pinyon forests on the southern slopes of Cold Spring Mountain, and the gorges at the upper end of the park might stem the floods of cattle that threatened to engulf and ruin them. They did not fear invasion from the southwest. Beyond those mountains were the Mormons. A tenet of the Mormon belief was that even the small settler should have an equal chance to work out his destiny. It was not likely they would countenance the movement of vast herds through their domain when it was known that such movement would mean the ruin of many small ranchers.

Profiting from the example and advice of another rancher, an ex-English nobleman sold his cattle and bought a band of sheep. These were run north and east of Brown's Park, thus forming a living barrier on that side against the encroaching cattle herds. Middlesex stubbornly left many of their cattle on the same range with the sheep. That winter, the sheep survived, but the hills were dotted the next spring by the carcasses of cattle that had perished.

Thus began the "range wars" in our county. Wars that would lead to bitterness, hatred, death to animals and to men. Seeing the determination of the settlers, representatives of the Middlesex outfit went to them with offers to buy them out. Although all offers were refused, the company persisted.

Middlesex herds were handled by an army of cowboys. The cattle were moved from the summer range along the state line into the Green River valley in winter. In the spring they were shoved northward. After one such "shove-up," Ann Basset found in a willow clump a tiny calf whose mother had been forced to move with the herds. In such a movement there was bound to be a calf overlooked here and there. Usually they fell victims to the coyotes and bobcats. This one Ann cared for and fed without telling her parents. She knew they would insist that the owners of the calf be notified.

You would have to be an eight-year-old girl in a country and in a time like that to understand at all the episode to follow. This was in Brown's Park, this was the year 1886, and the child was little Ann Bassett.

Knowing that the secrecy concerning the calf could not go on indefinitely, she contrived, by strategy and blandishments, to get her father to take her along on a trip he was to make to Rock Springs. In that town, she steered her parent to the office of Mr. Fisher, the manager of the Middlesex Cattle Company. While her father listened in amazement, she explained the matter of the calf to Fisher, not stopping even to take breath until she concluded by offering to trade one of her father's purebred yearling steers for the almost valueless waif calf.

Caught in such a position, Bassett could only agree to the trade. But Mr. Fisher must have been a magnanimous man, for he assured the little girl that he would not consider such a one-sided trade but instead would make her a gift of the stray calf. So now, to her unspeakable delight, Ann was the owner of a genuine Texas dogie. A hired man, Slippery Jim, whom she had taken into her confidence, had assured her that this breed was the best. Slippery was caring for the calf during Ann's week-long absence.

Back at the ranch, Ann devoted her time and bestowed her affections on her "herd." She had named the calf "Dixie Burr." Everyday she fed it and brushed it and noted its growth and improvement. Then, one day when she went to feed the little waif, it was gone!

After scouring the country, she found only the tracks of a small herd that had been driven along the Bassett outer fence. She rode to the house and consulted Slippery. It was late, so Jim advised her to get a good sleep and to be on the trail in the early morning. This she did. Here is the way she related it later:

"I overtook the herd on its way. A rider who brought up the rear was dragging my Dixie Burr behind the herd and lashing her with a rawhide rope. I went "hog wild." I began whipping him over the head with my quirt. As I look back on the incident, I can't blame him, for the only brand on the calf was that of the Middlesex outfit. But at the time his resistance and rough declaration that he would take the calf seemed outrageous to me."

"The other cowhands had gathered around to watch the fracas. One of the men was Joe Martin, even though his real name was Joe Blansit. He had worked for a man named Martin and so was known by that name. Joe was repping for himself and some of the ranchers over on Bear River, whose cattle had strayed to the park."

"Finally Joe Martin said to the Middlesex foreman, Roark, the man who had my calf and whom I had quirted, 'Why not just let the kid take the calf and settle the ownership later?'"

"Joe's innocent suggestion touched off Roark. He went for his gun. yelling as he did so, 'I didn't ask fer your advice, you.'"

"It proved that Roark was just a would-be gunman. Joe beat him to the draw, took away his gun and getting off his horse laid aside his own gun and hat. Roark did the same and the fight was on. For awhile I was uncertain how the fight would go. But Joe came on fast and soon had the other man down, for the final count."

"I jumped off my pony and began to kick him. Joe Martin grabbed me by the arm and said, 'Shame on you Ann. That's cowardly to jump on a man when he's down.' Those words brought me up standing. I have never forgotten them."

The first thing Ann did after returning the calf to the ranch was to sneak it out in the brush, build a branding fire, and with a hot iron convert the brand by making brands into a "Pigpen." Later, the calf was taken to the Bassett camp in Zenobia Basin.

Joe Blansit or Joe Martin as he was usually called, we knew well. He sometimes rode with the Two-Bar. We got to know this quiet, bashful, and well-mannered young Texan well.

The incident of the calf owned by Ann Bassett was to set going a chain of events of grave consequences to almost all residents of the county. The man Roark must have been eager to earn his salary and to get in solid with his employers. He often rode alone, literally spying on the ranchers.

"He never showed up to talk matters over," Ann told us. "He just coyoted through the brush. During one of father's absences from the Basin, Roark found Dixie Burr. The job I had done was a sloppy imitation of brand blotting. (Me heap savvy now.) When Roark found the brand so obviously changed he lit out for Hahn's Peak, the county seat of Routt County, over 100 miles from Zenobia Basin. He swore out warrants for the arrest of everyone in Brown's Park excepting father. Father was one of the county commissioners and was at a meeting at the county seat at the time. Roark made no exceptions in the wholesale arrests. He included men and women alike."

"Sam Walker of Hayden was sheriff. He came to the park with his bundle of warrants and was treated as any guest would have been treated. But the serving of the warrants was received with amazement. A roving Englishman, who roamed the world, was in the park at the time and had built himself a cabin and shared the life, without really being a part of the community. He was astounded when presented with his warrant and hadn't the least idea of what it meant. The most innocent and law-abiding lady, Mrs. Sears, viewed her warrant with a mingling of astonishment and consternation."

"However, all the recipients of these warrants reacted as any good citizens would and appeared in court when the case was called. The case was immediately dismissed for lack of evidence. Its instigator may have foreseen this conclusion, but a deeper purpose, no doubt, lay behind his move—a hope to discourage the occupants of the park from remaining there. Judge Rucker was on the bench. As a result of my child effort to protect a cherished pet from brutality, Brown's Park was branded as a home for rustlers, and a lying rumor was widely circulated that no good can come from Brown's Park."

Judge Rucker threw the Brown's Park case out of court. He made an observation that was to become a prophecy fulfilled: "If such methods continue to be used by the big cattle companies, those companies are bound to fade from the scene."

His prediction was all too true. The Middlesex company failed in its attempt to intimidate and drive out the small ranchers. Its holdings were sold to Ed Rife. He promptly stocked the range with sheep, forming an additional bulwark against the encroachments of other big cattle companies. The settlers now lived in peace and security. It was only when another cattle company, owned by Ora Haley, came into the area that their troubles began again.

To quote Ann Bassett, "Some of Cassidy's Wild Bunch were hard cases. But among them were a good many who under different circumstances might have been good boys. One such was Elza Lay."

"When haying time drew near," related Ann, "Father sent a man with wagon to Rock Springs to get some hay hands. When the crew of haymakers arrived at the ranch, among them was Elza Lay, a young, well-bred appearing fellow with a winning smile and perfect manners. He was a capable workman, strong and active, with a gentle good-nature that won the hearts of old and young alike. Elza remained on the ranch for a year and he was the only Easterner we knew who was never bitten by the cowboy bug. He had no desire to be a top hand."

"Young men by the score came to the Western ranches. At one time father had for "adjustment" a Clark and a Converse, sons of well-known railroad people, boys who had gotten out from under parental control by having too much money to spend. They were all good boys, but none were so generally liked as Elza Lay. When the year was up he went back to Rock Springs. Not long afterward rumor circulated that he had joined forces with Butch Cassidy and they were carrying on a series of bank and train robberies."

Ann continues, "Elza and Butch returned to Brown's Park at times, but we did not pry into affairs concerning their private lives, for we were not the instigators of their shortcut to riches and we did not channel the course they set."

"Friendly relations between the Brown's Parkers and the bank robbers caused a great deal of comment. The question has frequently been asked, how could a people permit themselves to harbor the committers of a crime without becoming involved in the deals? The answer is simple. We were in a constant struggle to protect our own interests on the range where our living was at stake. Bank robbers were not a menace to our personal interests, and we had no reason to carry the ball for the banks and trains. We had a fair size job to do in itself. Law officers were elected and paid by the taxpayers to assume jurisdiction over legal matters of the country."

When after a year or two Elza Lay returned to Brown's Park, the young people welcomed him enthusiastically, the older ones with more reserve. At a dance in his honor he met a beautiful girl from Vernal, Utah. Attraction must have been mutual. After a clandestine courtship, aided and abetted by the young people of the park, especially the Bassetts, a wedding was in the offing. Without the help of Mormon elders, and with the opposition of the girl's people as an obstacle, it took much strategy to accomplish this. The girl, Mabel, rode her swimming horse across Green River and made her way to Big Springs in Yampa Canon where Lay was in hiding. Later the bride-to-be rode her horse many miles to find a minister willing to make the trip and to perform the unorthodox ceremony. He too had to swim his horse across the Green. So, on a high mountainside, under a broad pine, with Ann Bassett as witness, the still dripping divine united in marriage the determined girl from Utah and the unreforming member of Butch Cassidy's Wild Bunch.

Lay had told the girl of his way of life and even after marriage he did not change. Like most such people, he "justified" his lawless life by explaining that rich men had defrauded his widowed mother of a rich inheritance. His way of reprisal was to rob other people of their money.

Unlike most stories of outlaws, that of Elza Lay had a happy ending. In later years he abandoned the outlaw trail, became a solid citizen in southern California and raised and educated well a large family.

In 1886, shortly before the arrival of our family in the county, there had been considerable excitement in Brown's Park over a horse race between one of the fine animals owned by Charlie Crouse and a horse belonging to Ken Hatch, of Vernal. The race was run on a circular track originally laid out by the Indians on land owned at the time of the race by Valentine Hoy.

Everybody in the Park turned out for the ride. As his jockey, Crouse had the services of a young chap who, having heard rumors of the coming race, came over from his home in Utah and volunteered to ride Crouse's horse. The shrewd and horsewise Crouse tried the boy out and decided he was capable of the job.

The Crouse thoroughbred won the race by lengths. The Brown's Parkers were wildly elated. A big dance was given that night to celebrate the victory of Colorado over Utah. The young people swarmed on the hero of the hour, the jockey from Utah. They found him quiet, not timid, not very communicative. About all he told of himself was to say his name was Ed Cassidy and that his folks lived a piece beyond Vernal! After supper, and when the festivities began, young Cassidy—went to bed.

Before many years had passed these people were to come to know Ed Cassidy as "Butch" Cassidy, leader of the Wild Bunch. Even in the days of his greatest notoriety, when his name was on every tongue and front page, he remained the same quiet, soft-spoken but very determined man.

Of him, Ann Bassett had this to say: "He worked for Charlie Crouse for a year. He was always well-mannered. I never saw Butch Cassidy wear a gun—in sight. I have no personal knowledge of any of his deeds of outlawry. I do know that he never lived in Brown's Park when he was wanted by the law."

"Occasionally he came that way, stopping for a meal at various ranches, but took no part in the social life nor even attended a party after that one following the race. He never harmed or bothered the people of our community. If the law officers had come to the park for him not one hand would have been raised to protect an outlaw. Everyone knew that a large reward had been offered for the capture of Butch, dead or alive. I am proud to say that not one of us wanted that kind of money. We had no commendation, no excuse for his 'profession' but we knew that his life was a hard, unhappy existence. He was often seen in towns such as Baggs, Wyoming, and Vernal, Utah, and other communities."

And so, this was life in Brown's Park. It was to such a life that Ann Bassett was born and on which she left her mark.

The ebullient Ann proved too much of a problem for her father to face for long. Her adventures kept him unsettled and guessing every moment. So, on the advice of friends he sent her to Salt Lake City to be schooled by the Catholic Sisters of Charity.

It might be concluded that the restless and daring pioneer girl from the cattle ranges of Brown's Hole would stir up a tornado in the environs of the gentle nuns. To the surprise of everyone, including herself, Ann "gentled down" like any well-handled bronc and not only gave the Sisters no trouble, but became endeared to them for her always merry ways, her diligence in study, and her kind heart and generosity. It would have delighted her mother, could she have seen the progress Ann was making toward "being a lady."

Came the time when this "making of a lady" progressed even farther. Herbert Bassett, with his background of education, culture and idealism, sent Ann to a "young ladies finishing school" in the East.

Ann had respected and loved the Sisters. But this finishing school was a different proposition. It came near to "finishing" not only the young student, but some of the instructors. She made no pretense of conforming. Informed of the situation, her father welcomed her back to the life she loved.

Back on the ranch she took up life where it had been interrupted. The family had cattle. As always, the range was threatened by the big outfits. By now, it was the Two-Bar, ramrodded in this area by Hi Bernard. Bernard, the tall, sandy-haired, slow-spoken Texan, was cattleman all through. It has been said that Hi was a gentleman. Just what that may mean is debatable, but in those days it was taken to mean a man who in everyday life showed none of the roughness, profanity, vulgarity, immorality, or other vices but who was gallant to women, kind to children, generous to adversaries and charitable to the unfortunate. Strangely enough, the general idea was that a man could be a hell-raiser on wheels most of the time yet be "a perfect gentleman" when in the presence of ladies, children, or preachers.

That was Hi Bernard, I guess.

The high points in the life of Queen Ann Bassett from that time on included her marriage to Hi Bernard. It was an example of the theory "if you can't beat 'em, join 'em." Only in this case, it was the foreman of the enemy Two-Bar outfit who joined the Bassett side. The Two-Bar was using every stratagem to inch its way into Brown's Park. The Brown's Parkers had successfully resisted this move by presenting a united front to the encroachment. A blow, that was almost a disaster, fell when J. S. Hoy sold his holdings to the Two-Bar!

It must have been that by this time, the feeling between Hoy and his neighbors had become strained and raw. Almost any of the main ranchers in the Park could have, and would have, bought Hoy's holdings in order to maintain solidarity.

The marriage of Ann and Bernard must have been a desperate move to offset the problem of a Two-Bar stronghold right in the community. Hi was no match for Queen Ann in any department. He was a smart livestock man, but for him to match his thinking power against the keen intellect of Ann Bassett was to match a pigmy against a giant.

The eventual advantage of this union was never demonstrated, because of rapid changes that ensued. Bernard was replaced as Two-Bar foreman by Bill Patton, who had been working for Haley at his ranches near Laramie, Wyoming. Patton was a good cattleman, but had no talent for getting the last lick of work from the men. Nor was he as well liked as Hi had been.

The general belief was that Patton's chief assignment was to get Queen Ann Bassett Bernard off the range. Whether true or not, in the summer of 1912 the whole country was electrified by the word that Queen Ann and a cowpuncher, Tom Yarberry, had been arrested for killing a Two-Bar steer. It was said the meat and hide of a beef had been found in the Bassett buildings where Ann dwelt. This was not denied, but it was maintained that the beef came from an animal owned by the Bassetts.

The first trial resulted in a divided jury. As long as two old-timers live, the question of the guilt or innocence of Queen Ann will be debated. The only reason and basis for an opinion I have comes from putting the question direct to the one person who really knew the answer.

"Court week" in Craig in that day was a big event. Court officials and attaches and the many jurors doubled or tripled the population of the town. The restaurants were crowded and saloons did a thriving business. At night there was a dance at the theater building.

At the dance the night before the trial closed, among the dancers were most of the distinguished residents and visitors, including Queen Ann and also Hon. John T. Shumate, judge who presided over the trial. To the horror of the gossips who lined the benches in the dance hall, the courtly white-haired judge asked for and was granted "the pleasure of a dance" with the personable and handsome lady who, on another day, he might have to "send over the road."

A few dances later I danced with Ann.

"What are you trying to do, corrupt the judge?" I kidded her. We had a little fun out of the incident. Presently I asked Ann how she liked Two-Bar beef.

"I thought you had a better opinion of me," she laughed. "Do you think if I really killed a Two-Bar critter I'd let myself get caught?"

The jury didn't think so, for next day they brought in a verdict of acquittal. It was widely approved.

Over the years, vast changes had taken place. The country was filling up with homesteaders. The big cattle companies no longer dominated the scene. It was hard for Ora Haley to accept these changes, so long had the old "Cattle King" had much his own way. His foreman, Bill Patton, was not liked. I worked under him only a few weeks one spring on the horse roundup.

An incident that didn't enhance Patton's standing with the waddies was the arrest of Bill White for cattle stealing.

Bill White was a professional horsebreaker, or "bronc peeler" as they were known. He had worked every spring for the Two-Bar for years.

This summer a Two-Bar calf got mixed in with White's cattle at his Lily Park ranch. The Two-Bar cattle had crossed on the ice. Bill hazed them back to the north side and up the Vale of Tears. Later, he found this one calf among his cattle. The ice had gone out of the river by then so he could not risk drowning the calf by making it go to the other side. Somehow Patton learned of the calf and had Bill

White arrested. The whole thing turned out to be a fiasco as the justice threw the case out of court. It didn't hurt Bill White, but it lowered Patton's standing another notch, so when the Queen Ann trial came on, Patton and his boss already had two strikes against them. If a clincher was needed, Haley supplied it.

On the witness stand in Queen Ann's trial, he testified to the number of cattle he had on the range. When the defense attorneys introduced another statement to which he had sworn as to the number of his cattle for tax purposes, the jury got the message. The difference in the two numbers was too great to be an accident or error.

It was too bad. To us, Haley was a man of great ability and a welcome visitor. But greed had ruined him in his later years and led him to go to any lengths to save money on taxes and to evade the charges made by the Forest Service for ranging cattle in the high country. It was suspected that he brought here Tom Horn, said to be a hired killer, and finally the bringing in of Patton and the arrest of Bill White and the Queen Ann affair sunk him.

The Two-Bar was indeed at a very low tide in its fortunes. The sun of the cattle kings was setting, the homesteaders would soon rule, and they in turn would give way before the silver horde.

The sheep were coming.

★
Epilogue: The Demise of the Two-Bar Rooster

by Irby H. Miller

I knew it was about to pour rain and I was goin' to get wet, which made me wonder why I hadn't tied my raincoat on the *outside* of the bedroll behind my saddle, instead of rollin' it up inside the blankets.

Most folks would've thought about the weather when packin' a bedroll. And I thought about it too, as the rain started pourin' down by the bucketful, drenchin' me and Snort, my old horse.

I pulled back on the reins. Snort put on the brakes and turned his head sideways, tryin' to see me, and I could almost hear him say, "What now, you lunkhead?"

I twisted around in the saddle and untied everything to get to my slicker. By the time I got it on, I was soaked, my blankets were wet, and old Snort was drippin'. I think any fool would have tied the slicker on the outside of the bedroll.

Me and Snort had been travelin' east for the better part of three days, headin' towards the Pot Hook cattle spread up by the Colorado-Wyomin' border. I'd thought I might land me a job there, as I'd heard that Shorty Temple was needin' cowhands.

Even though I hadn't had too much experience, I figured he might hire me on. I needed a job, and I hadn't had much to eat the last several days. My belly was flappin' against my tailbone every time Snort took a step. The old wagon road we were followin' was more of a trail than a road, and it was turnin' to mud before my eyes.

I'd left Ora Haley's Two-Bar outfit a few days ago, in circumstances outside my control. My troubles there started with a mangy, worn-out rooster that had called the Two-Bar home for at least 10 years. But I reckon, thinkin' about it, that the rooster wasn't really my trouble. It was his demise that was my undoin'.

It started out that I was havin' a hard time bein' a cowboy. I hadn't even seen a real cowpoke until a few months before I hit the Two-Bar.

I'd been back in the Missouri Ozarks, cuttin' hardwood for the new railroad that was comin' through the country. My pa and me would walk about three miles to the timber stand, then work about 10 to 12 hours, sawin' and cuttin' and hewin' the ties with a broad-ax. That was just about all we knew to do, which was just as well, seein' that loggin' was about all the work there was back in the Ozarks.

So, I finally took leave of my folks, promisin' that I'd write them once in awhile. With the clothes on my back and a $5 gold piece (a present from my folks) sewn to the inside of my longjohns, I headed for Colorado.

Knowin' that gold piece was ridin' around in my longjohns was a comfort. I reckoned that as long as it was there, I wasn't in any danger of starvin'. But as soon as I got to the wide open spaces, I realized it wasn't goin' to help me much unless I could barter it for somethin' to eat. Money ain't worth nothin' unless there's somebody around to trade with, and coyotes and prairie dogs don't understand or care much about human needs.

But after much determination, I made it to western Colorado. There were plenty of big spreads scattered around the country. A good many cattle had been trailed up from the Texas plains over the Goodnight-Loving trail to the Colorado Rockies.

I'd heard from a cowpuncher I'd met on the trail that the Two-Bar outfit was runnin' around 40,000 head, out near the Utah border. That's a lot of cattle to keep track of. I headed that direction.

I finally found myself walkin' up a dusty road towards a good-sized ranch near where I'd figgered the Two-Bar might be. I needed a drink of water bad and was awful hungry. Some of the cowpokes were out near the pump, washin' up for the evenin' chow.

They all had their old beat-up hats on, covered with trail dust and grime. They'd remove their hat when it came their turn to wash up and hang it on a fencepost near the pump. They'd then roll up their sleeves to the elbow, grab the piece of lye soap, and splutter while they soaped their faces and arms with the cold water and scrubbed off the day's dirt. The old hat went back on as soon as they were finished and they'd dried off with an old dirty towel.

Their clothes were about worn out, some of their shirts had the sleeves threadbare with their elbows stickin' out, and their britches were patched and ragged, held up at the waist with a belt made from either leather with a harness buckle, or a rope tied in a knot. Some had on leather wrist cuffs, which they removed while washin'. All wore runover low-heeled boots with turned-down spurs buckled on. The rowels tinkled with a musical clink when they walked.

It was evident that the cowboys of the Two-Bar spread weren't goin' to win any fashion shows anywhere. And they could've cared less.

I sauntered up, tryin' to get my courage tightened up enough to ask for somethin' to eat and drink. They turned, first one with a red walrus mustache, then a long lanky one, then the others, one by one, and stared at me.

I looked down at my clothes, held out my hands, and tried to figger what they were lookin' at. It was only then that I realized that I must be lookin' like one hard customer. I was still wearin' my old, worn-out bib overall and run-down work boots. They looked me up and down for a spell, and then a smile cracked one's face.

"Reckon I might bother ya fer a drink of that water?" I asked, eyein' them right back.

The grizzled old cowboy with the walrus mustache said, "Help yerself, kid." He gestured toward the rusted old pump with a banged-up tin dipper hangin' from it.

I walked over and pumped that dipper full of the coolest, clearest water I'd ever seen in my life, then swigged it down. That done, I guzzled another.

The old cowpoke said, "When'd you eat last, boy?"

"Yestiddy mornin'."

His tobacco-stained mustache quivered a little while he tried to hide another grin, but he muzzled it and said, "Whyn'tcha get washed up and join the rest of the boys here for supper."

I knew he was feelin' sorry for me and makin' sport of me all at the same time, but I knew too that I wasn't gonna get a second invitation to put somethin' in my belly, so I moved on in.

We et quick, and the fellers were so busy stuffin' their faces that they didn't pay me much mind for awhile. And after a meal of fatback and beans, with gravy and hot biscuits, all washed down with plenty of hot black coffee, my innards felt a good deal better. Which propped up my courage some, because I found myself sayin' to the old feller with the mustache, "You got any need for a cowhand?"

He scowled at me and looked me over again, a forkful of beans halfway to his mouth.

He asked, "You know anythin' at all about cowboyin'?"

"Reckon that depends on what you want me to do," I replied.

"Can you ride a horse? Know which end the bridle goes on?" He stared me down till I felt like I was goin' to wilt right there, and finally he pursed his lips and twirled that mustache again.

Finally, Mr. Lytton (for I was to learn later that this was the foreman himself) twirled that dusty mustache once more, then said, "I reckon we could use some help. I'll put you on fencin' at first. If you make a good hand, we'll hire you on as cook's helper when the roundup starts this fall. $15 a month plus board."

I woulda jumped up and yelped, but the cowpokes just kept lookin' at me, most of 'em still fightin' off grins.

Still, it sounded good, the idea of eatin' on a regular basis. Havin' the company of a bunch of bow-legged misfits might not be too bad. I found out as I got to know them a little better that some of 'em were soft-hearted and would give you the shirt right off their back if they thought you needed it.

After chow, some of the cowboys went about doin' ranch chores. I learned quick that they all hated to do any kind of work involvin' their back muscles or their brains. They grumped that they were hired out as cattle wranglers, not ranch hands.

I was sittin' back learnin' what I could when I heard Heck Lytton tell one of the cowpokes, "I'm a man of few words. When I say come, you come!"

The old cowpoke stiffened his back and piped right back, "I'm a man of fewer words, and if I shake my head, I ain't comin'!" The foreman just shrugged his shoulders.

The ranch had a few head of milk cows and some layin' hens for the breakfast eggs, and a couple of old tough-as-shoeleather roosters—includin' the one that was to be my undoin'.

That old reprobate rooster refused to bunk down in the henhouse, so he usually roosted on top of a pole that run across the two long gateposts down by the road, up off the ground about 15 feet. He was an independent old cuss, and his eyesight was awful poor. He'd attack anyone or anything that got in his way, includin' the boss himself.

After I'd come to know his miserable habits, I watched him one evenin', just about dusk, shortly before his time to roost on the pole. He jumped into the middle of a tumbleweed that was blowin' across the yard in an evenin' breeze. The weed had blown in from across the fence and was doin' a purty good clip, when "Old Buzzard" (that's what everyone called him) spotted it and gave chase.

He caught up with the whirlin' weed and jumped it right in the middle, stirrin' up a ball of dust so we couldn't see him for awhile. But the tumbleweed musta got the best of him, 'cause before long he was caught right in the midst of it, squawkin' and tryin' to untangle himself.

His old sharp spurs stuck out a good two inches, sharp as porcupine quills, and they kept gettin' caught on the dry stems of the weed. But he finally pulled loose, shook off, then stood there and glared at the weed as it took off rollin' down the lane and out the gate. He flopped his wings, stuck out his scrawny neck, and gave out with a screechin' squawk that was supposed to be a tri-umphant sound of victory.

Even though Old Buzzard treated the cowpunchers like he had that tumbleweed, Heck warned the boys to lay off the old cuss. He'd told them he was fond of the old rooster.

Since the bunkhouse wasn't too roomy, I put my bedroll on the floor in a corner near the door. This left my feet stickin' out in the doorway, where the late-comers had to step over them. This posed some problems durin' the night, whenever someone would have to get up and "go look at the moon." I learned quick not to get bedded down for a night's sleep when the boys went into town for "refreshments," which usually happened around payday. Most of them would saddle up their cow ponies and ride the 12 or so miles to the nearest waterin' hole. If they didn't get thrown into jail, they'd show up back at the ranch in the middle of the night.

Well, you can imagine my problems when they started to come in the door of the bunkhouse, with my bedroll booby trap waitin'. An unwary cowboy would step in the middle of my shins and then sail across the room and land on the bed of an innocent sleeper. Then things came alive, and business picked up consider-ably.

"Ozark, you dad-blamed clodhopper, why can't you hunker up a little bit and draw your feet up when I come in the door? How do you expect me to remember that you're layin' there sprawled out like a bullfrog in a haystack?" They had started callin' me "Ozark" when they found out I was from Missouri.

By the time the cowboys would arrive back at the ranch, most of the effects of the firewater had worn off, and they were so tired and rumdum that they couldn't think straight. I've seen some of them come in and pull the bridle off their horses and turn them loose with their saddles still on. The next day they'd wonder who'd saddled up their horses.

After I'd been on the Two-Bar a couple of months, Red, one of the cowboys, asked, "Ozark, have you ever been in a snipe hunt?" Red was the bowleggedest cowboy I had ever seen. "Snipe huntin' is a real honest profession," he said. "Sometimes you can make good money and have a good time while you're doin' it."

Well, I wasn't about to get snookered on that one, for I knew the game. "Matter of fact," I said, makin' my voice sound as casual as his own, "I've hunted a few snipes back in the Ozarks. It was sorta like a cattle roundup out here in the West."

I shifted around so I could dead-eye him and told him flat out, "I made lots of money on them snipes 'till we hunted 'em all out."

Old Red grinned and paused, then said, "Well, I reckon since you've already been snipe huntin' you probably don't want to do it again for a while. Reckon that don't make no nevermind, though. We got another job cut out for you, and it fits you to a 'tee.' You're just skinny enough to make a good job of it, too."

I was suspicious, but eager to please these old cowpokes, too, so I said, "What you got in mind?"

"You remember that mangy old rooster?"

"Yeah, I remember."

Red leaned forward and frowned, like he was about to share an important secret with me. "I want ta let ya know, there's sometin' dreadful wrong with that old skinny-legged cousin to a buzzard."

"What's that?" I asked. He had my ears wide open.

"Well, every mornin' just about daylight, he sets up the most infernal racket you ever heard, out there on that pole across the gate.

He acts like there's somethin' hung up in his throat, from the way the screechin' sounds. Could be too, that one of his back teeth is loose and half chokin' him."

Another puncher by the name of Barney had come in while we were talkin', and now he spoke up. "That rooster eats so danged many grasshoppers that his gizzard is likely all messed up. I thought of that a time or two myself."

"Thing is," Barney added, "we got a can of that Black Draught laxative here in the cupboard. If we could mix up a batch and force-feed him about half a teacup-full with a spoon, he'd likely snap out of it in a day or two and quit wakin' us up with that terrible croakin' every mornin'."

I began to feel half sorry for the old bird. He was, without a doubt, the sorriest specimen I'd ever known to be called a rooster. And he was a sore sight to look at, too. In front, where his craw stuck out, was as bare as a board in a hog pen, and the feathers had been worn off his breast many years before.

Barney and old Red could see it, I could tell by the mournful looks on their faces, and I was beginnin' to see it too. I reckon that old bird had an unhappy childhood as a young feller.

And sure enough, while I was thinkin' that way, Barney and Red took to speculatin' on that very thing and talkin' about how to give the old reprobate a better life.

Red said, "You gotta remember that the boss is sorta fond of that old geezer, and we don't want anythin' to happen to him. So you'll have to be careful. Since you're so skinny, we figgered you could shinny up that gatepost without wakin' Old Buzzard up, then grab him around the neck and force some of that Black Draught down his craw. Might not hurt if you looked down his throat and checked to see if anything is hung up down there, while you're at it."

The plan sounded right to me, and I was pleased that they'd look to me for help. So I agreed to carry the plan out as soon as the timin' was right.

I laid there after the coal oil light was out, thinkin' about what they were trustin' me to do. I figgered that them cowpunchers were softhearted after all, to be so concerned about an old worn-out rooster.

My work on the Two-Bar up till then was all fixin' fences. Heck had given me an old crow-bait for a horse, and I filled up the saddle pockets with staples and hammer and rode the range. I'd had a hankerin' for quite awhile to own my own horse, along with a saddle, bridle, spurs, chaps, and lariat. Any respectable cowboy wanted to own his own outfit. It was sort of a sign of wealth, depending on how good your outfit looked.

I had saved most of my last two paychecks. Good horses were hard to come by, unless you wanted to break your own. But I didn't hanker to have all my bones busted at the same time. The boys had tried their level best to entice me on broncs, but I always managed to squirm out of the deal.

One evenin' the discussions turned to ownin' your own horse. I mentioned the fact that I'd like to get a decent horse, but I didn't want just any crowbait that was about to lay down and die, but rather a sensible, fairly young cow horse that I could depend on.

The boys were goin' into town the next day, bein' it was the time of the month that the boss let them off.

They usually took several days before they got back to the ranch and got their brains straightened out again. I asked them if it would be possible for me to ride into town with them and look for a horse. It was a long trip, and it meant that they would have to put up with me for quite awhile. They began to hem and haw and give me excuses as to why they couldn't do that.

Finally, Barney said, "Ozark, I'll tell you what we'll do. If you'll trust us with $30, we'll check at the livery barn or at some ranch and see if we can buy a horse. For that money, we should get you a fairly good saddle horse that's green broke and in fair shape. We even might get some kind of saddle and bridle thrown in. They won't be fancy, though."

"Well, I hope you know that's two month's wages for me," I answered. "You boys get twice that much for your work. How do I know you won't get into a crap game and lose all my money?"

Antelope answered, "I tell you what, Ozark. I'll take the responsibility for your roll. I'll guarantee you'll get the best buy for your money. These other hombres know I keep my word."

The other boys agreed. Even Bill Flannigan nodded his head. The two cowpunchers I respected most were Bill and Val FitzPatrick, as they were off the old block, and their word was as good as gold.

"Well, alright," I answered. "Try and get me a good one."

I handed Antelope a $20 and a $10 gold piece, figurin' that I was a fool to give my hard-earned money away like that. Still, I wanted a horse bad and decided I'd have to take a chance.

The next few days went by slow. I didn't do much around the ranch. I was anxious for the boys to get back with my saddle horse, to see what they had come up with.

Finally, the Two-Bar bunch come in around midnight and seemed to be in good shape. At least they had enough sense to pull the bridles and saddles off before they turned the horses loose. They came in the bunkhouse and lit the lantern and woke me up.

They looked tired. Antelope said, "Ozark, we shore got you a good deal on a horse. Got a nice saddle and bridle too. Even brought you some money back."

He fished around in his shirt pocket and drew out the $10 gold piece I had given him a few days ago. I was dumbfounded. I wondered what kind of horse he'd bought with a $20 gold piece. I wondered what kind of crowbait he'd led back to the Two-Bar, that probably would die in a day or two.

He said, "Well, I'll tell you how it happened. It was day before yestiddy, and we started lookin' around for a horse. We went down to the livery barn, and what looked like a greenhorn dude probably from back East somewhere rode up on this tolerable lookin' saddle horse.

"We could tell he was a dude by the way he was dressed. Fancy boots and not a sign of sweat around his hat band. He led the horse into the barn."

"Well, Barney pulled out some Old Crow and offered the dude a drink. He at first declined, but Barney insisted and said somethin' about strangers resistin' the hospitality of the West. So he finally took a snort, and from then on it was purty easy. After awhile, we told him we'd like to buy his horse and outfit and wondered what he'd take."

"He at first said that they weren't for sale, but as the afternoon went on, he said we sure were good friends, was glad he'd met us, and began to agree with about anything we said. I don't think he knew he was in a horse barn or a king's palace and couldn't have cared less."

"We asked him what he wanted for the outfit, and he finally put a price of $100 on it. But we told him that according to Western standards, a saddle horse shouldn't have any more than a half inch sway in its back and this one had at least two inches. We measured it with a manure shovel handle."

"And, furthermore, the front legs were out of whack. We measured from withers to fetlocks with the shovel and showed him that the legs weren't straight. The knees bowed in about an inch on both sides. The dude kinda scooted over and layed on his back and sighted up one of the horses legs and agreed."

"Well, we allowed that he should reconsider his price and handed him the bottle again. Everytime he took a snort, the price came down. Some of the snorts were good for a $10 discount, and by the time the deal was over, and he was still sober enough to sign a bill of sale, the price was down to $20."

"The last we saw of him, he was bedded down on a pile of hay in the barn, not botherin' to even pull his boots off. Here's the bill of sale, and old Snort is out in the horse pasture. Guess that you'll have to wait till mornin' to see him."

I couldn't believe that these characters would pull somethin' like that on a greenhorn dude. I was concerned about him gettin' the law on all of us.

Barney spoke up, "Don't worry about that. He probably will be so ashamed of himself that he won't say anything about it by the time he sobers up. And you have a legal bill of sale. He doesn't know any of us from Adam, and probably by the time you ride back into town in a few weeks, he'll be back East again, tellin' of his brave Indian fightin' in the West and how his horse was shot out from under him."

The next mornin', just about daylight, I headed out to the horse pasture to see what Snort looked like. I had to walk about a half mile from the ranch house to find where the horses were grazing.

Snort was grazing by himself about 100 yards down a draw. I walked over to him, expecting him to take off. I was surprised to find that he stood still and let me walk up to him. He wasn't a bad lookin' horse either. He let me rub his neck and pat him, acted like he plumb enjoyed it. It was a pleasant, unexpected surprise for me.

And as far as his bow legs and swayed back, you'd have to look close to notice them. I knew that old Snort was goin' to be a good horse for me. He had a Two Circle Bar brand, which was owned by the Cary Brothers up in the Bear River valley, about 75 miles to the east.

I pulled the bill of sale out of my shirt pocket, but couldn't quite make out the name of the gent who had so generously parted with his horse. I wanted to know who he was, just in case I met up with him sometime, and he accused me of horse stealin'.

Barney was out at the pump washin' up, and I asked him if he knew the dude or had ever seen him before. He said, "Never laid eyes on him before. We asked around town before we left, but nobody knew him either. One old puncher said he thought that he'd seen Snort a few weeks earlier up on the Pot Hook."

Antelope added quietly, "The signature is Billy Sawtelle's."

Old Snort and I spent most of the summer with my job of fence repairin' and had become acquainted with just about every gully and cedar-topped hill in a 50 square-mile area, with the Two-Bar ranch in the middle.

I had ample opportunity to view the country from the saddle. The sandy hills were covered with pinyons and sagebrush, with some willows down in the shady washes where seeps and sometimes a good flowing spring would be found.

Range grasses were plentiful, and the Two-Bar cattle grew sleek and fat throughout the summer, grazing the public domain. The roundup season was nigh at hand, and the cattle were scattered from the Utah line as far east as Fortification Creek and Black Mountain and as far south as White River. I wondered if the boss still wanted me to help the cook with the chuck wagon chores.

One evenin', after we had bedded down in the bunkhouse and the usual lies and tall tales had made their rounds, the conversation dwindled down somewhat.

Antelope spoke up, "Ozark, do you remember you said you was gonna check that old rooster out and see what ailed him? His infernal screechin' hasn't slowed down one bit. He still sounds like there's somethin' caught in his throat. He must be sufferin' purty bad."

Barney added to the conversation, "Yeah, you need to do somethin' soon, we're goin' to be on the roundup before long, and he may die before we get back to the ranch. Then we'd never find out what was wrong with him."

I asked, "How do you expect me to shinny up that 15 foot gate post after dark without raisin' the dogs? If they start barkin', the boss is bound to wake up and come out with that old scattergun, thinkin' there's a skunk in the chicken house. I shore don't hanker to have my rear end loaded down with buckshot."

"Well, we've thought quite a lot about that very thing," answered Barney. "We've thought it out and come up with a plan. The evenin' before you climb up the gatepost, we'll loop a couple of lariat ropes over the top pole and tie 'em to a cedar fence post. You can sit on it and we can pull you up to the top with a couple of saddle horses, maybe before the dogs see or hear us and start raisin' Cain."

I replied, "Well, I guess that might work. But it's dangerous to be out at night if those dogs bark. Heck don't see too good after the sun goes down. But we can give it a whirl. The moon's up around two and if we can get ourselves woke up, I'd be willin' to try it if you boys'll help me."

Antelope answered, "What about it, boys, do you reckon we can help Ozark get that old rooster cured?" Most everyone agreed to help to their utmost capabilities.

If there was a trick more lowly ever pulled on an unsuspecting, innocent cowboy, I've never heard about it. And I thought most of those two-legged varmints were my friends. At least they acted like my friends when they wanted a favor or wanted to borrow a buck when they went to town.

"Ozark, here's what we'll do," said Antelope. "We'll get up around three, the dogs should be purty well asleep by then. If they start barkin' we'll drop everything. We'll saddle up a couple of horses and tie them up at the barn. Then when we're ready, we'll lead them up to the gate and tie the ropes to the saddle horns. You make yerself comfortable on that cedar post and we'll snake you up to the top of the gate right quick. Then you can grab Old Buzzard around the neck before he gets awake and sort of throttle him so he won't squawk. Take a bottle of Black Draught mixed with water. If the moonlight's just right, maybe you can look down his throat and see what's hung up down there."

"Well," I answered, "I want you boys to take it easy when you pull me up. Just pull me up 'till my arms are about level with the crosspole."

"Don't worry, Ozark, we'll be mighty careful. Just be real quiet."

A thunderstorm was buildin' in the west, with a lot of sheet lightnin'. It looked like it might rain durin' the night, although we didn't particularly want that to happen.

The worst part of the whole deal was gettin' out of the sack at three in the mornin'. This should have warned me, when your "buddies" will go that far to pull a joke.

At 2:30, Barney got up and lit the lantern and woke everybody up. "All right you bowlegged cow cussers, you've checked your eyelids for holes long enough. Let's get this job of mercy finished."

Antelope rubbed the sleep from his eyes. "This is the dadburnedest scheme I ever heared about to cure a worthless mangy rooster who don't care if he's cured or not. And we're goin' to get soaked."

The lightnin' put on a display through the open bunkhouse door as we watched from our bedrolls. Thunder echoed across the rollin' hills that stretched from Diamond Mountain and Ladore Canyon. The moon tried to shine out from the scuddy clouds to the east, but it wasn't too long after we got up that the clouds drifted over the moon, and it was as dark as the inside of a cowboy's boot at midnight.

The only light that we had was the lightnin' as it flashed from the west as the storm approached the Two-Bar ranch. We wondered if maybe we hadn't made a mistake in the time we'd picked to liberate Old Buzzard from his throat ailments.

Antelope and Barney led the horses up from the barn and got them into position near the gateposts. They mounted and grabbed the lariat ropes that were hangin' over the pole across the gate. They whispered to me to "get ready to be hoisted up to the top," sorta like riggin' up a sail on a schooner.

Old Buzzard set docile on top of the pole, never movin', weatherin' the storm. I had just walked under the gate and wrapped my legs around the cedar post when a bolt of lightnin' split the heavens and arced down and hit a cottonwood tree about 100 yards from us, down towards the horse corral. If it had hit where we were, I wouldn't be tellin' this story.

The thunderclap sounded like a Civil War cannon. The dogs woke up barking. Heck woke up, skunks in his dreams. They were skunks alright, but the two-legged kind.

Heck grabbed his old twelve gauge scattergun and slammed the door. The horses spooked and started runnin', not carin' that I was at their mercy, ropes dallied around the saddle horns with the other ends holdin' the fence post I was hangin' on to for dear life.

I sailed up and grabbed the top of the gate, the top pole broke, and Old Buzzard flew down to the ground, landin' in the yard about 50 feet from the ranch house. Heck, now at the door, spotted Old Buzzard in the light from the next lightning flash, took aim, and blasted him to Kingdom Come, or wherever old worn out, half-blind roosters go.

The feathers flew, and Heck by that time realized that skunks don't have feathers. It must have been a moment of revelation to him, realizin' that he had just killed his pet rooster, thinkin' he was blastin' a skunk.

Meanwhile, I was havin' my Waterloo, tryin' to get untangled. The horses were pullin' one side of that post towards the west and one towards the east, with me suspended in the middle.

Antelope and Barney finally got their dallies untied about the same time, and I wound up in a big sagebrush near what was left of the Two-Bar gate. Fortunately, about all I lost was a whole lot of dignity.

Meanwhile, durin' the lightnin' flashes, Heck Lytton was takin' in the whole proceedin's, and it didn't take him very long to put things together. He went back into the house and slipped on his boots and came back out in the yard. I wondered if the old shotgun was ever used for anything other than killin' skunks.

I'd managed to get back to the yard, and Antelope and Barney had got the horses quieted down.

Heck roared at us, "You knuckleheads, just what in Hades are you doing out here this time of night? Have all of you gone crazy?"

Before anyone could respond, the heavens opened and a frog drownder hit us in full force. We were soaked in just a few minutes, and Heck was still runnin' around in his drawers.

He yelled, "Get to the bunkhouse!" We had a hunch then that we were in a heap of trouble, for no respectable foreman of a large cattle outfit talks to his crew in the bunkhouse at four o'clock in the mornin' durin' a rainstorm in his underwear with the trap door flappin' open.

The other boys in the bunkhouse had the lantern lit, for they realized that sleep was out of the question with the racket from the thunder and lightnin'. Heck burst in behind me, his old walrus mustache a quiverin', sort of like it did when I asked him for a drink of water when I first came to the Two-Bar. But this time, it was quiverin' from a different reason. I never saw him that mad before or since and I hope never again.

Barney and Antelope came in a few minutes later. Heck stood in the door.

"Well," he started, "Just who in this outfit can tell me what happened to this bunch of misfits that call themselves cowpunchers? What in the name of Jehosaphat is going on with you runnin' around out here in the rain in the middle of the night? Antelope, I'll start with you. Can you tell me what in tarnation has happened to the sanity of this bunch?"

Antelope was a little bit uneasy. I should say he was a whole lot uneasy. He shifted his gaze back and forth from Heck to me and to the rest of the bunch. I think he figured that anything he said would further implicate him, and he chose his words with all the care that he could muster.

"Well sir, Mr. Lytton," he began, "It's sort of a long story, and one which you probably won't believe anyway. But I guess that somebody will have to tell you, and I suppose that it might as well be me, although I wish somebody else would do it."

"It pains me considerable to have to relate to you the sad story of the fall of a noble man who just recently joined our gallant group, one to whom we've looked up to and held in very high esteem these last few months and has been an example to all of us."

Heck interrupted him with a bellow, "What in the name of Jehosaphat are you talking about? And *who* are you talking about? You sound like a Philadelphia lawyer that's been samplin' loco weed. Do any of you boys know what he's jawin' about?"

Everybody quickly shook their heads in the negative.

"Ozark," asked Heck. "What do you know about all this?"

I was on the hot seat now. I didn't have the savvy that Antelope had, and I figured that if I tried a snow job, I'd probably get caught anyway. So I tried the only way that I could think of, and that was to tell the truth.

"Sir, I was only tryin' to help out an old scrawny rooster that had somethin' wrong in his throat. The boys convinced me when I first came here Old Buzzard had somethin' hung up in his throat, or maybe a loose tooth that was half chokin' him. We were tryin' to catch him and give him a dose of Black Draught to clear out his innards and the top pole broke across the gate and started this whole mess," I answered.

"You was goin' to do *what*?" bellowed Heck.

"Yes sir, that's the truth," I answered. I could see my job with the Two-Bar disappearin' like the rain clouds when the sun came up in the next few hours. Heck turned around and cradled his head in his left arm as he leaned on the door frame. He pounded the wall with his right fist.

"I can't believe that I've hired such numskulls," he muttered to himself. Finally gaining his composure, he turned and looked at me.

"Ozark, we'll talk more about this later this mornin'. Have you got a slicker I can put on to get back to the house? I'm wet enough now, without gettin' any wetter."

"Yes, sir. I'll get it for you," I answered. Heck put on the raincoat and headed back for the house in the rain. We still had about an hour before we had to get up and start the chores, so we blew out the lantern and tried to get an hour's worth of shuteye. Our night's rest sure had been ruined, and I was so sore from my landin' in the brush that I had a hard time just tryin' to get down on my pallet.

We rolled out of the sack about 5:30 and did the mornin' chores. Breakfast was waitin' for us at the main house, and we washed up out by the pump. The night's rain had stopped and everything was clean again, with the last few week's accumulation of dust washed off. The sun was up and just a few ragged clouds were driftin' in the east.

Old Buzzard was still layin' out in the yard where he was pumped full of buckshot by Heck a few hours before. I sorta felt a pang of conscience about him when I saw him out there, even though I didn't pull the trigger.

We filed into the dining room, where Heck had seated himself at the long table, drinkin' a hot cup of black coffee. We filled our cups from the coffee pot on the stove, and the cook piled our plates down with flapjacks and fried eggs.

It would have been a good mornin' to be alive, except for the ruckus of the night before. None of us had much to say as we ate. Heck was quiet too, glancing at me once in a while. I wondered what he was thinkin'. It probably wasn't very good.

We'd almost finished breakfast when Heck broke his silence. "Boys, I guess that we'd better finish the business we started earlier this mornin'. I want to know just what was goin' on last night around here. You know that I don't allow or approve of such foolishness. When you boys bed down for the night, I expect you to stay bedded down and get some rest, so that you can give me a good day's work. I don't want a bunch of groggy cowboys stumblin' around here in their sleep, tryin' to do their work and gettin' hurt or maybe killed."

He spoke in a whole lot gentler voice than he had the night before. Almost like a father chastisin' his sons.

"Now, I'm going to ask you all again what happened and let's see if we can get to the bottom of this. Ozark, is what you told me last night the truth?" he asked.

"Yes sir, it's the truth," I answered. "I must've been a fool to listen to these hombres."

"Well, I'd say so. You should've had more sense than to fall for such a harebrained scheme. I'm afraid that I'll have to let you go. Pick up your gear from the bunkhouse, and I'll pay you what I owe you. When you grow up and get some sense, come back and maybe I can find a spot for you."

Barney spoke up, "Mr. Lytton, could you reconsider? It really wasn't Ozark's fault any more than the rest of us. Except Bill and Val. They didn't have anythin' to do with it. We shore didn't plan for things to get out of hand like this. If you'll not fire Ozark, we'll make it up to you, won't we boys?"

Everybody vowed that they would. I don't think Heck believed any of them.

Antelope said, "That's right, Mr. Lytton. Ozark really should-n't have to carry the whole load by himself. I shore wish you'd give him another chance."

Heck replied, "I don't think that I can give him another chance. He's responsible for me killin' Old Buzzard. I wouldn't have harmed that old bird for anything in the world. Him and I were a whole lot alike. We're both mean old cusses."

"I raised that old geezer from the day he hatched out almost 10 years ago. He's like one of the family, and you shore don't shoot one of the family, either accidentally or on purpose. I'm sorry, Ozark, but get your old horse saddled and head out."

I felt bad. It's bad medicine to be out of a job out in the boon-docks with no friends around. I didn't consider any of them varmits my friends. I could see that they had a little remorse towards me, but not nearly enough. If ever the chance presented itself, maybe I could repay them somehow.

"Ozark, before you leave, I want you to get a shovel and carry Old Buzzard out in the horse pasture and dig a hole and bury him. I think that should be your job," Heck said.

I said, "Yes sir, I'll do that. I'm sorry for all that's happened. I'll get old Snort saddled and pick up my bedroll."

"Before you leave, I have your pay and a note I want you to be sure and show anybody who might want to give you a job. Everybody in a 250 mile circle knows Heck Lytton."

I buried Old Buzzard down in the horse pasture. While I was rollin' up my bedroll and pickin' up my stuff at the bunkhouse, the boys were real quiet.

Just before I headed out the door, Barney spoke up. "Ozark, I'm really sorry about what happened. A lot of it was my fault. I'd like to make it up to you. Here's a $5 gold piece to help tide you over for awhile."

Antelope said, "Yeah, Ozark, that goes for me too. Here's another $5. I wish you well, and maybe our trails will cross again sometime."

The other boys said "so long" to me and we all shook hands, and it seemed to me that Bill Flannagan and Val FitzPatrick squeezed my hand a little harder than the others. I took the money from Antelope and Barney, thinkin' it might help to even up the score a little bit. I said "so long" and headed out the door.

I stopped by the main house for Heck's note, no doubt meant to warn off anybody who might hire me. He met me at the porch and handed me a folded piece of paper. He shook my hand and said, "So long, Ozark. I'm sorry that I had to let you go, but I didn't have much choice. You had me backed up against a wall in front of the boys. Good luck to you."

He handed me a $20 gold piece, which was a little more than I had comin' in pay, and I rode down through the main gate and by the top pole layin' on the ground. I figured it would be fittin' that Antelope and Barney got the job of repairin' it.

I never looked back. At least I was quite a lot better off than when I first saw the Two-Bar a few months ago. And not nearly as hungry. I slipped the piece of paper out of my shirt pocket and read it. "To Whom It May Concern: I would like to recommend the bearer of this note, namely, Ozark Johnson, for a job as a cowhand. He is still a little green, but he is worth $30.00 a month in salary. Signed — Heck Lytton."

Well, that seemed to make a lot of bad things right again. It sort of took the edge off and helped me to square my thoughts about the Two-Bar. Maybe, I thought, some day I could return to the Two-Bar and get a job again.

So, here we were, Snort and I, headed for the Pot Hook spread in Wyomin' Territory, tired and hungry.

We had followed the Little Snake River from the Two-Bar headquarters towards the northeast as it meandered through the juniper and sagebrush covered hills.

The day was gettin' along, and it would soon be dark. I hated to think I'd have to spend another night on the trail with no supper. It seemed like that was gettin' to be regular fare, even though I'd stopped this mornin' at the George Baggs ranch and they gave me breakfast. George was an old worn-out cowboy that had managed to carve out a niche for himself on the Little Snake, along with the help of his wife, Maggie.

Maggie was somethin' else. Her talk would blister the bark off a cedar tree and would start a grass fire once in awhile. It sure turned a lot of cowboys' ears red.

Just about dusk, we topped a little hill, and down in the valley below us, about two miles away, we could see the dim coal oil lights of a ranch shining like a beacon in the dark. Old Snort quickened his pace, and we clipped off the distance in short order. About a hundred yards from the buildings, the dogs of the Pot Hook spread heard us and began barking.

As I rode through the board gate, a man stepped out on the porch of the main ranch house. I rode up to him in the dusk and asked him if he was Shorty Temple. He said he was, and asked what could he do for me.

I handed him the note that Heck had given me a few days before. He read it and asked me if I was lookin' for a job. "I need some help. Fall roundup time is on us, and I need a chuckwagon flunkey bad. I'll give you $30 a month and your keep. I'll get some of the boys to take care of your horse, and you come on in and have some chow while you're thinkin' about it."

Well, I really didn't need any time to think about it. But I sort of held back, I didn't want to seem too eager. I couldn't believe it, gettin' a job that easy, with twice the pay that I had at the Two-Bar.

After I washed up, the cook dished up some leftovers from the evenin' meal, which tasted bettern' any banquet. I began to feel a whole lot better.

"Well, what do you say, Ozark?" asked Temple. "Can I put you on the payroll?"

I answered as discreetly as I could. "Yes sir, I'll take the job and will do the best for you I can."

We went down to the bunkhouse, where the cowpunchers were sittin' around, not doin' much in the lantern light. Some had a card game in progress, others were readin', and some were on their cots restin'.

We stepped in and Shorty said, "Boys, I'd like you to meet a new hand. Name's Ozark. He's goin' to start work for us in the mornin'."

"I want to introduce you to the boys, Ozark. Here's Chick Bowen, and over there in the corner is Ed Miles, and there's Art FitzPatrick, and behind him is Whitey Hindman. And over there next to the stove is Billy Sawtelle. Everybody else is out with the cattle."

Everyone spoke or nodded their heads toward me. I got my bedroll and found a place for it. At least I didn't have to sleep with my feet stickin' in the door, like I did at the Two-Bar. For the first time since the shootin' of Old Buzzard, I felt pretty good.

Then I remembered the bill of sale from the little horse-buyin' trip. I looked at Billy Sawtelle. He sure didn't look like no Eastern dude to me.

Billy looked back with a steady gaze and nodded his head. "I noticed you ridin' up on a pretty fine horse," he said dryly. Everyone else had gone back to their cards.

Even though the bill of sale was legal, I decided that I'd better write a letter back home and let the folks know that I probably would be buried on the Pot Hook Ranch in southern Wyomin' Territory.

I also wondered if I should tell someone not to bury me 'til they took that $5 gold piece out of my longjohns and sent it back to my folks. Then I remembered the other gold pieces that Antelope and Barney had given me.

"By the way," I said to Billy, "I have a message for you from the boys over at the Two-Bar. They send you their best and say that next time you're over their way they'll settle up whatever else you think that old horse is worth and not to worry, they're good on their word."

Sawtell relaxed and look a little amused. "Sounds like the honest thing to do. I shore appreciate that. I kinda wondered who them boys rode fer. Might just head on over there tomorrow."

His smile broke into a grin as he took a tin cup off a shelf above the ancient stove where a black coffeepot boiled away. "Now then, kid, how's about a cup of them Arbuckles?"

Things were lookin' up. I decided that bein' a cowboy might be alright and that old worn-out roosters weren't too bad after all.

★ Acknowledgments

Thank you to Irby H. Miller of Montrose, Colorado, a quintessential western Coloradoan who knew first-hand some of the people in Val's stories as well as Val himself, and who graciously provided his editorial assistance, as well as contributing his story *The Demise of the Two-Bar Rooster*.

Harold Babcock of Colorado Springs generously shared the story *Dogies, Dust, and the Drink* from his private collection of Val's works.

George Davidson of Craig, Colorado, graciously provided copies of Val's "Last Frontier" series, now out of print and difficult to find.

John Foster's editorial expertise helped polish the book till it had the sheen of a fine cowpony.

Without Marjorie Miller's vision and tenacity, this book would never have made it out of the chute.

Alice Sjoberg of Sjoberg Graphic Design in Carbondale, Colorado, contributed her talents for the book and cover design.

Maya Kurtz rode point on the herd, preventing stampedes when the storms came through.

And a very special thanks to Ron S. Riddick and the Greenwich Workshop for permission to use Ron's superb painting, *The Muddy Arbuckle Cafe,* for the cover of this book, as well as the inside title page.